HABITS
OF MIND

HABITS OF MIND

Fostering Access and Excellence in Higher Education

William B. Allen
Carol M. Allen

Transaction Publishers
New Brunswick (U.S.A.) and London (U.K.)

Library of Congress Catalog Number: 2002043000
ISBN: 0-7658-0184-1
Printed in Canada

Library of Congress Cataloging-in-Publication Data

Allen, W. B. (William Barclay), 1944-
    Habits of Mind: fostering access and excellence in higher education / W. B. Allen and Carol M. Allen.
        p. cm.
    Includes bibliographical references and index.
    ISBN 0-7658-0184-1 (cloth: alk. paper)
        1. Education, Higher—Aims and objectives—United States.   2. Moral education (Higher)—United States.   I. Allen, Carol M.   II. Title.

LB2322.2.A46   2003
378.73—dc21

                                                                    2002043000

*To the many students whose continuing studies and sustained
loyalty have taught us what it means to teach*

Contents

Acknowledgements

The authors are grateful for permission to republish material that has appeared previously. Some material that appeared in the article, "Taking the Final Step in Raising Academic Standards" (published by Virginia Polytechnic Institute and State University in the winter 1998 issue of its journal *Virginia Issues and Answers)* has been incorporated into chapter 1. Portions of chapter 2 were published in an article on "The Challenges of Academic Leadership" in the November/December 1999 issue of the *Clarion* (published by the Pope Center of Higher Education Policy) and in the proceedings of the Conference on Statistic, Science and Public Policy, held on April 26-29, 2000, at Herstmonceux Castle, Hailsham, England (edited by A. M. Herzberg and I. Krupka) under the title, "Excellence in Judgement: The Curriculum." A longer version of the essay, "On Becoming a Liberal: Guidance of George Washington," which is included in the epilogue, was published by the Locke Institute in the summer 1999 issue of *The Locke Luminary.*

We also thank the Educational Testing Service for permission to reproduce the tables in chapter 3, which were originally developed for the Testing Service and published in the 1998 report, *Growth in School: Achievement Gains from the Fourth to the Eighth Grade* (authored by Paul E. Barton and Richard J. Coley). We also appreciate the assistance we received from the staff of the Albert and Shirley Small Special Collections Library of the University of Virginia and for their permission to quote from the "Petition to Abolish Tariff on Scientific Books Imported from Abroad," which was made by the Rector and Visitors of the University to Congress in 1821.

Finally, we thank all those persons whose assistance has been instrumental in bringing this project to a fruitful conclusion. Too long to list, these include our editors at Transaction, and several of our former staff at the State Council of Higher Education for Virginia, with special notice to Belinda Anderson, Donna Brodd, Laura Ford, Fletcher Mangum, Cora Salzberg, and Karl Schilling. Priscilla Walker provided excellent proofreading skills, for which we are grateful.

Foreword

> Here I understand the expression "morals" in the sense that the ancients attached to the term *mores*; I apply it not only to morals properly so-called and which one may call *habits of the heart,* but to the different ideas that men possess, to the diverse opinions that are current among them, and to the totality of ideas that constitute the *habits of mind.* I include in this term the moral and intellectual condition of a people.—Alexis de Tocqueville, *Democracy in America*

With this book, we introduce a new beast into the higher education menagerie—a beast that speaks administration-ese yet defends high culture.[1] It embraces greatly expanded access to higher education, even nearly universal higher education, yet it insists upon high standards of academic excellence. It rejects the industrial corporatist model for the university, yet it insists upon managerial efficiency. It defends faculty control of the curriculum in the face of trustee activism, yet it insists upon the fiduciary capacities and responsibilities of trustees. Is it hopelessly conflicted, irresolute, the expression of divided counsels? No, it rather insists that these apparent contradictions in fact constitute the single path of prudential advance in higher education. Rarely in the mass of commentary and prognosis for higher education can anyone be found to sustain such a fusionist thesis. To the contrary, much of the commentary is mired in an "either-or" paradigm, championing *either* access *or* excellence, calling for *either* complete and unfettered faculty governance *or* intrusive trustee oversight, dashing blindly toward a corporatist, virtual future *or* yearning to return to a mythical, golden past. Unlike many another, this book is not predicated upon dire prognostication for higher education's future. Rather, we urge that the progress of higher education thus far justifies a hopeful, conscious, and deliberate provision for its future hereafter.

Just how do we propose that such a fusion of competing perspectives might be achieved? Moreover, why do we proclaim its necessity? Well, our thinking is informed by the view that habits of mind are far and away the most influential determinants of human con-

duct in our time, and nowhere are habits of the mind more pro-
foundly shaped than in institutions of higher education. Harry V.
Jaffa observed in 1972, in the new introduction to his 1958 classic,
Crisis of the House Divided,[2] that,

> I was aware that I was a member of that comparatively small class, the university
> professoriate, that today is the decisive source of the ruling opinions in our country.
> Primary and secondary teachers, the mass media, and the elected officials are usually
> the retailers of ideas that come in the first place from universities, and in particular from
> the graduate schools. Here is where the teachers of the teachers are taught. We have
> become the ultimate source of change in the regime.

Jaffa's view was not then novel, for it echoed the carefully articulated view of Alexis de Tocqueville, reflected in the epigram of this
volume. Tocqueville spoke of "habits of mind" as having supplanted
"habits of the heart" in shaping human moral experience. Despite
his very clear formulation, commentators since have seized upon
the expression, "habits of the heart," as though Tocqueville had meant
to recommend that as a paradigm for social interpretation. In fact,
though, Tocqueville meant to describe a phenomenon that emerged
with the democratic and anti-religious revolutions of the late eighteenth century—the emergence of the "intellectual" as the moral ar-
biter of society. Edward Shils, a fine reader of Tocqueville, conveyed the message as late as 1990:[3]

> The status of universities in society has also changed markedly and that has occurred
> partly in consequence of the triumphs of the Humboldtian idea of the university in the
> creation of new knowledge and the education of young persons. From having been
> wards of a particular church, the universities have to a large extent supplanted the
> churches.

They were mainly the "intellectuals" who spawned the revolution
in France in 1789, and they were the intellectuals in the nineteenth
and twentieth centuries, increasingly and eventually almost exclusively operating from universities, who became the standards of moral
and political judgment in a way that clergymen once had been.[4]
    Although this very articulate distinction clarifies greatly the us-
age of the eighteenth century, commentators since have preferred to
describe the "habits of the heart" as the focus of Tocqueville's work.
Tocqueville, however, sought to convey by "habits of mind" a new
and advanced understanding of terms of analysis central to our
evolved political and moral universe. What this means for *any* analysis of higher education is that, in order to be appropriate to the task,
such an analysis must undertake to identify the broader responsibili-

ties of higher education, including its moral responsibilities, and not merely the personal opportunities it affords to students. For higher education will, willy-nilly, form the habits of mind that will constitute our most decisive collective possession. For that reason we have a responsibility individually and collectively to judge and hold higher education accountable. This, we believe, is the deeper meaning of Maritain's observation that "the man of our civilization *is* the Christian man, more or less secularized"(original emphasis).[5]

What, then, is the basis of judgment we employ in judging higher education? What is the content of the concept, "habits of mind?" Well, here's an example. When the conversation about excellence comes to be replaced by methodologies of excellence—Total Quality Management, Continuous Quality Improvement, Peters, Naisbitt, Covey, Machiavelli et al.—*without* any articulate understanding of the goal, means have driven out ends and habits have driven out intellection. Managers have driven out leaders or statesmen. It is the same as supplanting musicianship with musical taste. Musicianship requires disciplined habits of mind shaped by articulate ends; for musical taste habits of the heart suffice. In short, where a mere focus on the means or management of higher education can and usually does disguise tacit ideology, we propose explicit judgment and analysis of means in light of a specific view of the ends of higher education.

In this volume we pass judgment on higher education, but we do so by means of a thorough discussion of the "ways and means" of higher education. That is, we believe that it matters how one makes provision for higher education every bit as much as it matters how one organizes a curriculum. Accordingly, the topics of liberal education and strategic planning are alike fundamental in meaningful assessment of the present condition and future prospects of higher education. So, too, must we be attentive to issues of access, for it matters who receives higher education just as it matters what they receive in the process.

The most fundamentally shocking paradox of higher education today is that it is free (and thus far immune to coercion) to select whom it will teach while, at the same time, not being required to account for what it will teach them (and thus far open to prostitute its services to high bidders). Adam Smith described it precisely in 1776: "the discipline of colleges and universities is in general contrived, not for the benefit of the students, but for the interest, or more properly speaking, for the ease of the masters..."[6] The reforms described in these pages are predicated upon the thesis that higher education is too important and too powerful for colleges and universities to be permitted arbitrarily to select the students they will teach, and that, because higher education is so important and so powerful, colleges and universities should be required to teach the students they receive and not merely to mouth the pieties of interested educational and research sponsors. Nor is there room for affirmative action in this view, for a vapid sketch of multiculturalism cannot provide the required standard of intellectual rigor. What this book does, then, is to chart a course out of these thickets for higher education, thus allowing the path of sound habits of mind to become clearer.

Notes

1. It is a beast found neither in The Academic Bestiary of Richard Armour (1974) nor in Academic Animals: A Bestiary of Higher Education Teaching and How It Got that Way by Lois Raney (2001).
2. Harry V. Jaffa, Crisis of the House Divided (Chicago: University of Chicago Press, 1959, 1982), 10. Lord Keynes said as much in his General Theory, but without much moral focus: "the ideas of economists and political philosophers, both when they are right and when they are wrong, are more powerful than is commonly understood. Indeed the world is ruled by little else. . . . Madmen in authority, who hear voices in the air, are distilling their frenzy from some academic scribbles of a few years back." John Maynard Keynes, The General Theory (New York: Harcourt Brace, 1936), 383.
3. Edward Shils, "The Idea of the University: Obstacles and Opportunities in Contemporary Society," in The Calling of Education, 237-38 [reprinted from Minerva XXX/2 (Summer 1992), Kluwer Academic Publishers].
4. Tocqueville undertook usefully to define the extraordinary French term, moeurs. That word has so many and varied meanings that it has for nearly the whole of the nineteenth and twentieth centuries baffled commentators. Tocqueville, however, cut through the bafflement with an explicit definition of the term at the outset of his chapter, "Concerning the influence of morals in the preservation of the democratic republic in the United States." The definition Tocqueville provided was "habits of mind," which he specifically contrasted with those "habits of the heart" that might most characteristically be thought to be the meaning of moeurs. Tocqueville's point was to demonstrate what had happened to the world that had been altered by the écrivains—the intellectuals—who had transformed the world in the eighteenth century by a revolution that altered not politics only but also the "entire moral and intellectual condition of a people" (Tocqueville, De la démocratie en Amérique, vol. I, chapter IX, sec. 4).
5. Jacques Maritain, Education at the Crossroads (New Haven, CT: Yale University Press, 1943 [1978]), 6.
6. Adam Smith, An Inquiry into the Nature and Causes of the Wealth of Nations, "Of the Expence of the Institutions for the Education of Youth," edited by R. H. Campbell and A. S. Skinner (Indianapolis, IN: Liberty Classics, 1976), 764.

Introduction
The Multiversity at a Millennial Crossroads

A habit of mind is formed which lasts through life, of which the attributes are freedom, equitableness, calmness, moderation, and wisdom. . .
—John Henry Newman, *The Idea of a University*

In 1998 and 1999, the senior author, William B. Allen, served as director of the State Council of Higher Education for Virginia (SCHEV). In doing so he initiated a series of reforms, which are discussed in chapter 5 of this volume. These reforms were premised on several underlying assumptions, which are developed in the first four chapters. Virginia's experience is used, then, to illustrate an approach to educational reform. Or, to put it differently, had we not gone to Virginia, this book would not have been written.[1]

During the initial weeks of this tenure the Council gradually outlined its goals. First and foremost it aimed to instill as widely as possible a deeper understanding of and a new respect for liberal education within the Commonwealth of Virginia. The new administration planned to continue in-progress efforts to curtail the cost of higher education and, more importantly, to develop a rational basis for budgeting. It aimed to engage academic leaders, legislators, and policymakers in a serious conversation about what constitutes quality in higher education, and how to measure and reward it. Moreover, it aimed to reduce administrative bureaucracy and place academic decision-making in the hands of academic leaders, governed by well-informed, lay trustee boards. The director sought to lead the Commonwealth to a new level of understanding of, and in the spirit of George Washington, a renewed commitment to, a long-standing, implicit goal to make higher education available to all high school graduates. Last, and far from least, we asked at every possible opportunity that those concerned with planning, funding, overseeing, or delivering higher education in Virginia ask themselves, "What is the purpose of higher learning?"

1

The thirteen and a half months this project lasted produced a number of initiatives aimed at a comprehensive reform of higher education in Virginia. The Council developed an innovative proposal to replace the erratic, ad-hoc decision-making of the past four biennia with a rational process for developing and reviewing the colleges' and universities' budgets. Tied to this funding proposal was a plan—breath-taking in its scope—which promised to free academic leaders from the knots of administrative red-tape that bound their hands and limited innovation and excellence. The funding proposal included a sizeable component of "pay for performance," offering financial incentives for Virginia's institutions of higher learning to achieve new levels of excellence, year after year. One of the most creative aspects of the funding proposal was its intention to measure the quality of an institution not relative to its peers or based on reputation, but rather dynamically—that is, based on the extent to which the institution added value to student learning.

In addition to developing the funding proposal—possibly the key accomplishment during our tenure—and a plan for a new approach to approving academic programs, the Council also led a statewide process of developing a six-year strategic plan for higher education in the Commonwealth. Although the state code directs the Council of Higher Education to present such a plan to the governor and General Assembly every other year, no such plan had been developed for at least a decade. The strategic plan presented in April 1999 offered a glimpse of other radical changes to follow this initial effort. The most far-reaching aspect of the plan was its insistence that the Commonwealth has both a practical and a moral obligation to articulate and to realize the implicit promise it had long made to its citizens: namely that it would provide higher education to all high school graduates. The success of the nation in setting the high school diploma as the universal minimal standard for education during the twentieth century emboldened us to ask why we should not set a college degree as the universal minimal standard for education during the twenty-first century. Certainly there are indications that a college degree is already a requirement for the majority of occupations that offer a decent salary today, and this trend seems likely only to accelerate and widen in scope.[2] Yet few planners in Virginia or other states seem to take seriously the question of whether, how, and when they might set universal higher education (logical end of the multiversity) as a real and realizable goal for their citizenry. Fewer still have given serious thought to how to fund such widespread access.

This volume recreates the lively discussion of these and other questions by academic leaders, elected officials, planners, and politicians in the Commonwealth of Virginia. Often described by the media as "controversial," these discussions nevertheless were based on the premise that academic leaders and the lay boards that governed them could do more than simply play the political game of fund-seeking and the promotional game of media rankings. These discussions had as their foundation a firm belief in the urgent purpose of higher education and in the moral responsibility placed in the hands of those who would lead the academy.

The Story of Higher Education in Virginia: The Promise

To paraphrase former Governor Gerald Baliles, "Yes, Santa, there is a Virginia, a distinct polity, with a distinguished history. Not perfect, by any stretch, but always rich in possibilities. . ." Governor Baliles's apothegm illustrates especially well the history and future of Virginia higher education.[3] And he went on, in a celebration of Governor Mills Godwin, silently to prove his point about Virginia's imperfections and its promise in a dramatic misquotation of Thomas Jefferson's most intriguingly contentious assertion, that "the earth belongs to the living." "Life belongs to the living," Governor Baliles rather anti-climactically proclaimed, and "each generation of Virginians must accept its responsibility to the next," which was James Madison's retort to Jefferson's original thrust.

Thomas Jefferson, of course, founded the University of Virginia, acting as chair of the board of commissioners who planned the University and as Rector on its initial board of visitors. In designing the University Jefferson leaned heavily on James Madison, who led him to include *The Federalist Papers*, for example, along with the "Declaration of Independence," as fundamental documents to be used for instruction in the nature and structure of republican government.

The founding of the University of Virginia was the Commonwealth's first, fully conscious expression of a commitment to public education, primary and higher. It entailed a vision far broader than the vision for the University itself, one that has sustained the growth of a system that reflects remarkably well those original ambitions despite having been detoured by the "earthquake" of the War of the American Union and, since, the tortured history of Jim Crow and racial segregation.

If one examines this history with the eye of an evolutionist, one will be impressed with the extraordinary progress made toward a clear goal in somewhat less than two hundred years. That would be wrong and misleading, however, for the real story of Virginia, as with its now vibrant economy, is how much has been accomplished in not quite thirty years. That is, Virginia progressed principally since the era of "massive resistance," an era that carried anti-miscegenation statutes in the laws as late as 1967. It is only since the end of the 1960s that the entire community college system has been created, that the system of public colleges and universities has expanded sufficiently to make the promise of access for all citizens seem a real possibility, that Virginia's information technology industry emerged into national and world leadership, and that Virginia's public colleges and universities have come to be recognized as among the best in the country, public and private.

Nor does recognizing the most recent accomplishments of Virginia higher education imply neglect of prior accomplishments. The historically black colleges and universities played a unique role in preparing the citizen body that could advance beyond the early years of racial division and now undertake important efforts to realize a truly unified system of higher education.

Virginia today offers higher education for 350,000 students enrolled in public, private not-for-profit, and private for-profit institutions. Moreover, since the turn of the twentieth century, when only 3 percent of Virginians had attained any college education, we find over 50 percent of the adult citizens having had at least some college—a dramatic mushrooming not only of higher education but also of the role of higher education in shaping other aspects of Virginia life, including its robust economy and its increasing political sophistication.

From the beginning of the prior century (when the Virginia General Assembly finally began to embrace the goal for which Jefferson had so much labored in frustration: public support of education) to the present hour, Virginia has erected an educational foundation that bears all the insignia of cultural preservation and economic development. The growth of its institutions reflects this not only in continuing public support—which necessarily responds to the ups and downs of political and economic circumstances—but also in the increasing growth of private support for colleges and universities. As the 1996 report of the General Accounting Office relates, Virginia ranks sixth nationally in attracting private support for public institutions of higher education.[4] Today, billions of endowment dollars help to support its colleges and universities.

Her colleges and universities are also economic drivers, not only pumping $2.3 billion dollars into the economy every year, but also providing the knowledge basis for the increasingly important knowledge industries that drive economic growth. In the era in which business needs change with increasing frequency, the strengthening of educational fundamentals through continuous quality assessment, as well as the provision of unique skills, creates an effective spine along which run the nerve endings of economic progress.

That Virginia shook off the incubus of a troubled racial past and educational backwardness to produce such dramatic progress in not quite thirty years is a remarkable story, which tells far more about Virginia's prospects for the twenty-first century than its pre-1960s history could ever convey. For while Virginia began well with the leadership of true founders, that genius flowered elsewhere in the United States far more fully than it did in Virginia—at least until now. When Governor Baliles skillfully corrected Jefferson's apothegm into a life affirming commitment to Madison's version, he identified Virginia's best as Virginia's standard. The challenge for Virginia leadership in higher education is precisely to realize and accept the true account of its success and not an antebellum myth of Virginia's lost virtue.[5]

Virginia's "local" story is related to the national story and the global story, namely, to the emergence of the multiversity in response to deliberate public policies. In undertaking the arduous efforts we pursued in Virginia, we were highly conscious of the opportunity afforded the Commonwealth to make significant strides in providing in a coherent and progressive manner for the support of higher education. The evolving notion of the "charter university" expresses quintessentially the direction in which we pointed Virginia policy. Thus, chapter 2, "Excellence in Judgment," draws on the strength of our success in Virginia. In short, the two missions we undertook in Virginia continue, and we now seek to further those missions for higher education in general.

The Story of the Multiversity: The Reality

The century just ending produced the efflorescence of the modern university—the multiversity.[6] The flowering of the multiversity took the form of massive and constant differentiation. The aspects of life and learning in the multiversity are so many-sided that only with difficulty may one consistently identify the wholes to which the diverse parts or units belong. John Francis and Mark Hampton have aptly substituted the metaphor of a flotilla for the more familiar "great ship" metaphor to describe the modern university.[7] Their usage reminds us not only that the multiversity is constructed out of articulable or modular units, but also that it is still presumed to seek a common destination.[8] This presumption challenges Clark Kerr's view of a "confused. . .uneasy balance" in the research university.[9]

The century now opening poses the question whether a common destination or vision for the multiversity can survive the inertial momentum of large-scale differentiation. The millennial crossroads is defined as the choice between further differentiation (looking backward) and enhanced integration (looking forward).

We engaged all of Virginia higher education in posing this question in its several guises, and the chapters that follow reflect the nature of the multiple conversations and their suggestions for further connections.

This discussion is mindful of the particular economic and technological, in addition to educational, premises currently driving concern about the future of higher education. We do not, however, discuss these pressures programmatically for we believe that to speak of the multiversity requires the magnifier more than the telescope. Accordingly, this book develops contexts and visions and not merely prescriptions.

To illustrate how far we move away from the direction of parsing activities in university silos, we acknowledge in the first chapter, "An Idea of the University," that we are neither unfamiliar nor unconcerned with the educational "boutique"—the residential liberal arts college. We highlight it early in order plainly to identify the question this work does not purport to answer: whether there is a future for the liberal arts college per se. That institution clearly perceives and responds to the familiar pressures of the day, but it does so without internalizing the forces of differentiation (some would say disintegration) that beset the multiversity. Moreover, the liberal arts college may still depend on a reality that will not alter no matter how greatly we enlarge and redefine the market for higher education: the core constituency will continue well into the future as the cohort of 18 to 24 year olds for whom study "at college" in some form will be far preferable to study in the "virtual university" from Mom's and Dad's study.[10]

While we expect residential, liberal arts colleges to continue to struggle with changing economic scales and to encounter new sources of competition, we do not think the concerns addressed to the multiversity necessarily engage the liberal arts college. For that reason, we distinguish them clearly in the opening chapter, and proceed thereafter to address the world of the multiversity, which includes entire systems ranging from doctoral/research institutions to the community colleges that articulate with them.

Our discussion of the multiversity seeks to answer a few critical questions and to suggest a broad framework for reform. We begin in chapter 1 by acknowledging that the university today has lost all sense of any central, organizing idea of itself. We analyze the six major trends that have contributed to this confusion and offer, within that discussion, some general suggestions for restoring an idea of the university. Chapter 2 emphasizes that this work rests on the shoulders of academic leaders and hones in on the chief attribute needed in these leaders—excellence in judgment. We explain the centrality of excellence in judgment to the life of the university, arguing that its raison d'être is to develop such judgment. Further, we demonstrate the essential role of the curriculum in fostering excellence in judgment. Chapters 3 and 4 unfold the fusionist core of our vision of education reform. Chapter 3 focuses on access; it identifies the chief obstacles to access and offers broad recommendations for removing those obstacles. In chapter 4, the role of evaluation and assessment in fostering excellence is developed. Both chapters taken together convey our central message: the democratic university of the twenty-first century cannot choose between access and excellence but must deliver both. Chapter 5 describes how we embarked upon a plan to do so in Virginia. Finally, an "epilogue," chapter 6, illustrates fusionist rhetoric at work.

Before turning to our discussion of an idea of the university, it will be useful to focus on a specific aspect of our approach, which is not singled out elsewhere in the book, but which is foundational to our overall thinking.

One Coin Obverse and Reverse: Teaching and Research

We stand now more than a decade into the latest national conversation about the "crisis" of higher education. At this point it is fair to say that something of a consensus has emerged around a few central principles, namely: (1) excellence in undergraduate teaching requires to be re-emphasized and deepened into a controlling norm of university community; (2) teaching and research excellence need to be envisioned as reciprocal rather than competitive; (3) shared governance must be redefined to safeguard its centrality in the face of exigent standards of public accountability; (4) demands for public accountability will increase rather than recede; and (5) colleges and universities must accommodate an environment of evolving social, economic, and technological demands without sacrificing autonomy.

In the face of this impressive and well-documented orthodoxy may not a stray, contrarian voice be raised in the defense of the ivory tower and its unchanging central mission? We hope this may be so, lest the consensus of reform refigures the details of higher education at the cost of higher education itself. That is the danger implicit in neglecting the fact that education's central task is to address ignorance, which is a more powerful rationale than the work of assimilating cultural expectations. At the same time, and unfortunately, much of the evolved consensus aims to accomplish the latter, albeit without disparaging but nonetheless imperiling the former. To take the most powerful example, Robert Coles' researches that led to development of the concept of "learning communities" clearly preserve the work of addressing ignorance as an organizing conception.[11] At the same time, however, the specific reforms grafted onto this stock do not clarify the continuing relevance of intrinsic age-old concerns.

The following reflections invite reconsideration of what works and does not work in higher education. That goal leads to a contrarian view of some practices that have been called into question in the general discussion of the "crisis." We suggest that some expenditures now considered wasteful are not so, that some conceptions of discursive community actually fall short of producing one, that at least some organizational principles in the research university work to undermine the goal, and that in some respects what is too casually regarded as intellectual arrogance is a necessary shield of inquiry.

Jean de la Fontaine defended the moral fable as "making men better." In the fable called "Education" he described this as the work of cultivating their specific and intrinsic excellences as opposed to the work of encouraging their inclinations (which are merely responses to momentary temptations). Universities address ignorance to the same end, to cultivate specific and intrinsic excellences. For that reason, the single, unchallenged piety of higher education is the ubiquity of ignorance. Every learner presents herself as ignorance awaiting assault. The unique character of this piety is that it invites attack rather than worship.[12] Accordingly, the discursive community it fosters will be characterized less by the saccharine characteristics of tolerance and respect for others (though these belong) than by the robust, negative values of skepticism, redundancy, and remoteness (from the urgencies of generalized desire).

Likewise, the best faculty will adopt a probing, often skeptical approach to their teaching, an approach that Jacob and Noam Neusner aptly capture in their account of the "good teacher":

> What makes a good teacher, then, is clear. A good teacher is someone who can enter the mind of another person and bring life to the mind of that person. A good teacher does the work by arguing, pressing, asking questions, challenging answers, asking more questions. The life of the good teacher is expressed in giving life to ideas, imparting meaning to what appears to lie entirely beyond the intellect, making the obvious into a problem, turning the world of settled truths into an adventure. A good teacher is argumentative, disorderly, prepared for confrontation everywhere, all the time, with everyone, on everything—all for the sake of the vital mind, the freely inquiring spirit.[13]

Importance of the Negative Values

Although we have come to describe the university exclusively in terms of positive virtues (curiosity, intelligence, free inquiry, charity, etc), negative values play the critical role of directing its essential functions. They are the means to the ends that do, indeed, give rise to more positive virtues as their consequences.

It is skepticism about every piety—and all the prejudices with which learners enter their vocations—that produces the motivation to penetrate to the sources and true bearings of things. As such, the discursive community is better fostered wherever skepticism is practiced as a right—expected—rather than as the mere force of an extraordinary personality. To that end, the university can not go too far in support of skepticism. If the United States is generally regarded as the apogee of political progress, let it be challenged by radical inquiry into its foundations. If Martin Luther King, Jr. is universally embraced as a prophet, encourage every doubt of his wisdom. These are the moments from which universities crop their glories.[14]

Nor can such moments be so generally enjoyed without healthy doses of redundancy. For it takes different voices parsing Shakespeare to scare up meaningful discussion of the true bearings of his work. Learners must confront choices at every step of their inquiry in order to feel seriously the challenge of skepticism. Where one seminar in Shakespeare is good, two will always be better (though not always possible). The industrial model of reducing all processes to the fewest productive motions is inappropriate to higher education. Economies are imposed on universities by necessities. But a smarter choice is to calculate the fewer areas in which an institution can concentrate meaningful redundancies rather than to seek universal coverage of all areas of inquiry by unique iterations. Better Shakespeare done well than everything done poorly! Our current consensus drives us in the latter direction, thus universally sapping the soul of education rather than heightening the excellences that could well be differentially accomplished in different institutions.

So, too, it goes without saying that the university that is not going to serve every conceivable purpose (satisfy every putative stakeholder)—one that recognizes that to "make men better" in a few ways serves better than the commitment merely to "serve men better"—must benefit from a shield against the pressure to indulge every popular passion. There is no better shield than remoteness. Remoteness further serves the purpose of protecting the society from the robust conversations that must characterize a properly skeptical academy. Moreover, the faculty who must engender these conversations benefit from being called to account only by those who share in their vocation and are immediately affected by it. As Oakeshott expressed it, "a university is not a machine for achieving a particular purpose or producing a particular result; it is a manner of human activity."[15] The true learning community distinguishes among learners primarily by the length of their terms within the community. Call them customers or stakeholders if we must, but they are all really disciples for whom a special asylum—a gilded exile—has been created.

Gilding the Ivory

Most of the questions raised in the current atmosphere of crisis challenge us to defend the cost of conducting higher education in the manner it requires to be effective. Rather than to embrace cost-cutting as a principle (as opposed to a necessity), higher education needs an articulate defense of the ivory tower—one that can make manifest why even the ivory needs gilding.

To this end we begin by noticing that the defense of tenure on the basis of academic freedom fails to hit the mark. While tenure may incidentally foster a degree of candor, insofar as we mean by it to protect faculty from external accountability for opinions expressed, this conception concedes too much—namely, that the audience of academic discourse lies beyond the learning community. And insofar as we mean to protect faculty from one another, not only does tenure commonly fail to deliver, but it assumes a learning community in which vocation—the moral relation in which disciples stand to one another—inadequately structures their interactions.

On the other hand, where tenure represents a specific economic trade-off in which faculty opt for long-term gains over higher, short-term gains, tenure works (functionally securing a desirable remoteness and a stable community of discourse). That is, we must pay something to entice the needed, long-term members of the learning community to participate, and tenure is the price that we fittingly pay.[16]

The economic defense of tenure presupposes, of course, that decisions here are made in the market place—at the margin—and that, accordingly, compensation ought to reflect the price pressures that prevail in the market. Thus, not only ought faculty to be enticed into the ivory tower, but that should be done by means of relatively competitive and hence, richer, compensation. As noted above, tenure is one element of that enhanced richness. Naturally, in such circumstances performance reviews (every contract has two sides) would be normal. Nevertheless, for more than three decades "accountability has been a suspect term to academics, in whose interest it is to embrace the term."[17]

Similarly, if redundancy is a key value, it will follow that the cost must be accepted.[18] While it is true that one person can teach Shakespeare to a single class of forty students, the gilding that will offer two classes of twenty students more surely serves the mission to "make men better." It provides the means more surely to constitute the learning community. The competition of ideas within the academy is necessary apart from competition of goods within the marketplace.

Finally, the operational aspects of the university must perform consistently with the goal in view. Since the university—the learning community—is not designed as a place to repair for momentary consumption or use, thence to return to the comforts of home, it must be so built as to make it possible for people to be at home within it. Conversations that spill from classroom into "living room" do so only where adequate spaces for living are maintained. It requires capital expenditures and conscious design to maintain such spaces—just as it does to assure that classrooms harbor rather than obstruct conversations.[19]

Auxiliary resources will be no less affected. In an era in which it becomes increasingly clear that the library must benefit from clear-headed thinking to fulfill its central role in this large mission, not only must money be spent on "information technologies" that capture the functions of libraries less dependent on central housing, but also the evolving role of the whole library as a "special collection" will necessitate more spending. As the "circulating" function of the library migrates more and more to electronic and bookstore forums, the library will focus more and more on the unique uses that benefit from central housing. Designed interactions with specially valued text sources play a key role in higher education. More and more the entire library must serve as only smaller special collections departments have served before, intensifying the use but augmenting the costs. This gilding is part of building the tower itself, and central to the mission of the university, as we suggest in the epilogue.

The Future University

The learning community built on the foregoing model offers a distinctive characteristic in the context of current conversations: there emerges no viable distinction between teaching and research. Teaching and research are not merely reciprocal but identical in this model. For the particular discourse privileged in this model demands the one no less than the other. To be sure, certain "industrial," "assembly line" approaches present in the research university are excluded from the discussion in these terms (even in equipment dependent technological areas of research and study). But that is just another way to say that research universities must avoid the category error that holds that whatever a university performs is intrinsic to the mission of a university.

When we try to identify every component activity of the university—Therbligizing—as a key to dealing with the present crisis, we end by demystifying teaching (treating it as no more than one function among others). That is what leads us to imagine that it is separable from research. When, instead, we reason from the central mission, we gain indirectly the power to distinguish essential from non-essential activities (which is not to say that nonessential activities, from accelerators to zoospheres, are not of value). The upshot of this observation is modestly to suggest that different management principles may be appropriate for functions truly different. In the larger business organization that is the university, it may be appropriate to distinguish meaningfully the educational from the industrial endeavors. When we have done so, we will finally have arrived at a true understanding of the distinction between teaching and research in the multiversity: obverse and reverse of the single coin, education.

Notes

1. Whereas his predecessor left office by publishing a screed in which he questioned the competence and seriousness of his employers, William Allen rather believed, upon his withdrawal, that he retained the capacity and authority to speak to the aims of higher education. Gordon K. Davies, "Education is Not a Trivial Business, a Private Good, or a Discretionary Expenditure; It is a Deeply Ethical Undertaking at which We Must Succeed if We Are to Survive as a Free People: Twenty Years of Higher Education in Virginia" (Richmond: State Council of Higher Education for Virginia, 1997), <http://www.schev.edu/wumedia/gordon.html>. (April 13, 2001).

2. Robert Zemsky, Susan Shaman, and Maria Ianozzi, "In Search of Strategic Perspective: A Tool for Mapping the Market in Post-Secondary Education," Change (November/December 1997): 23.

3. Gerald L. Baliles, "In Mills Godwin's Legacy: Lessons for Today's Virginians," The Virginia Newsletter 74 (July 1998): 4.

4. Higher Education: Tuition Increasing Faster Than Household Income and Public Colleges' Cost (Washington, D.C.: General Accounting Office, August 1996), 43-44.

5. It was a great personal disappointment when we were forced by the Council in Virginia to delete candid references to "Jim Crow" and the "Civil War" from the principle strategic document in which it was important to cite the history. The decision reflected a distasteful squeamishness we had not expected at that date.

6. We use the term as it was given currency, though not first introduced, by Clark Kerr. Clark Kerr, The Uses of the University, 3d. ed. (Cambridge: Harvard University Press, 1982), 135-50.

7. John Francis and Mark Hampton, "Resourceful Responses: The Adaptive Research University and the Drive to Market," The Journal of Higher Education 70 (November/December 1999): 625-642.

8. We presume a common destination despite the fact of an origin and development which, we suspect, "just growed that way," Topsy-like. For as Christopher Lucas observes: "The hegemony of the multiversity as a regulative idea is well-nigh complete, but its preeminence does not seem to have come about as the outcome of principled decisions or any discernible process of rational choice. On the contrary, it appears to have been the inevitable result of an academic system seeking to garner popular support by attempting, in most times and places to be all things to all people." Christopher J. Lucas, Crisis in the Academy: Rethinking Higher Education in America (New York: St. Martin's Press, 1996), xiv.

9.   "A university anywhere can aim no higher than to be as British as possible for the sake of undergraduates, as German as possible for the sake of graduate [students] and research personnel, as American as possible for the sake of the public at large—and as confused as possible for the sake of the preservation of the whole uneasy balance" (Kerr, 1982: 18).

10.   Cf. Zemsky et al., 1997: 36. Their model of market segmentation authoritatively demonstrates the solidity of the market for residential, liberal education. "At the other end of the spectrum is the 'brand name' part of the market, dominated by rite-of-passage students. . . . they attend full-time, living in on-campus residences. . . . What these students and their parents purchase are holistic experiences, . . . which are preparatory experiences in their continuing pursuit of extended education."

11.   Robert Coles, The Call of Service: A Witness to Idealism (Boston: Houghton Mifflin Co., 1993). " Coles's method of imparting moral truths through service learning is to assign some of the classic works of enduring writers and then send his students into the community." OP-ED, The Washington Post (1 April 1995, Saturday, Final Edition): A15.

12.   In which spirit the "mission" of Brigham Young University, quoting Joseph Smith, takes on still deeper and more urgent meaning: "Thy mind, O Man! if thou wilt lead a soul unto salvation, must stretch as high as the utmost heavens, and search into and contemplate the darkest abysses, and the broad expanse of eternity—thou must commune with God." Brigham Young University, The Mission of Brigham Young and the Aims of a BYU Education (Provo, UT: BYU, 1955), 4.

13.   Jacob Neusner and Noam M. M. Neusner, Reaffirming Higher Education (New Brunswick, NJ: Transaction Publishers, 2000), 2.

14.   "Universities are uniquely placed to have opportunity to teach these future leaders how to think honestly and clearly, how to deal with problems in an intelligent and responsible way without resorting to unexamined ideologies or prejudices. A failure of the university to cultivate thinking skills in students and faculty is a lapse in its community responsibility." Noel B. Reynolds, "On the Moral Responsibilities of Universities," in Dennis L. Thompson, ed., Moral Values and Higher Education: A Nation at Risk (Provo, UT: Brigham Young University Press, 1991), 99-100.

15.   Michael Oakeshott, "The Idea of a University," in Timothy Fuller, ed., The Voice of Liberal Learning: Michael Oakeshott on Education (New Haven, CT: Yale University Press, 1989), 96.

16.   Economist Charles Smith speaks to this understanding of tenure in a way that is rarely encountered. Acknowledging that "Few academic practices have been more fiercely and universally attacked as academic tenure," Smith nevertheless goes on to build a cogent case for it as an "unfunded fringe benefit," whose benefits greatly outweigh its costs. Charles W. Smith, Market Values in American Higher Education: The Pitfalls and Promises (Lanham, MD: Rowman & Littlefield Publishers, Inc., 2000), 32-35.

17.   "The demand for and the reaction against accountability will continue to produce tension in higher education. The general public and the various constituencies of the university will continue to demand accountability in the abstract. The task facing higher education practitioners is to define accountability in acceptable terms and provide measures for accountability which will benefit students, provide for critical scholarship and offer better service to society." Lynn W. Lindemann, "Why Faculty Object to Accountability in Higher Education," Liberal Education 60 (May 1974): 179.

18.   Nor may the cost of such redundancy, or of a college education in its totality, be so great as is often represented. Smith compares the cost of various types of postsecondary education such as the training provided by the United States armed forces and that offered to business executives and finds that even the "least expen-

sive" of these programs costs more than the "$1,250 a week at the most expensive private colleges" (Smith, 2000: 4-8).

19.   The point here is not particular to the residential or brand-name college. It is no less pertinent to the world of on-line universities, which require effective electronic forums for each class in order genuinely to invoke the dynamic of the learning community.

1

An Idea of the University

Nel mezzo del cammin di nostra vita
mi ritrovai per una selva oscura,
che la diritta via era smarrita.
In the middle of the journey of our life I found
myself in a dark wood,
for the straight way was lost.
—Dante, *The Divine Comedy of Dante Alighieri*

A growing number of friends and critics of higher education, within and outside the academy, have lately concluded that the colleges and universities in this country have lost their way. Too many campuses wander about in a dark wood—mistaking workforce preparation as their chief goal, seizing technology as their primary strategy for successful competition, lowering academic standards in a misguided belief that access and excellence are incompatible goals, and pandering to those who would teach prejudice under the guise of multiculturalism. Surely such institutions are in need of a compass—one might even say a moral compass—if they are to find their way back to the light, back to the original destination.[1]

But what is the destination? Do we, either as a society or as a profession, have a common understanding of the aims of higher education? Many would answer, "No," as does Christopher Lucas: "...if there is a true crisis in American higher education today, it is chiefly a crisis of purpose."[2] We must start the work of rebuilding our moral compass, which is to say the work of fusing what appear to be opposite poles into a single axis around which educational thinking can revolve, by laying "bare the questions hidden by the answers."[3]

We might most fruitfully begin by asking why we care about education in the first place.

17

What is the Value of Liberal Education?

We care about education on account of the young. Although we accustom ourselves to speaking of the contribution education makes to our lives, our economy, and our civic practices, we actually mean to avow an unconditional commitment to posterity—to lives, economies, and civic practices that we adults will know only indirectly at best. It is worthwhile to ponder why one generation forms this bond with succeeding generations.

The most prominent version of the commitment to posterity has been conveyed in the Preamble to the United States Constitution, in which "we the people" pray for the "Blessings of Liberty" not only for "ourselves" but also for "our posterity." Unborn successors always formed part of that larger conception, society, in the minds of the architects of American nationhood.

Our posterity takes place first as our young, our offspring, and in a moral community all the young are our offspring. When we pray for their future accomplishments we pray not to prescribe them but to ready the young to accomplish them as their own work. That is the reason our prayers take the form of provision for their education. We see in the education of the young the only gift we have that properly expresses our unconditional love. We know that before they can enjoy the "Blessings of Liberty" they must first enjoy liberty. Nor can they enjoy or benefit from liberty unless their souls first grow into able agents. They must grow to govern themselves, to attain such moral command of themselves as to be at liberty to structure their lives in accord with the "Blessings of Liberty."

If we, the present generation, perform our work well, our posterity will perpetuate the way of life we know not because they will have inherited it from us but because they will see and embrace its virtue. Accordingly, this very abstract account of the reason we care about education is, in fact, the most concrete way we have to remind ourselves of what we seek in building schools, faculties, education partners, and communities in which the young see themselves as both cared for and directed.

Try to imagine writing a letter to a young friend or relative, providing guidance for his future educational choices. Then, the particular things you might say to him will manifest the general principles we have developed here. For example, you might say to a youth that education would provide valued skills, extensive knowledge, and enduring discipline to serve throughout life. However, it is still more likely that you would discuss the acquisition of character and judgment that would strengthen the youth's confidence in his own decisions. The cultivation of good habits of decision on sound moral and religious grounds is the single most important gift that education conveys. Insofar as we are able to offer such a gift, we have a moral duty to do so. The best schools, the best education, provide exactly such a gift.

Chapter 2, "Excellence in Judgment," stresses that the chief productive goal, or outcome of education is proficient humanity, which is characterized by excellence in judgment. The work of developing excellent judgment is fundamentally the work of replacing prejudice and accepted notions of the world and oneself with the capacity to see beyond the ground on which one stands, and even to comprehend within one's vision one's own ground, one's own prejudices, one's own point of view. In fact, you might go so far as to say that your education doesn't amount to a hill of beans unless it gives you the power to look at yourself with a penetrating, critical eye, to understand why you stand where you stand and why you do what you do. James Baldwin describes the centrality of judgment to the work of higher education with these words:

> The purpose of education, finally, is to create in a person the ability to look at the world for himself, to make his own decisions, to say to himself this is black or this is white. To ask questions of the universe, and then to learn to live with those questions, is the way he achieves his own identity.[4]

Our aim is not just to inform students, but also to help form them. We have no trouble recognizing that young children are not fully developed. We readily accept that a major function of elementary and secondary education is to contribute to the overall growth and maturation of these students. We sometimes overlook, however, that the 18-to-24-year-old youths, who still constitute the majority of undergraduate enrollment at four-year colleges, are yet in their formative years.

The challenge of undergraduate education is to stimulate our students' growth in both intellect and character. It is not enough to fill their heads with knowledge and skills. By the time they graduate, our students should feel that their education has challenged every segment of their being. And, the best way we know to offer students this challenge is through a robust, liberal education—one that exposes students, with appropriate depth, to a general education in literatures, mathematics, history, science, philosophy, and the arts.

A growing number of colleges and universities across the nation have recently re-embraced the notion that one of the fundamental purposes of education, including higher education, is to create the informed citizenry that is the bedrock of our democracy. Often this notion is taken up under the rubric of "service learning," although it takes other forms as well. Yet at many, and perhaps most, institutions, this vital connection between education and democracy is overlooked in practice, however much it may be touted in college catalogs and mission statements, which still speak of "preparing students for responsible citizenship" and "developing future leaders." It was surprising to encounter this phenomenon even in Virginia, where statesmen such as Washington, Jefferson, and Madison articulated the connection between education and democracy from the very founding of this nation.

Our public discourse about higher education too seldom touches on this connection. And, as we describe more fully in chapter 2, an earlier age than ours expected that the work of making youth ready to participate in our deliberative democracy would be substantially completed by the end of their secondary education. Yet just as the colleges and universities of this age have had to shoulder remedial education in such basics as composition and mathematics, there seems to be a need for them to provide remedial civic education as well.

As Jeffrey Wallin, president of the American Academy for Liberal Education, writes, the purpose of liberal education with regard to civic education is "neither to venerate nor to subvert, but rather to inquire about the most important matters, regardless of where answers to them may lead."[5] Our aim must be to help students grow in intellect and character so that they are "well able to engage in the most serious issues we face as men and women and as citizens: What is the best way of life? What is the best regime?" Surely the rising generation will face unforeseen challenges and opportunities as they fashion their own answers to these vital questions. And they may surprise us by answering these questions in unexpected ways.

If they are fortunate, our students will also encounter the unexpected in the evolution of their own interior lives. We aim, through a liberal education, to convey to students that an "examined life" is the only sort worth living. We point them toward the philosophic, literary, artistic, scientific, religious, and political avenues they might travel to grow in understanding of themselves and the world around them. In this journey toward understanding, the most important of our lifelong learning pursuits, we learn not by treading the safe waters of the known but by venturing into the unknown, perhaps even by seeking the unknowable. The best gift we can offer our students is to start them on this odyssey. We may hope, in return, to hear from our students an appreciation like that Susan Saltrick expressed in a talk she gave to a regional technology, teaching, and learning roundtable in November 1997. "My teachers gave me the world; and they honed my faculties to appreciate it, and in doing so, they gave me myself."[6] But whether or not we hear such appreciation from our students—or from others—we can take satisfaction in knowing ourselves the enduring value of our work and in seeing its cumulative expression in the lives of successive generations.

The value of liberal learning not only endures but increases throughout our lives. James O. Freedman, former president of Dartmouth University, conveyed something of the value of a liberal education when he wrote:

> A liberal education acquaints students with the cultural achievements of the past and prepares them for the exigencies of an unforeseeable future. . .
>
> [A] liberal education conveys to students a sense of joy in learning—joy in participating in the life of the mind; joy in achieving competence and mastery; joy in entering the adult world of obligations, intimacies and relationships; joy in engaging in the converse among our several generations.[7]

Why Have We Not Realized the Value of Liberal Education?

Put most simply, we fail today to realize the value of liberal education because we have lost sight of the *idea* of the university. The staggering growth of American colleges and universities through processes of accretion and differentiation during the past century brought with it so many new markets and missions that our universities have, by and large, forgotten their true purpose—their original destination. It is outside the scope of this book to analyze every development that has led to this consequence; however, six trends stand out:

1. The notion that the primary purpose of a college education is to prepare students for careers.[8]

2. Over-reliance on technology as the main tool for improving student learning and for enhancing the competitiveness of the institution.

3. A lowering of academic standards, mistakenly adopted as the means for expanding access to college.

4.   A preference for measuring quality based on inertial growth rather than dynamic growth.

5.   An incoherent curriculum, particularly within the general education program.

6.   A perverse emphasis on multiculturalism and diversity in all aspects of the college experience.

Each of these trends has damaged the core of the university. Some analysis of their impact must precede our discussion of how to restore an idea of the university.

Work to Live, or Live to Work?

John Kenneth Galbraith had it right when he predicted that, at the end of the twentieth century, universities would become what banks were at its beginning—the major suppliers of the nation's most needed source of capital.[9] Throughout the nation, colleges and universities compete to generate that capital, and to capture increased revenue in the process. Even before Gary Becker first identified the economic return (in the form of higher wages) on the student's investment in a college education, the academy had begun an inexorable expansion of its role in preparing young men and women for careers. As community colleges became major providers of postsecondary education and as the Perkins Act and successive United States legislation provided funds earmarked for vocational education, colleges and universities significantly ramped up the work force preparation aspect of their work. During the past decade, the clamor from business and industry for employees with computer expertise and other technological skills spurred the academy into new and ever closer alignment with employers, and still greater emphasis on the vocational aspects of collegiate study.

While it may be true that what is good for General Motors is good for a country, it does not necessarily follow that what is good for training automobile mechanics to work on today's computerized vehicles is good for the college curriculum. W. E. B. DuBois cautioned educators about this underlying tension between vocational education and liberal education early in the century when he urged college faculty to impress upon their students the truth that:

... life is more than living—that, necessary as it is to earn a living, it is more necessary and important to earn a life; that is to do for the world—its thought, its aspiration, its human value—so much that the world will not always continue to ask if life is worth living.[10]

The first-time students entering college this fall will have careers that extend well into the fourth decade of the twenty-first century. They are likely to lead active, productive lives well beyond the year 2050. These young women and men not only will constitute the work force, they will be the political and religious leaders, artists and scholars, citizens, and parents whose thoughts and actions will shape this century. Their college education must do more than simply equip them with a set of vocational skills whose half-lives may be shorter than the duration of a politician's latest promises.

Those who would mold the college curriculum to fit current, pressing needs for specific technological skills would do well to remember how quickly these specific needs can change. Consider for example, these two predictions, which were not nearly so accurate as that of Galbraith's. In 1943, Thomas Watson foresaw a world market that would need no more than five computers. Forty years later, Bill Gates stated confidently that "640 K ought to be enough for anyone." Hutchins limned the inherent limits of providing job training under the guise of a college education:

> My contention is that the tricks of the trade cannot be learned in a university, and that if they can be they should not be. They cannot be learned in a university because they get out of date and new tricks take their place, because the teachers get out of date and cannot keep up with current tricks, and because tricks can be learned only in the actual situation in which they can be employed.[11]

Education—as opposed to job training—should last a lifetime. It should carry graduates successfully through the whitewater rapids of technological and economic change. Further, education must prepare our youth not only for a life of work, but also for the work of life.

The truth is that if we adopt a fusionist approach, we do not really need to choose between educating students for life and for work. A strong liberal education will equip students with the important skills they will need in the workplace. A liberal education will develop students' skills in speaking, writing, thinking critically, and reasoning ethically, along with other skills that employers across many job sectors say are essential.[12] Even those who emphasize career preparation in collegiate education recognize the central importance of the broad skills and abilities that liberal education has long conveyed. For example, Craig Swenson, then vice president of the University of Phoenix, cites these as the skills our graduates need to become "productive as knowledge workers": "the ability to write clearly and persuasively, to articulate and present ideas to others orally, to work capably and in group and team settings, and to analyze and think critically about problems."[13]

More important still, a liberal education will also guide students in developing the excellence in judgment that can lead to proficient humanity. Billy Wireman, the president of Queens College, aptly describes the dual and blended transformation that liberal education offers:

> Two concepts are keys to the future of the human race: productive careers and noble lives. We must design academic programs and institutions, which unite the two powerful ideas and use them to transform our students' lives. Either concept, alone, is an orphan. Together, they can become a forceful theme for liberal education in the 21st century.[14]

It is our hope that liberal education may yet become the theme and destination of higher education in the twenty-first century, and the chief purpose of this book is to advance that hope.

We do not deny that there remain many excellent liberal arts colleges and a number of comprehensive universities, which offer students a liberal education of this nature. Tucked within the residential college programs at some research universities, similar opportunities can be found. Nevertheless, the sad truth is that the majority of colleges and universities at all levels—from community colleges to doctoral/research institutions—offer students only the slimmest exposure to liberal education. Campuses today chiefly attempt to offer this limited exposure to liberal education through the general education curriculum. However, as is explained in more depth in chapter 2, the structure and content of most general education programs are ill-designed to nurture a student's growth in judgment.

A Fruitful Tension

We believe the chief reason many perceive a tension between practical and liberal education derives from the third aim of the 1862 Morrill Act. But these tensions have been dramatically resolved in some instances. One example is Virginia State University, which as a historically black institution and as a land-grant university is grounded in two important emancipations within American education. The nation's HBCUs (Historically Black Colleges and Universities) tell an important story about the stunning rate at which exslaves, so soon after slavery, launched themselves into paths of education. The schools that followed—pre-collegiate and collegiate—grew at an unparalleled pace as long pent-up energies and curiosities broke free. Within thirty years, we went from virtually none to more than one hundred and twenty HBCUs—and America found students and professors to fill them. One such student was Emma B. Delaney, who put the education she had earned to use in missionary service in Africa by the opening of the twentieth century.

The early success stories of these colleges were marred by the chapters written by the Jim Crow laws that followed. Although Jim Crow impoverished black higher education as it did so many other dimensions of black life, black colleges continued to offer students a wealth of learning. Throughout their history, and to this day, the black colleges of the United States have given more than just degrees to their students. As Samuel D. Proctor describes in his essay on "Land-Grant Universities and the Black Presence," HBCUs have offered their students "dignity, overlook, overview, perspective and fortitude."[15]

The story of the land-grant vision within American education is a compelling one. Not yet fully realized, the educational and political ideals that shaped Justin Morrill's vision when he introduced the original land-grant legislation in 1857 can and should inspire us yet today. He modeled that Act on Michigan State University, where the daughters and sons of ordinary American families could receive the benefits of a rigorous liberal education and flower into works of genius.

> Signed into law in 1862—at a time when the United States was in the midst of a fratricidal war—the Morrill Act had three purposes: First, to train the manpower needed in a swiftly developing industrial nation; second, to open up postsecondary education to those who were part of what was called at that time "the industrial class;" and, third, to guarantee that all classes of society had the opportunity to receive an excellent education. What was meant by an "excellent education" was the opportunity to pursue a liberal arts education rather than to be limited to vocational training. [16]

Over 130 years later, these three purposes—workforce development, access to education, and quality education—continue to be defining goals for higher education. Virginia State University has been dedicated to achieving these purposes from the time of its founding in 1882 through the addition of a land-grant purpose to its mission in 1920 and up to this day, despite encountering obstacles that have at times blocked it from fully achieving the goals.

The Morrill Act, which was amended in 1890 to provide support for black institutions, envisioned a curriculum that would combine liberal and practical education. There is a built-in tension between these dual aims that has at times been a source of conflict within the land-grant mission. This same tension has, at other times, been a source of creative vigor.

Maxwell Goldberg describes this "fruitful tension" as the "great ongoing dialectic between liberal arts and other educative components" within the land-grant system. He goes on to say:

> In spite of this historical and logical contradiction...the paradox "liberal and practical" works in actual operation. It has proved an effective formula for implementing the great historical venture to which American higher education committed itself, namely, to combine the personal and social strengths and benefits characteristic of an aristocratic society at its best with the corresponding strengths and benefits characteristic of an egalitarian society at its best. This paradox is summed up in the Jeffersonian ideal of a natural aristocracy of character and intellect...[17]

Education that is worth its name lasts a lifetime and indeed develops one's appetite and aptitude to become a lifelong learner. We do a great disservice to our students if we focus too much on developing specific job-related skills. These skills will have shorter and shorter half-lives as the rate of technological change continues to accelerate. For many students today, the general education program is their primary exposure to the aims and programs of liberal education. It is, therefore, vital to form a coherent, shared understanding of those aims. The aims certainly may, and should, vary from one institution to another. But these aims should be based on objective principles that may be judged by independent observers.

Developing this shared understanding of the aims for general education is an essential step toward raising academic standards. While we have never ceased to claim academic excellence as our standard, published research and our own experience tell us that American higher education has experienced a decline in acceptable levels of accomplishment across broad subject areas. Restoring excellence as our standard will require a team effort within and across institutions. It is the theme of this book.

Fire, Not Tricks

We are now two decades into higher education's frenzied love affair with technology, and there is no indication that the passion has cooled, nor that it is likely to do so. The promise of the moment may fade and mutate: from the early, unrealized expectation that technology would save money (or, at least, reduce the rate at which costs escalate), to the still fervent conviction that technology will improve student learning, to the latest dream that nearly every institution of higher education has the potential to capitalize on its faculty's talent by developing and selling the "killer" distance education course in a given subject. But, the underlying belief that technology is the number one survival strategy persists, unaffected by any evidence to the contrary or by the wisdom of the faculty.

Our message is not that of the Luddite. Technology is not only inescapable in today's world, but offers much to us as individuals and as a society. The academy correctly takes up its responsibility to prepare students not only to use technology but to use it wisely—to understand its transformative capacity and to mold it to our purposes rather than allowing it to shape us unawares.

The dangerous opportunities of technology must be exploited within as well as outside the academy. These opportunities include accessing voluminous information in library databases and on the Worldwide Web, harnessing the power of the computer for research and analysis, modeling laboratory experiments online, and connecting students and scholars worldwide. As a report from one technologically advanced institution (Virginia Tech University) points out, advanced technology, if used correctly, can "free faculty for students, not from them." Similarly, technology should enable us to intensify rather than to replace the traditional strengths of academic capital. Our library collections, for example, can become more rather than less significant learning opportunities, freed by online methodologies to operate almost entirely as special collections centers. Such centers would reinforce the importance of the bookish arts—where the study of books, their contents and their production, can take center stage—beyond the superficial search for supportive references (a task easily relegated to online resources).

Through avenues such as these, faculty and students put technology to use *in support of* teaching and learning. We underscore the words "in support of." We ought never lose sight of the understanding that technology is a means to an end, not an end in itself. For all the exciting opportunities that these new technologies offer to enhance learning, we do well to remember Parker Palmer's admonition that "Tips, tricks, techniques are not the heart of education—fire is."[18]

That fire is to be found in the dialog between text and reader, between teacher and student, between student and student, and—especially when faculty come together to debate and forge the curriculum—between teacher and teacher. That fire can be found in the dialog between past and present, when—in the best tradition of a liberal arts education—we introduce students to the voices of the past as well as the present. That fire leaps forth when we kindle in ourselves and in our students the appetite for discovery and reflection, the desire to seek the truth, and the determination to know ourselves in the context of a conversation that spans ages no less than communities.

Our souls must be ignited by the fire of knowledge and heated by the passion for liberty and truth it inspires, and our characters must be forged by industry, discipline, and the desire to learn if we are to achieve proficient humanity. The best way we know to light these fires is through liberal education.

Excellence *and* Access: Taking the Final Step in Raising Academic Standards[19]

Carolynn Reid-Wallace, a member of the Boyer Commission on Undergraduate Learning, writes that

> . . .the sort of defeatism that makes some people reluctant to enforce high academic standards is premised on a false dichotomy between access and excellence. Specifically, many assume that achieving excellence requires limiting access for low-income and minority children, and that providing access requires compromising excellence. These people are wrong. Access and excellence are in no way antithetical—they represent two noble goals that are both worthy of our best efforts.[20]

It is necessary, however, to distinguish strictly between the impact of mere numbers and the true impact of democracy upon formal education—namely, democracy separates the tacit and unnecessary identification of aristocratic merit with formal credentials. Thus, the observation by Leo Strauss that identifies liberal education with aristocracy does not directly oppose Reid-Wallace's observations:

> Liberal education [here and now] is the counterpoison to mass culture, to the corrupting effects of mass culture. . . . Liberal education is the necessary endeavor to found an aristocracy within democratic mass society. Liberal education reminds those members of a mass democracy who have ears to hear of human greatness.[21]

Reid-Wallace's analysis emerged in a consideration of the latest of the series of educational reform movements that have consistently punctuated American life. Of this last reform movement, though, she speculated that enthusiasm for reform was flagging. Perhaps it is true that the spirit of reform has flagged, but there has certainly been no remission in the appearance of works urging continued reflection. Most notably, those works have addressed some form of the question of "liberal education," the "core curriculum," or "general education." While it is true that education for a "global economy" receives its due share of ink or binary code, it remains the case that most informed commentary focuses on questions of general education. The reason for this is not hard to discern—education that is worth its name lasts for a lifetime.

Even a cursory review of recent titles reveals that the regularly recurring "crisis" of higher education marks our era no less than previous ones. Since the publication of *The Closing of the American Mind*, however, the conversation has bogged down over collateral issues perhaps best summed up in the expression, "culture wars." It is useful to reflect, therefore, that there are educational questions inherent in the debate that transcend the question of whose political ox is being gored. Among those questions none demands closer attention than the question of the adequacy of undergraduate learning. It would be foolish to haggle over "scientific" demonstration of the proposition when something so nearly like a consensus exists that we have experienced a decline in acceptable levels of accomplishment across broad subject areas. The more serious discussion of the current "crisis," therefore, ought to reconsider the demands we make upon our students—our expectations.

This does not mean simply making subjects like foreign languages, science, mathematics, or English more rigorous. It also means expanding what is taught in these subjects. It is not enough to learn the grammar and syntax of a foreign language; one must learn to speak the language fluently, and one must read great literature written in that language. Moreover, it is not enough for American students to explore the history and culture of foreign nations without a solid grounding in the history and culture of Western civilization.[22]

In the broad discussion of general education, it appears ambiguous whether folk mean a full-fledged liberal education or only some condensed version of what students would have received if they had pursued a full-fledged liberal education. This perhaps explains the standoff between advocates of "multiculturalism" and advocates of "Western civilization." There may be fewer questions of intellectual merit at stake (though there are surely some such questions) and more questions of depth and adequacy of coverage. Advocates of Western civilization certainly cannot say that they oppose "multiculturalism" inasmuch as so-called "Western civilization" is the true and original model of all multiculturalism. It would be very difficult indeed to conceive of an argument for the study of Western civilization that did not engage Western civilization's very pronounced and consistent exploration of world cultures. In fact, we can think of no model of multiculturalism at all that does not originate in fundamental premises, principles, or practices of Western civilization.[23]

This example should illustrate the nature of the question of education reform in our time. Insofar as we have been hesitant to embrace any full-throated articulation of educational goals because of anxieties regarding their collateral implications, then we have denied ourselves the opportunity to go as far as we might go toward assuring excellence. That is the reason we have deliberately used in the title of this section the expression "final step." That word, "final," is a red flag, designed to challenge people who defend themselves against all possible infection from supposed "absolutes" to rethink what is their best defense. Human ambition, at its best, aims for the most complete accomplishment, even while recognizing human fallibility. A premature decision to ignore any expression of complete ambition is tantamount to lowering levels and standards of exertion. It is far better to hear the word "truth" and retain one's ability to think than to shield one's ears from the word and lose the ability to think.

So, too, in education it is better to contemplate "perfections" and learn to recognize "failures" than to fail without acknowledgment because we refuse to entertain perfection. The practical implication of this apothegm is that higher education needs to delve more deeply into the discussion of undergraduate learning. Among the things to be noted, most certainly, is that this will remain the core of higher education. It does not diminish the significance of the research university to observe that its foundation is still the undergraduate program. Further, we must admit that our goal to make access virtually universal has challenged us to seek new ways to assure that standards of accomplishment can and will be met despite the variable preparations of students.

That the students graduating from high schools across the nation have received variable preparation for collegiate study is indisputable. Too many youngsters obtain the high school diploma without obtaining or demonstrating the knowledge and skills that the diploma ought to certify. In the face of this fact, we only want to ask a simple question: Have we bothered to ask our youngsters to do more? To rise to the greatest challenges? We may seem simplistic, and we do not mean to. But we have learned through time that the very young almost invariably respond to direct requests to perform at high levels. We have also found that they must be asked, directly. It will not do to categorize and program them. One must rather, and quite literally, put before them the large ambition, if one wants the joy of seeing their souls expand. When, then, students arrive at college less prepared than we wish to see them, we do not shrink from starting them where they should have been instead of merely where they are—although this gets harder as we age.

Students need and deserve to be challenged in their collegiate study, whether or not they have been fortunate enough to have been pushed to do their best during their elementary and secondary schooling. Nothing has so much deflected us from the task of challenging students to perform at the highest levels than the fear of failure. More specifically, we have bought the false hope that to protect our students from the fear of failure would reinforce in them a feeling of competence. In fact, nothing builds the feeling of competence so much as the recognition of high standards and working tirelessly to achieve them.

The senior author often remarks that he shall never forget the first year student who failed his course, "What is Political Power," a course reported in a national publication as the "toughest" at Harvey Mudd College. So stunned was this high school "A" student with high SAT scores that he returned to the course the next year determined to pass. And he did so, with an "A" grade. Moreover, he went on eventually to undertake Ph.D. study in political philosophy under this professor's guidance.

We believe that students, no less than the faculty, will always choose excellence in the manner that we understand it. Therefore, raising academic standards begins with raising our own understanding of what those standards should be.

Quality, Not Quantity, is the Measure of Excellence

If we set proficient humanity as the goal of a college education, it will not suffice to make excellence the standard for the academic performance of only the students. The colleges and universities *themselves* must also set excellence as their own performance standard. More to the point, we must also rethink the very terms on which we judge the performance of colleges and universities. Nearly every indicator that is typically used today to assess their performance fails to measure what is most important and, often, generates unintended consequences that divert institutions away from a focus on undergraduate learning. Indicators such as reputation (as determined by *U.S. News and World Report* or *Kiplinger's*), size, and student grade point averages do not adequately measure institutional performance nor do they reveal much about the extent to which the college or university adds value to students' learning.

Throughout the book, but especially in chapters 4 and 5, we affirm that the best approach to gauging and influencing the performance of colleges and universities is to measure their capacity to add value to student learning. An institution that seriously attempts to measure—and to improve—that value will define itself primarily in terms of its capacity for change—in terms of certain "habits of mind." The exemplar of this approach to measuring excellence is the residential college. Although the residential, liberal arts college is not the concern of this book, which focuses instead on the multiversity, a discussion of how the residential college assesses its performance offers insight into the overall question of how to foster excellence.

Residential Liberal Education

The processes of residential university education are characterized more by dynamic than inertial changes. We mean by this that success in the residential college depends less on growth in numbers (if at all) and far more on the constant refinement of procedures, resources, and facilities. Higher education emphasizes harmonized and coordinated functioning of dynamic and physical growth factors, and universities compete on the basis of dynamic growth. Program quality and efficiency, subject matter suitability and relevance, and discipline defining achievements (chief among which are graduates highly sought after) constitute the distinctive ways in which universities qualify themselves as educational exemplars.

This point may seem at first less than intuitive. If, however, you reflect that the character of the residential college experience entails a clearly discernible upper limit to the number of students usefully admitted in a particular program—whether that is the 500 students at St. John's College, the 1,000 students at James Madison College, or the 1,500 students at Pomona College—then you will agree that there may be some impracticality in the idea. No one can reasonably expect to provide a genuine residential college experience—with its concomitant requirement for meaningful faculty-student interaction in a context in which the collegial experience itself also remains visible and meaningful to all members of the college—in a setting of open-ended, infinitely expanding enrollments, inertial growth as opposed to dynamic growth.

Open-ended, infinitely expanding enrollment is the very soul of the large, research university, and particularly the public university. There productivity is far more routinely measured by growth in numbers—matriculants and dollars—than by any other factor. This inertial growth and the desire for it impose on the large university the logic of segmentation—some would say fragmentation. Within it the most specialized and the most growth-oriented units are the most successful. Thus, a college of social science prospers within a research university by the very logic of its mission and structure—to produce as many graduates (plus credit hours) in as many sub-specialties as possible.

Against that standard, how can a residential college—whose productivity must be measured dynamically rather than inertially—defend itself and prosper in the bureaucratic competition? This dynamic measures the quality of the academic life rather than the quantity of academic life. Better teaching? That means lower GPAs. More integrated learning? Abler students. Readier attainment of life-long learning as a reflex and not just as a slogan? Cultural richness. And most ineffably of all, superior understanding. Are not these all the virtues of education we strive for? Are these not also the very virtues sacrificed to the logic of inertial growth?

If we are right about these things then it appears that the residential college is the best hope for achieving the mission of higher education and, in the context of the public university, the least likely candidate to be recognized as fulfilling the mission of the university. The broad administrative challenge we must ponder, then, is how to privilege dynamic approaches to learning over inertial approaches. If we do this we can spawn a renaissance of residential colleges, even within public universities. But this will not be easy. It does not suffice to point out that more Rhodes scholars are sent to Oxford from dynamic programs than from inertial programs. That truth is recognized and, as a contribution to overall institutional reputation, even appreciated. Nonetheless, the implication that one could greatly multiply the number of near-Rhodes scholars by expanding the role of the residential college—and we don't mean a mere "living-learning center"—is stoutly resisted by the privilege accorded to inertial programs.

The Curriculum as Conceptual Map

Now the special virtue of the residential college is the intensification of the college curriculum. Without that intensification, in the multiversity, the entire burden of achieving dynamic refinement and improvement will fall on the unassisted curriculum. That is why there may be no greater obstacle to the goal of offering students the chance to develop proficient humanity through liberal education than the curriculum itself. And, the incoherence of the curriculum is nowhere more apparent than in the general education programs available at most college campuses today.[24]

General education should be a friend of excellence, not one of its enemies; however, some interventions in the curriculum work against excellence. Those who imagine that "workforce training" is not just a need of this economic era but also a component part of education for life make such a mistake. Similarly, those who believe that graduation is more important than learning (and that, therefore, to avoid failure is more important than to acknowledge ignorance) make a like mistake, and a still more dangerous one, for they treat the curriculum like a bolt of cloth to be tailored to figure faults. A good tailor can make a fine suit without improving the wearer!

Constructing a coherent curriculum for general education must start with a shared understanding of the aims of higher education, as discussed at the start of this chapter. The next step, once we reach clarity about the educational outcomes we intend our students to achieve, is to review our conceptual map for reaching that destination. Surely the curriculum ought to serve as the map that our students follow along their own educational journey. Yet, a key issue in today's curricular debate is precisely *whether* such a map is needed. This question is closely followed by that of whether all students need use the same map.

To begin to consider these questions, we pose two others. First, must we not agree that for any fixed starting point and any desired destination, there may be multiple routes for getting there from here? If that is so, then must we not also agree that the routes will not all be nor all need be equally "good," while many will be variably eligible? The appropriateness or goodness of the route—as distinct from the start and the destination—may in this case be more subject to prudential determination than to definition. Do we require, for some reason, the most direct route? The fastest? The one that relies most on expressways, or the most scenic? Most or least traveled?

We cannot discuss in any depth the means for reaching the end without also discussing the criteria we will use to evaluate those means. Or, to put this question a bit differently, can we discover a shared educational philosophy that we might use in deciding among variably eligible routes? At too many campuses in North America today, there is no real shared educational philosophy shaping curricular decisions. At a colloquy on the college curriculum held at Rollins College in 1997, Charles Anderson reflected on why we lack such a philosophy:

> To endorse an educational philosophy is to set priorities. It enables us to "economize" in the moral sense. It provides us with reasons for preferring this program to that [one], for putting resources here, rather than there. An educational philosophy would enable us to compare the worth of various subjects. This runs counter to the dominant temper of the academy, in which all existing disciplines are thought to be equally worthy and thus entitled to a share of the pie. The university as it exists today is the outcome of a very long truce. [25]

Unless this truce can give scope for folk to take heart and courage to re-enter the battle for the true, the good, and the beautiful, it is a truce to defeat the peace rather than to fructify the peace. For our situation today differs not from the challenge given to Danielle Allen as she set out in search of a college while yet a high school junior. "Within very broad limits, choose whatever you wish, only make certain that it is such a place as has the courage first to tell you what an education is."

During our tenure at the State Council of Higher Education, the Council undertook a comprehensive review of the general education programs at all public and most private colleges and universities in Virginia. The results of the study (and the debate it triggered statewide) inform some of the comments about general education in this book (see especially the discussion in chapter 2). One of the aims of the study was to move faculty in Virginia out of what is an uneasy truce at best and a self-defeating one at worst into an active re-engagement of important questions about the curriculum. It is the role neither of coordinating boards, such as the Council, nor of governing boards to shape the curriculum; that is the responsibility of faculty. But, such boards—and works such as this book—can serve as catalysts, spurring each institution to take up these questions anew. The resulting faculty discussions ought to light a path out of these dark woods, just as lone faculty or departmental foraging has led some astray.[26]

When they do take place, such discussions are not easy, nor are the rough spots limited to the ground trammeled by the culture wars of the past decade. Charles Anderson challenges us with these words:

> Now we can see precisely where our quest for an integrating theme for liberal education must take us. This is not a congenial, easygoing search for new ways of "packaging" the curriculum. The perils are epistemological and, in that sense, moral. We are going to have to assert that some ways of understanding are better than others; that some tell more truth, more reliably inform us about the world; that some are more seemly, or civil, or more effective as guides to action. To say this is to break the tacit truce of skepticism on which the contemporary curriculum rests. It is to say that colleges and universities are responsible for distinguishing between reasonable and unreasonable, the warranted and the unwarranted, the better and the worse, that it is their calling to distinguish among the possibilities of belief and comprehension, and to teach, to prescribe, the better habits of mind.[27]

These tough-minded distinctions between reasonable and unreasonable, the warranted and the unwarranted, the better and the worse—and especially the teaching of "habits of mind"—are the most fundamental and most important work of academic leaders. It is because these distinctions must be made, and because the consequences of how they are made (and whether they are made) are so great, that we argue in chapter 2 that excellence in judgment is the primary qualification we ought to require in those who lead and teach in our institutions of higher learning.

Suppose, then, we can settle on some useful answers to questions about the purpose of education, and can sort out reasonable from unreasonable ways of achieving the purpose. What next? We must articulate both the end and the means in terms that can be understood intersubjectively. We need to develop educational maps that can be fathomed by those outside as well as within the academy.

One reason that our desired educational outcomes are often stated in vague language is the academy's uneasiness about being held accountable for those outcomes. In a hard-hitting article in the *Chronicle of Higher Education*, Robert Diamond drives home this point, saying "...once you have stated your goals in measurable terms, you become accountable for assessing how well you are meeting those goals and for making difficult decisions if you are not doing so."[28]

Diamond admonishes us that if the faculty do not themselves take steps they may be set marching to alien orders. He writes:

> It is true that if we begin to describe in measurable terms what a college degree should represent, we will be held increasingly accountable for the substance of each graduate's education. But if we do not create our own framework of skills and measurements, then legislators, trustees, and others beyond our walls will not hesitate to impose theirs on us. The time has come for higher education to bite the curriculum bullet.[29]

Defining the purpose of higher education, deciding on reasonable means to achieve that purpose, articulating the end and the means in clear, objective terms, and evaluating whether the means achieve the end—these are the essential components of higher education reform.

Multiculturalism and Diversity: Destruction from Within

Even a casual observer of the modern-day college campus cannot fail to notice how thoroughly a rigid cleaving to the doctrines of multiculturalism and diversity has reshaped the landscape over several decades. After years of feeding on a potent mixture of multiculturalism, moral relativism, and deconstruction theory, faculty, students and, in particular, administrators have lost the ability to recognize and embrace their common humanity. The ivory tower, wherein the study of the humanities was once pursued as the best possible way to awaken students to the ennobling sense of shared humanity, has morphed into the battleground on which culture wars are waged in denial of that common bond. In the name of tolerance intolerant behavior, speech, and policy are not merely condoned but cited as models for emulation. Western civilization—the true original of multiculturalism—is spurned as the legacy of racists in favor of countless faddish pursuits that purport to expose students to "other" non-Western (and, therefore, superior) cultures.

The multicultural mindset has become so deeply ingrained in the ethos of the college campus that it is difficult to envision its eradication. However, if there is to be any hope of weeding out this indoctrination, the effort must begin with a clear understanding of the true nature and impact of multiculturalism and diversity, as they have developed within the academy.

Originally called multiculturalism, diversity, in strong alliance with deconstruction theory, has as its central objective to provide an advantaged position for peoples previously identified as marginalized in society—on campus, and beyond. That is the diversity movement, but the diversity movement did not begin in a vacuum. It has a long pedigree, leaning so powerfully as it does on the movement of multiculturalism.

The diversity movement expresses, ultimately, an abandonment of confidence in American liberty—a search for alternatives to American liberty; a belief that American liberty is mired in racism; a belief that, in this particular dispute, what is at stake is a question of justice and that justice cannot be guaranteed on the grounds of American liberty. While diversity begins as an attack on ethnocentrism, it ends by heightening ethnocentrisms.[30]

We can all recognize well enough the original, humane notion of multiculturalism—the notion that there is an underlying humanity on the strength of which peoples of differing backgrounds can nevertheless establish some degree of fellowship.[31] That notion is at risk today, if not lost altogether. That notion has been systematically pushed aside by debate, policy formulation, and classroom study in which there surge to the forefront understandings that there are, in fact, no common measures of human identity that translate from one cultural perspective to another.

This is the understanding behind the political correctness movement, launched at Stanford University and other campuses in the 1980s. A review of some of the arguments presented by Thomas Grey in authoring the regulations against "hate speech" at Stanford (and as developed in his essay "Civil Rights vs. Civil Liberties") illuminates this point all too starkly. Professor Grey begins his argument by noting that despite the typical belief of "American liberals" that "both civil liberties and civil rights are harmonious aspects of a basic commitment to human rights," recent experiences have shown us that "these two clusters of values have seemed increasingly to conflict."[32] He points out that the issue of verbal harassment on the college campus brings to light a practical and conceptual division that runs quite deeply in the fabric of liberal thought and practice.

The point, to be quite certain, is that we are struggling with an issue that goes beyond the feelings of individuals or groups, according to Professor Grey. We are struggling with an issue that lies full at the heart of those constitutional and social principles, which define the people of the United States as such. He goes on to observe that:

> ...there has been recently, an upsurge in the number and intensity of incidents of racist, homophobic, and sexist abuse in American universities. An extreme example would be an incident reported at the University of Wisconsin, in which white students followed

a black woman student across campus, shouting, "We've never tried a nigger." More ambiguous was the following exchange at Stanford University; after a dormitory argument in which a black student had claimed that Ludwig von Beethoven was a mulatto, two white students defaced a picture of the composer into a black-face caricature and placed it near the black student's room.[33]

The question, Professor Grey says, is what disciplinary action, if any, is appropriate in such cases? He poses this question while seeming to discount—or perhaps not even to perceive—the extraordinary distance between the two cases. One is the case of direct, intimidating, verbal expression directed to an individual in the middle of campus in full public view, while the other is at least a pseudo- or quasi-intellectual exchange between black students and white students about the genetic heritage of Ludwig von Beethoven. And yet, these two dissimilar incidents are assimilated in a single question—what disciplinary action, if any, is appropriate in such cases?

Professor Grey goes on in his essay, which is in essence a defense of the Stanford regulations he authored, to describe the problem. He begins his description by noting the first important case tried judicially, which arose at the University of Michigan; he says this about that case:

> Viewed through a First Amendment lens, a Michigan regulation now seen as a "hate speech" or "group defamation" rule rather than a harassment prohibition, was a dramatically over broad incursion into core areas of protected speech.

This appears from considering just *one* example of the kind of speech prohibited by the regulation taken from the guidelines the University distributed to students to explain the new policy. This provision follows: "A male student makes remarks in class like, 'Women just aren't as good in this field as men,' thus creating a hostile learning atmosphere for female classmates."[34]

From this, Professor Grey goes on to say, one can readily extrapolate to other statements that would violate the standard, whether made in the classroom or dorm hallway, saying for example, that low black IQ scores are genetically based, or that homosexuality is unnatural, or a disease, or that women are naturally less creative than men.

> The expression of these opinions is certainly experienced (the subjective reality, in other words) as "stigmatizing" and "demeaning" by many, probably most, students belonging to the protected groups. When cumulated to create a climate of opinion they might well foreseeably "interfere with the academic efforts" of the students whose basic humanity, or equal mental capacity, they deny.[35]

Thus, by degrees it becomes clear that what Professor Grey describes is an infringement upon the sense of common humanity that these students may have—not reflecting upon their particular, or idiosyncratic views of themselves, but upon their sense of belonging to common humanity. That observation goes back to his first observation, namely, that there is a tension in liberal democracy in which we seek to defend the individual, individual claims of rights against unjust incursions, but, then at the same time we give appropriate recognition to group distinctions. That is, we see as an ultimate expression of individual rights the freedom to form group identifications.

The question is—can a liberal democracy defend group identification without imposing upon individual right of expression? We know that vast numbers of students, faculty and administrators at campuses throughout this country endorse Professor Grey's answer to that question.

But, nevertheless, these are rules in which the fundamental distinction that is made is a distinction between what he has defined as protected groups, and all others. In terms of those rules, these are forms of ordinary speech, including not only the immediately intimidating and demeaning speech of students at the University of Wisconsin, but also that of the students at Stanford University for whom the rules were created in the first place, who placed the poster near the dormitory room of the black student.

These rules say that students are protected from such harassment, that it creates a demeaning and intimidating atmosphere, which undermines their claim to humanity, and the appropriate punishment extends all the way up to expulsion from the university.

It is important to note, however, that such rules prohibiting speech demeaning protected groups cannot be applied inversely, from protected groups to unprotected groups; if you were a black student and were to pursue a white female student across the campus at Stanford, and you were to say, "I've never tried a honkey," you would be guilty of harassment because of the gender provision of these rules. But if your sexual orientation were homosexual, and it were a white male, you would not be guilty of harassment for saying, "I've never tried a honkey."

The rules cannot apply to people who are not expected to have the sensitivities that make the relevance of demeaning speech an urgent issue on our university campuses.

When we speak about racism on campus today, it is essential to note that we are not talking about the lingering battle to desegregate American higher education. We are not even talking about the critical question of whether we can permit black campuses still to exist, historically black colleges and universities. Those are ongoing disputes in American law, but they no longer pose interesting questions.

The interesting questions today are, can we pay due heed, due regard, to people's differences—racially or otherwise—in such a way as to convey desirable protection to those whom we have identified as protected groups, while nevertheless excluding those protections from those not so identified? One of the difficulties is immediately evident. If you say, "Well, I can solve this problem; I will simply write the rules and say that anybody who says anything nasty about anybody gets kicked out of school," then, the difficulty with that, of course, is precisely that you now tread so broadly upon the First Amendment principles, that there is simply no way to escape the iron grip of the Constitution. Not only the Michigan judge, but every judge will throw you out of court.

You need a very special exception to write race-regarding, gender-regarding, and sexual-orientation-regarding rules, and that exception is a legal atmosphere created by the history of adjudication of the Fourteenth Amendment, through which it has come to be seen that there are protected groups in society—not protected individuals, but protected groups. And one earns title to these protections only to the degree that one creeps within the shadow of the protected group.

This is where the question of the loss of confidence in American liberty arises, for American liberty is predicated upon assuring protection to individuals. As John Moore reminds us, the ideal of American freedom is

> ... rooted in the Judeo-Christian tradition and its central values. It is in that tradition that the value of the individual human being is most strongly expressed, that the relationship between the person and the creator is understood, that the basis for thinking that every individual is important is laid down. Without that, there is no basis for arguing that individual freedom matters.[36]

The original, multicultural impulse was designed to say that we could, on the strength of protecting individual liberty, bring to the fore a flourishing of various cultures in the United States. In an essay on multiculturalism published by *The New Republic* in 1991,

Nathan Glazer proffers a defense of multiculturalism harkening back to this older view—in which he points out that surely there is no objection to broadening the horizon of our academic curricula. Such a broadening, in addition to all things else, would include material representative of African and, indeed, of the experience of American blacks; it would add material indicative of the experience of women; it would add material indicative of the experience of Hispanics; it would add material indicative of the experiences even of homosexuals—if one wants to insist upon segregating homosexuals as a group.[37]

No objection to that. This is regarded as wholly compatible with the idea of a university education. But, of course, Nathan Glazer himself, responding to an attack on curricular reform in the state of New York, goes somewhat beyond that critical verb we have used repeatedly, add. For now the prevailing wisdom is: substitute, not add. The thought is that there has been previously a predominant white, European, male-oriented view of the world, which is, in its principles, an act of oppression on people whose backgrounds and origins are not white, European, and male. And how does one improve the white, European male's point of view by adding to it? One can only improve it by replacing it.

The reason one can only improve it by replacing it is rather straightforwardly to be articulated: namely, cultural views are mutually exclusive. Cultural backgrounds are mutually exclusive. Ethnic heritages are mutually exclusive. There is not, as the leading thinkers in the movement of deconstruction argued, a notion of common humanity. In fact, the very notion of humanity itself is an instrument of oppression, which has been used to marginalize those who are not defined or described as fitting the stereotypical characteristics of what is called humanity. The only way to overcome the marginalizing impact of reason, the reason in accordance with which the notion came to prevail in the Western world, is to displace it altogether. Hence, now we talk of various, centric curricula: Euro-centric, Afro-centric, Hispano-centric, etc.—all mutually exclusive.

This question was posed to us in an interesting way by Allan Bloom in *The Closing of the American Mind*. Bloom's book was the first open challenge to what later came to be called political correctness. What Bloom's book did was to suggest that these notions, these criteria of relevance, were themselves incompatible with the function of the university. He argued that they sought to replace the objective of the university, which he described as "openness," with an objective of indoctrination. Bloom went on to suggest that political correctness, understood as cultural relativism, had prevailed in the United States and largely throughout the world. He made unmistakably clear the extent to which the understanding of humanity, which characterized the academic experience of those on campuses in the United States in the 1980s, was an understanding that accepted the premise that cultural backgrounds were mutually exclusive and not intersubjectively transmissible, intersubjectively communicable.

Given the clarity and forcefulness with which Bloom developed his thesis in *The Closing of the American Mind* and given the success of the book (at least in terms of sales), we then must ask: Why did Bloom fail? Why do we not automatically see today that political correctness founded on these notions of the mutual exclusivity of cultural heritages is simply wrong; and why is it that the debate over political correctness, reaches its full bloom only afterwards, rather than at the time of Bloom's book?[38]

We think this has something to do with Bloom's notion of the university as dedicated to openness. When he said that the purpose of the university is to cultivate a genuine openness,[39] meaning, of course, a liberation of each individual from his narrow cultural perspective, he was not saying something that was idiosyncratic. He was saying something that has been generally and normally understood to be the work of the university.

We appeal to young minds to escape the prisons of their narrow child rearing. In other words, that means to rise above their ethnic heritage, to rise above their cultural background—and in pursuit of what? Does Bloom tell us in pursuit of what? Here lies precisely the reason for Bloom's failure. For Bloom, in raising the promises of reason, the idea of truth, nevertheless, delivers us into nothing more certain than the prospect of nihilism by the end of his book. He defends the university's openness, but he ends without suggesting to any degree whatever how that openness might lead to a conception of humanity, proficient or otherwise. The reason he doesn't do so, apparently, is that Allan Bloom, too, believed the notion of humanity has been shot down, once and for all, by the modern assault on reason.

It is therefore, not impossible to explain why Bloom failed and political correctness blossomed. Multiculturalism merged with deconstruction to produce diversity, largely in the aftermath of

Bloom's book, because most diversity built on the strength of the argument that reason was incapable of leading to any objective standards, and Bloom ended precisely where diversity began—precisely where deconstruction began.

We struggle today with this political correctness movement, then, in large measure because a subtle transition has occurred in the academy of North America. Namely, there has been a transition from emphasizing cultural plurality, in which we honestly believed it was possible for us mutually to share one another's backgrounds, mutually to be enriched by various heritages, mutually advanced, therefore, toward a conception of common humanity—that is what we thought.[40] But we made a transition from that to emphasizing, instead, not common humanity, but cultural marginality. At every pen stroke, work devoted to proving the argument of cultural marginality drives a wedge into the argument in favor of plurality. The one argument is the enemy of the other. Ultimately, the diversity that succeeded multiculturalism is the destroyer of multiculturalism.

To state it in political terms, the argument in favor of diversity is the enemy of the notion of a common heritage in the United States as well as among all citizens of the United States. The diversity argument has been so thoroughly absorbed within the academy that Barbara Herrnstein Smith can write–without apparent irony or regret—in response to E. D. Hirsch's proposal to develop the "cultural literacy" of American youth, that

> The existence of an American "national culture" is by no means self-evident. Every citizen of this nation belongs to numerous communities (regional, ethnic, religious, occupational, etc.) and shares different sets of beliefs, interests, assumptions, attitudes and practices—and, in that sense, cultures—with the other members of each of those communities. There is, however, no single, comprehensive macroculture in which all or even most of the citizens of this nation actually participate, no numerically preponderant majority culture in relation to which any or all of the others are "minority" cultures, and no culture that, in Hirsch's term, "transcends" any or all other cultures.[41]

This shows up in an interesting way in a passage in Bloom's book, in the French edition, the title of which is *L'Âme Desarmée*, as opposed to *The Closing of the American Mind*. It is a passage that was written as a question in the English version, but in the French version as a declarative sentence, and this is what he said in the text:

> The social compact is impossible there, precisely where there is no longer any common good or common vision of a public good. [42]

Social compact means social organization, a view of the society as a whole. In the English, he made it a question; he said, "Is it the case that?"[43] but when he wrote for the French, he became more bold. When we declare that there is no longer an American common good, there is also no longer a ground of common identity on the strength of which Americans of various cultural backgrounds can claim to be one.

This observation by Bloom accurately describes the progress of the movement called diversity in recent years, which has succeeded to the movement of multiculturalism. It explains why, therefore, multiculturalism and diversity have had divergent goals—the one, aiming at assimilation to a common standard, while the other seeks to eliminate every standard whatsoever, insisting there is no standard of comparison between, say, American blacks and American whites.

This is a new era. When, therefore, we speak of diversity on campus, we must learn to speak correctly. What we are really talking about is the reemergence of ethnocentrism as a moral horizon with a vengeance and as the only legitimate reference to humanity. We no longer admit references to common humanity as prevailing moral authority. And, as a consequence, racial conflict and separatism have increased at many colleges and universities.

There is another, closely related aspect of the university's preoccupation with diversity, which must be highlighted—namely, the ironic truth that prejudice is fostered, not lessened, by this preoccupation. To the extent that institutions of higher education throughout North America have systematically promoted multiculturalism as diversity for several decades, our systems of higher education have failed in an essential aspect of their mission.

If we understand by education—as we think we must—a power that enables us to see with clarity our own circumstances, our own understandings—if we mean by education liberation from mere prejudice, then it is safe to say, today, that our education fails us. Rather, far from liberating us from prejudices it does little more than to demand faithful adherence to prejudices.

Two examples will suffice to make this truth plain—examples that are pertinent to our social and political reality but distant enough to foster a reasonable degree of objectivity.

In the troubles in Los Angeles in 1992—the riots or uprisings, as you prefer—something occurred on the morning after the riots, the first morning on which the schools reopened after the riot. It was very informative.

A school teacher in the Compton area—which is south of Los Angeles and which was involved in the general area of rioting—returned to her classroom to find 27 second-grade youngsters all dressed in new clothing. She looked out and thought there was a problem. Rather than to follow her lesson plan, she said, "Let's talk about this. Let's talk about the right and wrong of looting. Do you think it's right to loot, to steal from others?" She was surprised that the question was puzzling to the children. The question puzzled the children in the sense that, not saying the obvious things—such as, well, it's wrong but we did it and we couldn't resist it or everybody was doing it and so we did it, too—the students manifested genuine confusion about the application of moral principles in this context. They communicated that they were not certain how they were supposed to decide what's right and what's wrong. One student finally stood forth and said, "Well, Miss, it's right and it's wrong."

Now, the child had not become a politician already, learning how to speak out of both sides of her mouth. It seems to us, however, that the child meant this: for some persons in certain circumstances it is right to do wrong. This is a lesson that has been somehow inculcated and which is pervasive. People who see themselves as oppressed—as it is now popular to say—and who understand themselves to have suffered injuries, whether directly or only vaguely conceived, further arrive at the conclusion that people in those circumstances may abstract from the ordinary rules of morality and social engagement.

This is a lesson that we have delivered, not simply in our schools but in our education in a larger sense—meaning with respect to this very question that our education has failed to conserve clear-cut, well-articulated standards of right and wrong. This contrasts sharply with the experience of only a few decades ago, when, of course, oppression was no less manifest in our society, and when indeed the young William Allen experienced it personally.

His father at that time was captain of a commercial fishing vessel in a small segregated town in the south. He did particularly well because he was good at his craft—a craft in which one earned by virtue of one's labors. In fact, he earned in the early 1950s a salary that was so good that his son did not earn the equivalent until many years into his career as a university professor. In the year in which he earned that amount of money in a small southern town, it was deemed unacceptable for a black man to earn that much money and therefore to acquire that degree of independence within that social framework. So, powers that be intervened to deprive him of that employment.

The family eventually came to understand what had happened, saw it as an injury, and saw it as oppression. But they did not derive from that fact the conclusion that what they needed to do was to injure someone else in turn. Rather, they rededicated themselves to labor to vindicate the promise of this country and to demonstrate that such conduct was unjust and, in addition, that they were capable, through education, self-development, and other principles, of making a vital contribution not only to their own circumstances but to society in general.

Somehow in that day and age, in the early 1950s, people could experience oppression, could have a present consciousness of it and resent it, and yet still adhere to standards of right—not come to believe that the response was to do wrong. Nor did they think that to have suffered wrong became a justification for doing wrong to another. Now those are very personal examples. But the same messages conveyed in these examples are also found in the 1991 Civil Rights Act, where for the first time in the history of the United States distinct standards of justice for the same infraction were written into the law—standards different by circumstances. It is there said that if you are minority or woman, you must meet one standard of proof in filing a discrimination complaint under the law. If you are not, you must meet another standard of proof. This means, of course, different standards of justice.

We know that most of the debate over preferences in our society is a debate over the question of when it is right to do wrong to others. Is it right to do wrong to someone in order to make up for a past wrong to someone else? Therefore, this is not simply a classroom question, but an education that is pervasive through social practices generally maintained and rigorously argued for. But, do not make the mistake of thinking because we refer this to society in general, that it is not present in our classrooms. Ultimately, these kinds of standards only emerge out of what takes place in our classrooms.

Early in this century the political scientist, Arthur F. Bentley, formulated the argument in defense of a theory called pluralism—a common enough term today. We all speak of America as a pluralist society, and in which diversity is a rule. And we generally think that the term somehow is rooted in the founding experience. We have even heard teachers sometimes attribute the term to James Madison, and maybe even to the tenth *Federalist Paper*. But hearing something in a classroom does not make it true. You will not find the word pluralism anywhere in the *Federalist Papers*. Nor do we find the phenomenon described in *Federalist* ten to be what we call pluralism today.

What Bentley defined, and what he meant and literally said, was that "all politics is group politics." That is, there is nothing that takes place in the realm of politics that is not derived from group interest. Therefore, principles of affiliation, association, and identity are the foundations of politics. That simple argument has dominated our education ever since. Thus, we have persisted in inculcating notions of group identification, group enjoyments, and group sufferings above notions of individual rights and individual responsibilities ever since.

That is one of the reasons our education has failed us. It has left us with the impression that we do not need to confront ourselves as individuals—to ask ourselves what we believe, why we believe it, what we merit, and why we think we deserve it. Rather, it is sufficient just to check off on some standardized form the group to which we belong, in order to discern what our entitlements are. The 2000 census in the United States carried the tendency to its logical and, hence, absurd limit.[44]

That is what our education offers us. In disciplines ranging from literature to art to sociology, human choice and history are explained based on theories grounded in relationships of power. And what is meant by "relationships of power" in these theories? Relationships between groups—the oppressors and the oppressed. Or, if you speak of political science, or economics, or philosophy or anything else, the reality is that, we have been in the last several years particularly subjected to an onslaught of preaching about certain needs of mutual respect among groups, and which begin with the assumption of a mutual exclusivity of group identification.

Diversity means that every group must be taken on its own terms, and no group can pretend to understand any other group. This is at the root of most education that takes place in our country today. In fact, it appears that this term "diversity" is meant ultimately to replace the term, "university"—*di*, of course, meaning "two," substituting for the term *uni*, "one." "University": one turn, one turning, one ultimate foundation, being replaced by the notion of two or more foundations—the end of common humanity, and a straying into a very gloomy woods indeed.

Finding a Compass

These, then, are the chief obstacles that hinder higher education's attainment of its true destination. This book provides an ethical compass for the many concerned faculty, administrators, parents, and citizens who would seek to return our colleges and universities to the straight way. For, as Henry A. Giroux voices as a "commonplace," but no less significant assertion, ". . .the most important questions facing both the liberal arts and higher education in general are moral and political."[45] While we do not offer all the same answers to those questions as does Giroux, we affirm his classification of them as moral and political.

Will those who venture into the terrain of education reform encounter perils and phantasms along the way? Undoubtedly. But we urge them to remain stalwart pilgrims. We know there are guides we all can look to, for the ground of curricular debate and the path to uncovering the true purpose of education have been trod many times before. During the journey, we must bear in mind that we will not do all that can be done. Social revolutions never so completely alter the world as their resisters fear, nor so completely renew the world as their advocates hope. The senior author was much chastened when, visiting the chateau of the political philosopher, Montesquieu, many years ago, he discovered that there lived still on the family estate of that architect of modernity a class of dependents little removed in culture and habits from the hour of Montesquieu's own birth, though a full two hundred years had passed. We in this hour will also overlook some needed opportunities for change, and some of what we shall accomplish shall extend more shallowly than we would wish. But we can rely on the courage of our convictions to carry us over the rough places. We can take heart along this journey because we know it is not a trivial pursuit. If we make our way successfully, we know we can improve the excellence of many students' journeys through their undergraduate studies. For those students willing to make excellence their aim will find themselves, as Dante did, *disposto a salier a le stele*—ready to rise to the stars.

Notes

1. We offer here "an idea" of the University, in accord with Robert Maynard Hutchins's insistence on its importance to the entire enterprise: "An idea enables you to tell what is appropriate and what is not, what is to be included and what left out. The idea shapes the constitution, the external and internal relationships, and the activities of

the university. It holds the place together and defines and protects it . . . . All we have to do to decide whether we have an idea of the university is to ask ourselves whether there is anything imaginable that would seem inappropriate in an American institution of higher learning." Quoted in Christopher J. Lucas, Crisis in the Academy: Rethinking Higher Education in America (New York: St. Martin's Press, 1996), 78.

2.   Lucas, xiv.

3.   Robert A. Scott, "Lay Bare the Questions Hidden by Answers," The College Board Review, no. 184 (Spring 1998): 20.

4.   James Baldwin, "A Talk to Teachers," The Saturday Review 46 (December 21, 1963): 42.

5.   Jeffrey D. Wallin, "Is Civic Education Compatible with Liberal Education?" On Principle 5 (April, 1997): 3, <http://www.ashland.edu/ashbrook/publicat/onprin/v5n2/wallin.html> (August 6, 2001).

6.   Susan Saltrick, "Through a Dark Wood," paper presented at the Conference on Learning Communities, University of Miami, January 9, 1998. Distributed to AAHESGIT mailing list, November 20, 1997. <http://www.tltgroup.org/resources/rdarkwood.html> (April 20, 2001).

7.   James O. Freedman, Idealism and Liberal Education (Ann Arbor: University of Michigan Press, 1996), 1.

8.   While this is an understandable notion in light of the evolution of higher education, we should not forget José Ortega y Gasset's observation: "The higher education consists then, of professionalism and research. Without attacking the subject now, let us note in passing that it is surprising to find two such disparate tasks joined, fused together. . . . It is surprising, then, to find mixed together the professional instruction which is for all, and research which is for a very few." José Ortega y Gasset, Mission of the University, edited and translated by Howard Lee Nostrand (New York: W. W. Norton & Co., Inc., 1994), 35.

9.   Freedman, 1.

10.   W. E. B. DuBois, "The Hampton Idea," in Herbert Aptheker, ed., The Education of Black People (Amherst: University of Massachusetts Press, 1973), 14.

11.   Robert Maynard Hutchins, The Higher Learning in America (New Haven, CT: Yale University Press, 1962), 47.

12.   A liberal arts education remains as valuable today as it was in 1852, when Cardinal John Henry Newman delivered these words: ". . . the man who has learned to think and to reason and to compare and to discriminate and to analyze, who has refined his taste, and formed his judgment, and sharpened his mental vision, will not indeed at once be a lawyer. . .or an orator, or a statesman, or a physician, or a good landlord, or a man of business, or a soldier, or an engineer, or a chemist, or a geologist, or an antiquarian, but he will be placed in that state of intellect in which he can take up any one of the sciences or callings I have referred to. . . with an ease, a grace, a versatility, and a success to which another is a stranger" (Quoted in Lucas, Crisis in the Academy, 75).

13.   Craig Swenson, "Customers and Markets: The Cuss Words of Academe," Change 30 (September-October 1998): 34.

14.   Billy Wireman, "Productive Careers and Noble Lives: A New Mandate for Liberal Arts Education," Vital Speeches of the Day 63 (December 15, 1996): 136.

15.   Samuel D. Proctor, "Land-Grant Universities and the Black Presence," in G. Lester Anderson, ed., Land-Grant Universities and Their Continuing Challenge (East Lansing: Michigan State University Press, 1976), 20. The story of Virginia State University, and the other historically black colleges and universities of this country, underscores the value placed upon access to higher learning and its potential to transform lives. Virginia State University's story is eloquently told in Edgar Toppin's

history of the institution, titled Loyal Sons and Daughters.

16. Ibid., 21.

17. Maxwell H. Goldberg, "Liberal Learning and the Land-Grant System: Futures and Optatives," in G. Lester Anderson, ed., Land-Grant Universities and Their Continuing Challenge (East Lansing: Michigan State University Press, 1976), 157.

18. Parker Palmer, foreword to Mary Rose O'Reilly, Radical Presence: Teaching as a Contemplative Practice (Portsmouth, NH: Boynton/Cook Publishers, 1998), 2.

19. Parts of this section were initially published in William B. Allen, "Taking the Final Steps in Raising Academic Standards," Virginia Issues and Answers (Winter 1998): 18-21, and are reprinted here with permission.

20. Carolynn Reid-Wallace, "The Promise of American Education," in Lamar Alexander and Chester E. Finn, Jr., eds., The New Promise of American Life (Indianapolis, IN: Hudson Institute, 1995), 292. As an example of the adherents to this "false dichotomy" we offer Lucas' statement that ". . . in matters involving higher education, there seems to be an inverse relationship between democracy and distinction. Quantity and quality, forever mutually exclusive and irreconcilable, seem to be at war with one another" (Lucas, 1996: 91). The error in this view, as is shown below, is the confusion of inertial growth with the conditions for dynamic improvement.

21. As is true with the parables of Christ and similar remarks in the Old Testament, addressed to those who have ears to hear, this is a teaching for the masses. For the natural aristocracy cannot otherwise be nurtured. "Access and excellence" indeed are not antithetical. Leo Strauss, Liberalism Ancient and Modern (New York: Basic Books, 1968), 5.

22. Reid-Wallace.

23. While there may have been equally or even more dramatically universal cultures prior to and collateral with Western culture, the only surviving cultures that compete with Western culture have been exclusivist parochialisms. At times, shoots of Western culture have lurched in the direction of exclusivist parochialism. In fact, however, it has been overwhelmingly characterized by the triumphant form that emerged in the modern European Enlightenment. The modern European Enlightenment—and therefore Western culture—has consistently pursued the universalizing over the particular. In that sense it has been unfriendly to parochialisms but not at the expense of respect for the humanity of the particularists. That is why it is multicultural; it fosters respect for the peoples of every culture, if not for the mutually exclusive competing cultures. Moreover, it does so by means of its two component parts, the secular and the religious, the philosophical and the sectarian, Athens and Jerusalem.

 The tensions in Western culture are not inconsiderable. It may be figured as a ship severed stem to stern, its port and starboard halves (the secular and the religious) lying side to side rather than joined at the center. It will appear difficult indeed to progress in any journey in that condition. Yet, somehow, it remains afloat.

24. See the discussion on the goals of general education in chapter 2.

25. Charles W. Anderson, "Pragmatism, Idealism, and the Aims of Liberal Education," in Robert Orrill, ed., Education and Democracy: Re-imagining Liberal Learning in America (New York: The College Board, 1997), 111-12.

26. "In any university the faculty is the major key in these matters. If a faculty cannot govern itself well and accept the full responsibilities that fall upon it and the university, there is little the administration or the trustees can do to overcome the failing" (Reynolds, 1991: 170).

27. Anderson, 115.

28. Robert M. Diamond, "Broad Curriculum Reform is Needed if Students Are to Master Core Skills," The Chronicle of Higher Education 43 (August 1, 1997): B7.

29.   Ibid.

30.   The fundamental principles—and privileges—at stake in this critique are developed in W. B. Allen, "The Truth About Citizenship: An Outline," Cardozo Journal of International and Comparative Law 4 (Summer 1996): 355-372.

31.   "True multiculturalism—the study of the world's many cultures, including those of Asia, Africa, and South America—has a legitimate place in a core curriculum. But these courses should be taught in a context that includes Western civilization and that pays proper deference to historical accuracy. The goal should be to learn from, in the words of Matthew Arnold, 'the best that has been thought and known in the world'—whatever its cultural origins." New York Association of Scholars and Empire Foundation for Policy Research,SUNY's Core Curricula: The Failure to Set Consistent High Academic Standards (New York: The Association, July 1996), 20.

32.   Thomas C. Grey, "Civil Rights vs. Civil Liberties: The Case of Discriminatory Verbal Harassment," in Ellen Frankel Paul, ed., Reassessing Civil Rights (Cambridge, MA: Blackwell Publishers for the Bowling Green Social Philosophy and Policy Center, 1991), 81.

33.   Ibid., 84.

34.   Ibid., 87.

35.   Ibid., 87.

36.   John H. Moore, "Higher Education and the Burger King Society," Vision & Values 8 (November 2000), <http://www.gcc.edu/alumni/vision-moore2.asp> (December 8, 2000).

37.   Nathan Glazer, "In Defense of Multiculturalism," New Republic 205 (September 2, 1991): 18-22.

38.   The fact that the debate over political correctness and speech codes has abated somewhat in recent years reflects not the disappearance of these movements but rather how thoroughly they have become woven into the fabric of the daily life of the academy. The number of students, faculty, and administrators who still make the effort and take the risk to oppose the prevailing policies has steadily declined. This decline was detected as early as 1993, when Howard Dickman observed, "Those who remain 'politically incorrect' represent a beleaguered minority on university faculties, and those with the courage to speak out in defense of the liberal values that the academy once enshrined are a mere handful." Howard Dickman, ed., The Imperiled Academy (New Brunswick, NJ: Transaction Publishers, 1993), viii.

39.   Bloom discusses the concept of openness and the university's role in fostering it in the introduction to the work (pp. 25-43). He insists, accurately, that liberal education "does not consist so much in answers as in permanent dialogue" (p. 380). Allan Bloom, The Closing of the American Mind (New York: Simon & Schuster, 1987).

40.   The transition from what Diane Ravitch labeled "pluralistic multiculturalists" to "particularism" is well-nigh complete. Whereas "[p]luralistic multi-culturalists seek to enrich our common culture, to make it more inclusive and less parochial by incorporating elements of other cultures," adherents of particularism "reject the notion of a common culture altogether. . . . From the particularist perspective, education must recognize that students are culture-bound and teach them, not an oppressive or illusory common culture, but their own culture—or as academicians reconstruct it." Daniel Bonevac, "Leviathan U," in Howard Dickman, ed., The Imperiled Academy (New Brunswick, NJ: Transaction Publishers, 1993), 2-3.

41.   Barbara Herrnstein Smith, "Hirsch, Literacy, and the 'National Culture,' in Darryl J. Gless and Barbara Herrnstein Smith, eds., The Politics of Liberal Education (Durham, NC: Duke University Press, 1992), 77.

42.   "Le contrat social est impossible là où il n'ya plus de buts commun ni de vision commune du bien public." Allan Bloom, L'Âme désarmée, translated by Paul Alexandre (Paris: Julliard, 1987), 26.

43.   "But when there are no shared goals or vision of the public good, is the social contract any longer possible?" Bloom, The Closing of the American Mind, 27.

44.   Asking or permitting residents to check off multiple affiliations.

45.   Henry A. Giroux, "Liberal Arts Education and the Struggle for Public Life: Dreaming About Democracy," in Darryl J. Gless and Barbara Herrnstein Smith, eds., The Politics of Liberal Education (Durham, NC: Duke University Press, 1992), 119.

2

Excellence in Judgment[1]

The present argument considers the teaching of youth according to virtue—making them become both desirous of and passionate for complete citizenship—to rule and be ruled knowingly with justice. This is the nurture the argument is defining and also wants to proclaim alone as education.—Plato, Laws

Treating higher education on the model of corporate management has led to the misfortune of mis-identifying the goals of higher education. While there is no particular difficulty in conceiving a corporate chief executive officer who is unable to perform the discrete productive tasks that constitute the principal outputs of a major corporation, there is every difficulty conceivable in attempting to provide leadership in higher education without the leaders accomplishing in themselves the very goal of higher education. The reason for this plainly is that the productive goal or "principal output" of higher education is fundamentally identical with the capability required for effective management, and that is excellence in judgment.

It would be idle to insist that a university president must use his rostrum "or betray a trust," unless one could also expect an excellence of judgment that justifies the "heavy responsibility for explaining not only his own institution but also the cause of education generally." However, it is precisely excellence in judgment that qualifies one for "leadership as to ends and purposes and not as to methods and subject matter."[2]

Qualifications for academic leadership differ substantially from the qualification for directing the shipping and receiving operations of a major industrial enterprise. Although a shipping manager sits astride the very life-line of a major enterprise and must succeed in coordinating and regulating communications throughout the entire corporate body, much as the heart aliments the human body, she would err grievously who thought that particular talent a substitute for the brain. Nor does that observation bar the ascent of a talented officer from shipping manager to chief executive officer (CEO); it only insists that it is not the specific talent for coordinating system-wide communication that justifies the promotion to CEO. This observation reveals the inadequacy of Clark Kerr's original "moderator-initiator" formulation and its subsequent elaborations.[3] So what do we seek in an academic leader?

When we want to travel into space, we are well advised to place ourselves in the hands of technical experts who can get us there and back again. When we require brain surgery, we do well to consult neurosurgeons. Education is in many ways not different from such challenging initiatives; appropriate goal setting requires expert judgment. If we mean, though, to ask the public to pay for our space ships, our brain surgery, or our college education, then our space scientists, our neurosurgeons, and our higher education administrators must explain to the public exactly what it will get for its money. In all cases the fundamental commitment of public support turns on decisions that must be made by public bodies.

Technical experts provide the public information that constitutes the basis of sound decisions, enabling all stakeholders to play appropriate roles in carrying out these crucial missions. Lay boards are incompetent to declare what appropriate educational goals should be, but they are perfectly competent to say, "I understand," when presented with articulate formulations of those goals by college leaders. A University of Wisconsin trustee describes the lay board's responsibility sensibly:

> We do not fully appreciate our statutory responsibilities; we are insufficiently knowledgeable about our campuses and higher education and we spend time on peripheral items that fail to address issues central to academic quality, fiscal effectiveness and the public interest.[4]

Whereas a visible president from SUNY gets it wrong: "Politicians and political academic leaders cannot adequately safeguard academic freedom, because they are more concerned with . . . cleaning up academe. It is a mistake to fault them . . . they simply do not understand, because they come from a different culture."[5] It is rather President Bowen who does not understand his responsibility to articulate clearly goals and practices of the academy (assuming he understands the goals himself!). Effective lay leaders are not troubled by the fact that they might fail to understand a thing itself perfectly understandable. And why should they be? For they are typically experts in their own right in other fields—legal, medical, technical, or business. The trouble in higher education overall is that academic leaders fail to articulate goals not merely understandable but also appropriately elevated.

There are two reasons for this failure. First, the goal of university education has been "corrupted" by the proliferation of ancillary subject matters and demands for "skills certification" that we discussed in chapter 1. Thus, we get the "multiversity." Second, academic leaders have abandoned the true goal of higher education, proficient humanity.[6] Thus, we substitute "critical thinking," "values clarification," or "tolerance" for skill in moral judgment. While these may be tools of effective management, they do not answer to the central requirement or skill of excellence in judgment.

What does answer to that central requirement is a robust curriculum of general education. The goal of such a curriculum is a proficient humanity that is characterized by excellence in judgment. With the exception of teachers, it does not produce "professionals." Nor does it produce disciplinary adepts. It does prepare students to advance in graduate study in chosen fields. But what it does most is to build the character and knowledge more generally to be attributed to "statesmen, legislators, and judges" and, in this context, to leaders of higher education. For the best of these display a sure knowledge of human arts and culture.

Managerial Effectiveness

The efflorescence of the research university—the multiversity—is unmistakably a product of the century that just ended, although the term "multiversity" itself attained currency only with Clark Kerr's usage in the 1960s. One scholar identifies the emergence of the research university as decisive as early as 1910.[7] Note, though, that early views of the research university—and hence the management task—differ profoundly from views of the multiversity. Nicholas Butler defined a research university as, "an institution where students adequately trained by previous study of the liberal arts and sciences are led into special fields of learning and research by teachers of high excellency and originality, and where by the agency of libraries, museums, laboratories, and publications knowledge is conserved, advanced, and disseminated."[8] But this pristine view eventually yielded to pressures of growth and differentiation. Initially, those changes were positive, as captured in the view of Edward Shils: "The prestige of universities has grown throughout modern societies. From having been small institutions, with places for only a tiny percentage of young persons from the upper and middle classes of every European country and North America, they have reached a point where attendance at a university—or in the United States, a college—has become the norm."[9]

In chapter 1, we contrasted dynamic approaches to learning and to evaluating the performance of a college or university with the approach of massive differentiation and inertial growth. The latter is the very soul of the research university. Further, we make the case for the superiority of dynamic approaches in the educational work of cultivating excellence.[10] The broad, administrative challenge, then, is to privilege dynamic approaches to learning over inertial approaches. And the challenge of management effectiveness in this regard leads ineluctably to a focus on the fundamental area of leadership—the setting of curricular ends in light of which effective management becomes possible in the first place.[11]

Leadership: The Case of General Education

The very heart of the problem we are discussing is the noted failure of higher education to provide adequately for "general" or "liberal education."[12] Too many sources have identified this failing for us to ignore it. For example:

> In 1990 the American Association of Colleges issued a chilling report, *Integrity in the College Curriculum*, that found the typical curriculum to be fragmented, incoherent, and insubstantial. "As for what passes as a college curriculum," the report concluded, "almost anything goes."[13]

In the autumn of 1989 the chairman of the National Endowment for the Humanities in the United States, Lynne Cheney, had already begun the conversation with a report calling for "50 Hours: A Core Curriculum for College Students." That call sparked a flurry of interesting conversations focused above all on the question of how far the diverse institutions of higher education in the U.S. might or should aim for a common standard.

The NEH report naturally envisioned broad ranges of curricula reflecting diverse educational missions. What it invited educational leaders to do beyond their missions was to assess their respective obligations to offer and attain certain educational minima.

> The man who does not possess the concept of physics (not the science proper, but the vital idea of the world which it has created), and the concepts afforded by history and by biology, and the scheme of speculative philosophy, is not an educated man.[14]

In short, by the time of the NEH and AAC (now AACU) reports, the recognition of failure and the inspiration for reform were generally available.

Ten years later we saw in general continuing movement away from rather than towards "50 Hours." In other words, pieties about general education, core curricula, or more precisely, what it means to be educated, have not been accompanied by significant progress toward a curriculum to match the piety. At the same time, it is here that the academic leader will rise most surely to the task of leadership.

The spirit of general education reform in higher education advances the cause of integration against the continuing pressures of differentiation. In Virginia we responded in that spirit to accounts of deficiencies in the general education programs in the public colleges and universities in the Commonwealth. We surveyed the entire scene, public and private, and we concluded that, while Virginia averted the worst of the contemporary disasters in general education, it could still benefit greatly from giving more earnest attention to the subject.[15]

We do not often enough recall that general education emerged, at first, as a step down from the rigors of serious university education.[16] In the first thirty or forty years of the twentieth century, as institutions experienced an inundation of "unprepared" students, means were sought to provide some access to learning, if not the complete curriculum designed for a full "liberal education." That was certainly true of the initial general education program at the University of Minnesota. Nevertheless, elements of the Minnesota program paved the way toward the eventual embrace of general education as, in the advanced university, the equivalent of liberal education.

> General education is different from, and complementary to, special training for a job, for a profession, or for scholarship in a particular field of knowledge. Special training is important. Fine scholarship in a narrow line is excellent. Such training alone, however, is not enough to help get us ready for all our living. We spend less than a third of our lives in work. A much greater share of our time is spent in living with our families, bringing up our children, playing at our hobbies, relaxing in sleep or recreation, and attending to our rights and duties as citizens. . .[17]

General education was "extra" education in this conception. At the same time, the pressure to preserve liberal education from pre-professionalism was felt most strongly. The two streams of concern began to merge.

Many liberal arts colleges became largely pre-professional schools, especially in the big universities. Certainly it is hard for a student to secure a liberal education in four years when it has to be pieced together from many fragmentary specialized offerings. Luella Cole in 1940 wrote:

> The extreme degree of specialization indicated by the course offerings in large universities suggests strongly that these institutions are no place for an undergraduate to receive a general education, because he can hardly keep from getting into specialized courses before he is ready for them. . . . The number of courses in the largest institutions is simply staggering. This development is the direct result of two forces—the actual increases of human knowledge and the modern tendency to adapt college work to vocational demands.[18]

We invoke these mid-twentieth century paeans to liberal education and general education ever mindful of the anxiety expressed by W. I. Nichols: "Our passion for well-rounded education is such that we are in danger of manufacturing a nation of billiard balls."[19] Nichols's admonition goes unheeded in the published accreditation standards of the Middle States Commission, which insist that, "an institution must seek a balance between specialized areas and general education." Since every relation is a balance or some kind of balance, the failure to specify what the balance should be creates an admonition of balancing for the sake of balance, or a mere rounding off.[20]

Nonetheless, grounding our discussion in the prospects of democratic or republican life (we wrote in the Virginia report on "General Education") permits us to remain focused on the practical ends of education, without sacrificing the aim "to offer our brethren in every walk of life, all the blessings of broad, generous universal intellectual character."[21] In recent times practices in general education throughout the United States have been the subject of pervasive critique and profound skepticism.

Recent Concerns about General Education

Every academic calendar produces new and dramatic examples of this debate. Recently, the University of Chicago lay beneath the microscope of inspection, as a result of a thirty-year trend of changing core requirements and a then pending major renovation. In 1998, Brooklyn College of City University of New York underwent the same inspection, eventuating in retrenchment from a plan to broaden requirements. In most institutions the overriding question has been the departure from a sharply defined focus on the achievements of Western civilization in favor of standards loosely understood as multicultural. At the core of the debate we find far less an ideological stand-off between defenders of one culture versus defenders of plural cultures than a fundamental misunderstanding of the contents of the previous curricula and the intellectual justification of the newer standards.

The newer standards pose a challenge to a supposed "canon" of sources believed to be rather narrow in their focus. In fact, however, the fundamental rationale for a focus on Western culture has been its origin in the true original of multiculturalism. It has historically been Western science and Western civilization that have systematically advanced the goal of a broad understanding of humanity—as opposed to any particular culture—as the measure of intellectual progress. To that extent, a shift away from Western culture toward multiculturalism is, in fact, a contradiction in terms, as we discussed in some depth in chapter 1.

The Virginia survey did not directly produce a well-considered judgment about the level of intellectual leadership applied to this dilemma within Virginia colleges and universities. Nevertheless, enough dimensions and tendencies were revealed to afford opportunity to speak to the strengths or weaknesses of general education programs and, above all, to the apparent lack of real intellectual leadership on the subject.

While there is not a single college or university in Virginia that rises to the standard of the curriculum we will set forth at the end of this chapter (let alone the standard called for by Jefferson), it is nonetheless true, on the basis of a comparative assessment, that Virginia public institutions answered by anticipation many of the most damning criticisms. For example, perhaps no criticism of practices in general education is more persuasive than that which identifies a seemingly endless series of increasingly unrelated or over-specialized courses as fulfilling the very specific goals of a general education curriculum.[22] That criticism was true only of the University of Virginia in Virginia.

The Virginia patterns were appraised against the backdrop of general standards promulgated by national bodies. We derived from the American Academy of Liberal Education (AALE) and the American Association of Colleges and Universities (AACU) the general best practices in general education.

The published criteria emphasize not only subject or content areas but also the goals and management principles appropriate to general education.[23] These benchmarks were resolved into the set of criteria from which we derived a matrix on which we arrayed Virginia's institutions and assessed the extent of their accomplishment against the measure of these broadly recognized standards. In Virginia's study, however, we identified the goals of general education by seeking the first formulations of it in the official annals of the Commonwealth.

The State first attained the level of official and coherent expression of public goals in the "Report of the Commissioners for the University of Virginia" of 1818. More helpful, though, is the elaboration that followed the report, when the "Rector and Visitors" petitioned the Congress of the United States to eliminate the tariff duty on the importation of books. In that petition they signaled forcefully the range of subjects in which they thought it appropriate to offer general instruction:

> That the Commonwealth of Virginia has thought proper lately to establish an University, for instruction generally in all the useful branches of science. . . . That the difficulty resulting from this mode of procuring books of the first order in the sciences, and in foreign languages, ancient and modern, is an unfair impediment to the American student, who, for want of these aids, already possessed or easily procurable in all countries except our own, enters on his course with very unequal means, with wants unknown to his foreign competitors, and often with that imperfect result which subjects us to reproaches not unfelt by minds alive to the honor and mortified sensibilities of their country. That the value of science to a republican people, the security it gives to liberty, by enlightening the minds of its citizens, the protection it affords against foreign power, the virtues it inculcates, the just emulation of the distinction it confers on nations foremost in it—in short, its identification with power, morals, order, and happiness. . . are topics which your petitioners do not permit themselves to urge on the wisdom of Congress, before whose minds these considerations are already present, and bearing with their just weight.[24]

We find in this appeal three useful indices:

- First, comparative assessment of the standards of general education with reference to the attainments of those thought most advanced;

- Second, the public good expected to be realized from general education at the highest level; and,

- Third, the voice of a lay leadership that lays out the goals publicly identified and pursued.

That the fruits of general education may be expressed as "power, morals, order, and happiness" may appear less than intuitive to us, for we typically express the goals of general education in reference to individual rather than corporate attainments. But the "Report of the Commissioners" makes clear that, while education in itself targets the individual, it aims at the public good.

The first indication of this emerges in the consideration that the commissioners carefully distinguished the ends of general education at the higher level from the ends of education in general. Also known as the "Rock-Fish Gap" report, it distinguishes "primary" and "higher" education. The former provides for the citizen who "observes with intelligence and faithfulness all the social relations under which he shall be placed." Accordingly, it called for instructing "the mass of our citizens in [their] rights, interests and duties, as men and citizens." Wherefore one learns "to calculate. . .to express and preserve his ideas, his contracts and accounts in writing. . .[t]o improve by reading, his morals and faculties. . .to understand his duties to his neighbors. . .[t]o know his rights. . .and [t]o choose with discretion the fiduciaries of those he delegates"[25] This is the standard of lower or "primary" education. It is notable that, today, as at the origins of the contemporary discussion of general education in higher education, we often hear similar recitations (applied, however, rather to the *highest* than to the *primary* level of education).

What lay beyond this standard in the "Rock-Fish Gap" report was the goal "to form the Statesmen, Legislators, and Judges on whom public prosperity and individual happiness are so much to depend"— that is, a truly higher education. Students educated to this higher level were to "expound the principles and structure of government, the laws which regulate the intercourse of nations, those formed municipally for our own government, and a sound spirit of Legislation." People so educated would "harmonize and promote the interests of agriculture, manufactures, and commerce." They would, moreover, "develop the reasoning faculties of our youth, enlarge their minds, cultivate their morals." They would "enlighten them with mathematical and physical science, which advance the arts, and administer to the health, the subsistence, and comforts of life" and "generally, to form them to the habits of reflection and correct action, rendering them examples of virtue to others, and of happiness within themselves. . ."[26]

Thus, we see elucidated a series of professions to be prepared directly by general education at the higher level. Those professions entail law, agriculture, industry, commerce, and, most emphatically, teaching. In short, the end of general education at the higher level is to provide for education and support at the primary level. The goals announced for primary education will be attained only in proportion as advanced goals are attained in higher education. General education in higher education is the cement that makes possible a credible primary or pre-collegiate education that will, in turn, assure the development of able republican citizens who will act with intelligence and faithfulness.

Goal of General Education

Not the lesser goal of cultural familiarity but the noble goal of ability to direct and form culture (excellence in judgment) was the aim of general education as originally described in the official declarations of the Commonwealth of Virginia.

Much has changed since that time, including the massification of higher education. That has required us to revisit the definition of general education. Heretofore, however, we have done so only silently, accepting a tacit restatement that likens or reduces the goal of college and university education to what was previously envisioned as the goal of primary education—mere good citizenship. That may be a reasonable course to follow where ideals of access to higher education render less tenable the expectation that higher education will systematically produce "statesmen, legislators, and judges." But two questions must flow from such a conclusion for every genuine academic leader.

First, is there a successor to the former higher education, which assures the ability to provide the newly defined primary education? So much of the discussion of reform in teacher education addresses our deficiencies in this regard.

Second, do we adhere even to the more modest version of general education in our colleges and universities today?

Perhaps the most shocking remark a commentator could make about prevailing practices in general education in colleges and universities today, whether in Virginia or elsewhere in the United States, is that a tariff duty on foreign books would scarcely cause a ripple in our general education curricula. The pattern of offerings we discover upon review reveals little opportunity for comparative assessment with reference to the attainments of those thought most advanced.

To its credit we may say that American scholarship today is as frequently the intellectual standard as foreign scholarship. To our discredit there is little evidence that general education curricula foster much familiarity with cutting edges in scholarship, whether American or foreign.

To take the most obvious case, almost nowhere does there exist any general education curriculum in which the study of foreign language can be expected to foster anything more than a tourist's gloss on a foreign language. To be sure, many a foreign language major will have discovered an interest awakening in an elementary language course intended initially only to satisfy a general education requirement. That is something gained. The intensive study of foreign languages, however, is not a growth industry in the American academy.

Moreover, the evolution of general education courses as mainly the most general, introductory study preparatory to initiating specialized study in a major strengthens the presumption that there is no intrinsic virtue to general education itself—it is a means to the end of specialization more often than it is a substantive contribution to a student's understanding. Instruction in mathematics, like that in foreign languages, illustrates this ably. Indeed, a pervasive practice has emerged that isolates the handful of eventual majors in mathematics from all other students, who seldom acquire more than a sprinkling under showers effectively labeled "mathematics for the unfamiliar."

The guiding question in assessing general education is not how comprehensive is the list of offerings at a college or university. It is far rather, how effective an analyst of the structures of government the mathematics major is and how effective an analyst of mathematics the political science major is.

We cannot take great encouragement about the answers to those questions from contemporary performances. The importance of this stems from the fact that we read current practice in light of the requirement that general education produce, not proficient specialists, but rather "intelligent and faithful citizens" and, to the extent possible, "statesmen, legislators, and judges."

It has long been recognized as insufficient to think of "statesmen, legislators, and judges" as merely proficient specialists.[27] But a brief discussion of "critical thinking" will make clear the distinction between the civilizing talent—judgment—and mere talent. Proficient specialists are talented, indeed, but unless their specialties entail judgment across disciplines and needs, they are not talented enough to lead communities and they cannot qualify to lead colleges and universities. For this reason, we ought to ponder as well the goals and standards of higher education against the background of what it is not: mere critical thinking.

From Critical Thinking to Proficient Humanity

If we apply the case for general education as a test of academic leadership and excellence in judgment, we will encounter a further question that needs to be resolved: namely, why critical thinking is too narrow a goal for higher education. They err who place "critical thinking" in the role that has been reserved for "thinking" and "judgment." The point of higher education as opposed to any more utilitarian training is to enable the eventual adept to be able to distinguish in each case the good and the bad and the right and the wrong.

To the end of answering that question and illustrating the character of judgment that is most required for academic leadership, we lean on the important work of Ronald Barnett, *Higher Education: A Critical Business.* To place that work in its proper context, however, it is important first to comprehend the claims most generally made for "critical thinking," which now is frequently resorted to by academics in the United States and abroad as the most highly valued "transferable skill" provided by higher education. [28]

An example of the kind of understanding that attaches to the invocation of "critical thinking" is that provided by Martha Nussbaum in her *Cultivating Humanity.*[29] Her "political science student, Anna" found herself unprepared to work in China by reason of having failed to take courses that exposed her to a diversity of cultural practices: "Her imaginative capacity to enter the lives of people of other nations had been blunted by lack of practice." Nussbaum believes that the kind of "critical thinking" that would make one a more sensitive judge of different cultures is achieved primarily through "introduction" to cultural differences, as opposed to mature intellectual performance.[30]

This is where Ronald Barnett's work is significant, for he carefully differentiates "critical thinking" from "critical thought," arguing that excellence in thought and judgment is the true goal of education (rather than mere familiarization). Among the defects of the familiarization approach, he argues, is to "leave our students sensing that there is a givenness to the knowledge structures that they are encountering or that those structures are socially neutral."[31]

Barnett's agenda is to assure that higher education aim for the regenerative power of "symbolic creation" (or pushing the frontiers of knowledge) as opposed to the mere analysis or manipulation of symbols. This refocuses our thinking on the ends of education, and it is beyond the scope of these remarks to follow Barnett through his encounters with postmodernism and the forms of university organization in the contemporary world.

We do need, however, to pay close attention to two of his most striking conclusions. First, Barnett specifically maintains that deep familiarity with a "single intellectual field" is superior to a "superficial encounter" with diverse subjects or disciplines. If "cognitive transformation" is our end, as it should be, then our attention must be focused on levels of intellectual accomplishment more than on ranges of intellectual exposure. For that purpose, we require to identify and adhere to "critical standards."

Secondly, such intellectual maturity may be accomplished only on the strength of universal standards or principles:

> But these are large claims and they open up a number of large problems...it could mean that there are cross-disciplinary critical standards to which we could resort. The first possibility is that of linking territories together, if only in a piecemeal way. This is the Bailey's bridge route to critical reconstruction: creating new linkages but probably of a limited and temporary character. The second possibility is the cartographer's route in which we detect new connections in the map of knowledge, local territories being seen to be part of a new and larger map of the whole territory.[32]

The second possibility, that which envisions connecting the diverse strands of a continuing conversation across the ages, is the one that opens for us the door to a fuller understanding of the requisites of academic leadership. Higher education aims for each student to connect the conversations of fundamental inquiry or, as Oakeshott expressed it, to acquire a "language" and not just a "literature" of the disciplines.[33]

Moreover, it is plausible to maintain that the advance of society or civilization is directly tied to our ability to connect the conversations regarding being and knowing. In that regard, the multiversity cannot be allowed to descend further into "discrete academic subcultures" without rendering itself inert for the task of sustaining social momentum. While we acknowledge the truth of the wry statement that ". . .colleges are in the most unenviable position: one is a manager in a corporation which is trying to sell intangible value added assets,"[34] we nevertheless insist both upon the value of those assets and the responsibility of the university to maintain and even enhance that value.

It falls to academic leaders to express whether a relationship may be maintained "between transferable skills and critical thought."

> One response is that, in themselves, transferable skills are neutral in regard to critical thought. . . . Critical thought, after all, could be critical of transferable skills. But that view begs questions. . . . An individual might be—we can be charitable—skilled in her transferable skills, but will not be furnished thereby with the capacity to critique the surroundings. The skill lies in the competence to perform instrumentally and not in the capacity to form a deep understanding of her environment and to critique it. As policy and as educational project, critique is doubly written out of transferable skills.[35]

In permitting the emergence of transferable skills at the expense of "critical thought," universities permit the "instrumental, the technological, and the performative" to sideline the "hermeneutic, the liberal and the contemplative." What we see in the university, Barnett maintains, is a passing from "a hermeneutic mode of communication" to "an instrumental mode of communication." Now, our chief communicators are our academic leaders. Hence, the burden of justifying this change, or of arresting it, must fall to them.

It is also important to observe that Barnett does not fail to take into account the massive changes occurring in the modern university, including democratization, virtualizing, and consumerizing. The question, however, is whether in this age of change we must say, "goodbye, higher education as discipline; hello, higher education as play, as extension of popular culture."

It will now be clear why this discussion of critical thinking is pertinent to our discussion of academic leadership and the curriculum of the university. Nowhere is the instrumental view of critical thinking more consistently invoked than through the lips of university presidents. They, doubtless, do not see themselves participating in a postmodernist rejection of universal standards.[36] Perhaps, though, they can be led to see that they thereby abandon disciplinary standards and put at risk higher education's role in cultivating excellence in judgment as its distinctive contribution to society. For, as Maritain notes, ". . .supremacy of means over ends and the consequent collapse of all sure purpose and real efficiency seems to be the main reproach to contemporary education."[37]

What we require of academic leaders is that they be able to speak intelligently about this process of change that engulfs all of higher education, and that they demonstrate in their conversation about it the specific excellence in judgment that qualifies them for their offices. We recognize that they must perform this work in an environment of heightened transparency, as the organizational imperatives of modern university life have changed. They must provide the "accountability, efficiency, and responsiveness" the present demand-oriented environment provides for, even while practicing substantive, hermeneutic leadership.

> [Universities] have become organizations separately and they have become—in the formation of a state-sponsored system of higher education—a kind of collective megaorganization. Within universities, planning, management information, budgeting, target setting, efficiency savings, devolved budgeting and accountability measures become taken for granted as aspects of managing a modern university.[38]

We observed in *The 1999 Virginia Plan: Advancing the System of Higher Education in Virginia* that the state, the public, does not invent, albeit it certainly uses, higher education.[39] The point of that observation is to underscore the extent to which the university must transcend the political organization of the society and therefore the extent to which the academic leader must protect the university's integrity even while responding to the political imperatives that often drive planning in the modern university.

Higher education aims most comprehensively to eventuate in proficient humanity, and if proficient humanity entails not just the capacity for but also the practice of intelligent judgment across the range of human circumstances, then higher education must aim to foster such judgment.

Judgment on this order involves not only distinguishing the correct and the incorrect, the good and the bad, the fit and the unfit, and the right and the wrong across the extraordinary range of unique individual situations that constitute human life, but it also entails the ready expression of such judgments.

The ready expression of such judgments cannot result from any practice other than the application of consistent rules. Where any two particulars are separately equal to any third particular, the foregoing two must be equal to each other. No issue of taste, choice, background, or inclination may be allowed to intrude upon that rulebased conclusion. In that sense proficient judgment results from proficiency in thinking, and not the mere assertion of preferences even when preferences are informed by comparative awareness of the preferences of others or the consequences for others.

Because human situations are relative, it is all the more important that proficient judgment be rule-based. Judgment across the range of variable circumstances cannot be trusted if judgment may vary as the situations or circumstances vary. It is the purpose of the rule to support the adequacy of judgment in every particular circumstance.

Accordingly, rule-based thinking is the goal of higher education, and rule-based thinking may be contrasted with critical thinking wherever critical thinking is not formally understood to be rule-based thinking. An example of critical thinking that is not formally understood to be rule-based thinking is that which encourages protégés to express tastes, choices, or inclinations on the strength of broad information about all relevant tastes, choices, or inclinations but without requiring a demonstration of the propriety of particular tastes, choices, or inclinations. However admirable it may be that individuals would pay attention to the needs of other individuals before insisting on their own, it remains true that their own needs must still be defended by rational argument and are subject to be judged as fit or unfit, good or bad, correct or incorrect, and right or wrong. Only a firmly established habit of mind can secure such judgment.

Otherwise, critical thinking would eventuate in nothing more than the comparative weighing of the intensities of competing appetites. It is better to take competing appetites into account before insisting on just one appetite. But the one appetite is not better just for being the last one adhered to. Unless it can satisfy rule-based evaluation, it must be treated as mere appetite, irrational, and not worthy to be admitted. The prostitute that selects the healthiest of a number of prospective clients doubtlessly acts sensibly. But when it is clear that she would still select the most scrofulous if the only client, it is clear that her proficiency in comparing possibilities is not informed by a preference of good over bad and right over wrong.

The point of higher education as opposed to any more utilitarian training is to enable the eventual adept to distinguish in each case the good and the bad and the right and the wrong. The challenge of academic leadership is to demonstrate ceaselessly the centrality of this work and its enduring cultural value.

The goal of higher education, again, is to foster tough judgments under the guidance of high standards. The specific challenge to academic leaders is to apply such tough judgments and rigorous standards in their own work. Proficient specialists are capable of doing just this within the narrow range of disciplinary interests. Proficient humanity performs at this level across the range of human interests.

Higher education aims at proficient humanity via the route of integrated inquiry. That goal, integrated inquiry, needs to inform the mission of the university if it is to play its role in generating proficient humanity. To sacrifice that role to the liberal arts college (which disproportionately produces our research faculty[40]) may be a workable proposition, structurally, but it has consequences for vast numbers of our citizens that ought to be unacceptable to all of us.

Finally, in reply to the sensible inquiry, what, then would such a curriculum look like, we provide the following outline of a curriculum leading to excellence in judgment. The pre-supposition of this curriculum is an adequate pre-collegiate education, but it requires only further elaboration rather than abandonment in the face of different and more challenging realities.

A Course of Higher Education

Rather than to build on merely private motives or arbitrary conceptions of a higher education, and avoiding recourse to the merely classical, let us begin by recapitulating the standards conveyed in the "Rock-Fish Gap" report.

Providing for the citizen who "observes with intelligence and faithfulness all the social relations under which he shall be placed," it called for instructing "the mass of our citizens in [their] rights, interests and duties, as men and citizens." This meant each student would learn during his primary education how

> . . .to calculate . . .to express and preserve his ideas, his contracts and accounts in writing. . .[t]o improve by reading, his morals and faculties. . .to understand his duties to his neighbors . . .[t]o know his rights. . .and [t]o choose with discretion the fiduciaries of those he delegates."[41]

Let us make these, then, the givens with which every scholar begins a higher education. No university should have to expect anything less than this range of knowledges, competencies, and opening habits of mind in a fresh student.

Since "higher education" must build on this secure foundation, it surely aims at attainments considerably beyond these estimable ones. That makes it reasonable to aim "to form the Statesmen, Legislators, and Judges on whom public prosperity and individual happiness are so much to depend." Such persons will be able to "expound the principles and structures of government, the laws which regulate the

intercourse of nations, those formed municipally for our own government, and a sound spirit of Legislation." They know how to "harmonize and promote the interests of agriculture, manufacture, and
commerce." These results derive from studies that "develop the reasoning faculties of our youth, enlarge their minds, [and] cultivate
their morals." They "enlighten them with mathematical and physical science, which advance the arts, and administer to the health, the
subsistence, and comforts of life," and "generally. . .form them to
the habits of reflection and correct action. . ."[42]

It is not difficult to name the subjects of study that produce these
results. They begin with disciplined study in languages, arts, and
sciences, progress through advanced study in history and social science, and culminate in literatures, philosophy, and law-regulated
activities (which encompasses the professional disciplines from legal studies to physics to sculpture).

Throughout such a curriculum, students will write and speak frequently and extensively. They will have arrived prepared to do so
(or else must speedily be made capable of doing so).

The language study will be important, even when they have had
prior language training, for their grasp of foreign languages needs
to proceed apace with their increasing intellectual agility. In the arts
they must study the history of republicanism (in which United States
history must be central) specifically and human history more
broadly. Natural history will be no less important. And advanced
mathematics will bridge the arts and the sciences (or natural history). Students should have arrived with advanced algebra at a minimum, and be ready to proceed through probability, calculus, and
linear analysis.

In their second and third years they should continue and perfect
their introductory studies to the extent necessary, but should also be
engaged in rigorous historical and social scientific analysis (which
must include scientific as well as social architectures). Then in their
final year (assuming a four-year course of study rather than the five
that would be appropriate if students were to begin earlier or less
well prepared), they should seriously engage in integrative patterns
of study, which would emphasize close study of literature, the practice rather than the survey of philosophy, and the study (and/or practice) of what we choose to call "law-regulated" activities. These last
include the range of specifically human activities and professions
that are subject to disciplined development in accord with clearly

established procedures for validation. Here the student will rather study one or some than all of the possible disciplines, and to the extent the course of study permits it, such study may begin in the third year. Because the rudiments of these studies should have been well conveyed in the prior general curriculum, students should begin at levels appreciably advanced beyond current practice.

The goal of such a curriculum is that proficient humanity which is characterized by excellence in judgment. It does not intend to produce "professionals" (with the exception of teachers and of these it should produce generous numbers). Nor does it intend to produce disciplinary adepts. It does assure students well prepared to advance in graduate study in chosen fields. More importantly, it assures the aim of the "Rock-Fish Gap" report, namely, statesmen, legislators, and judges. For these persons are best prepared on the basis of general knowledge of human arts and culture.[43]

Notes

1. These remarks were first delivered at the Conference on Statistics, Science and Public Policy held 26-29 April 2000 at Queen's University International Study Centre, Herstmonceux Castle, Hailsham, UK and published in the proceedings of the conference under the title, "Excellence in Judgement: The Curriculum" (reprinted here with permission). They, along with portions of chapter 3, develop in-depth ideas previously sketched in W. B. Allen, "The Challenges of Academic Leadership," The Clarion 4 (November-December 1999): 12-35 (reprinted here with permission).

2. Harold W. Stoke, The American College President (New York: Harper & Brothers Publishers, 1959), 94.

3. "To make the multiversity work really effectively, the moderator needs to be in control of each power center and there needs to be an attitude of tolerance between and among the power centers, with few territorial ambitions" (Kerr, 1982: 39).

4. Phyllis M. Krutsch, "The Passive Culture of Public Boards," Trusteeship 6 (March/April, 1998): 23.

5. Roger W. Bowen, "The New Battle Between Political and Academic Cultures," Chronicle of Higher Education 47 (June 22, 2001): B14-15.

6. We share Lucas's regret for the passing of an earlier generation of academic leaders who were unafraid to express the work of the university in such terms. "Some of the lofty pronouncements of academics defining the purpose of collegiate education in an earlier day admittedly sound more than a little overblown to the modern ear. But for all their seeming pomposity, they did reflect a spirit of assurance, a sublime confidence in the formative powers of a liberal education less often advanced with the same degree of certitude today" (Lucas, 1996: 52).

7. "University builders anchored the research university as the primary form of American higher education by 1910." Laurence Veysey, The Emergence of the American University (Chicago: University of Chicago Press, 1965), 346-47, 369-70.

8. Nicolas Murray Butler, "A University Defined," in The Reference Shelf 7, edited by James Goodwin Hodgson (New York: H. W. Wilson Company, 1931), 48.

9.   Shils, 238.
10.   Cf., Krutsch, 22: "[Lay governance] should be concerned with dynamic improve-
      ments to a structure that is [presently] more responsive to faculty interests than to
      productivity or to the general education of undergraduates."
11.   Burton J. Bledstein, The Culture of Professionalism: The Middle Class and the
      Development of Higher Education in America (New York: W. W. Norton & Co.,
      Inc., 1970) Cf., p. 284 and 287ff. The common destination identified in chapter 1
      need not be ennobling, a different problem. Bledstein's exploration of
      professionalization and the middle class examined higher education's cultural impli-
      cations within a history of university leadership. Following Veysey, he accepted the
      "university builder" concept, describing these men as business-minded, bureau-
      cratic, focused on material establishment—i.e., raising money—and on improving
      institutional recognition. By improving structure, Bledstein believed, the "univer-
      sity builders" reinforced middle-class demands for an orderly environment in which
      to advance their status. The university made this new professionalism widely avail-
      able to the middle class.
12.   Recently we learned of another shocking example of the failure: Losing America's
      Memory documented the failure of the fifty-five most highly regarded colleges
      and universities in the United States. According to the report, released 21
      February 2000, students graduate from these institutions with a "profound
      historical illiteracy." Anne D. Neal and Jerry L. Martin, Losing America's
      Memory: Historical Illiteracy in the 21st Century (Washington, D. C.: American
      Council of Trustees and Alumni, 2000), 1, <http://www.goacta.org> (August 13,
      2001)].
13.   A Failure to Set High Standards: CUNY's General Education Requirements (New
      York: Empire Foundation for Policy Research and American Council of Trustees
      and Alumni, 1998), ii.
14.   Ortega ý Gasset, 31.
15.   General Education in Virginia: Assessment and Innovation—A Challenge to Aca-
      demic Leadership (Richmond: State Council of Higher Education for Virginia,
      1999) <http://www.schev.edu/html/reports/genedstudy.pdf> (February 12, 2001).
16.   Robert Nisbet does recall, but focuses too much on criteria of relevance and too little
      on qualifications of the students: "Whereas the. . .liberal arts phase [of the cult of
      individuality], declared disciplinary knowledge expendable, even injurious, the present
      and more radical phase declares all knowledge—knowledge, that is, in the tradi-
      tional university sense—expendable, injurious, and, in the word of the hour, irrel-
      evant." Robert Nisbet, The Degradation of the Academic Dogma (New York: Basic
      Books, 1971), 126.
17.   Ivol Spafford, Building a Curriculum for General Education: A Description of the
      General College Program (Minneapolis: The University of Minnesota Press: 1943), 1.
18.   Luella Cole, The Background for College Teaching (New York: Farrar and Rinehart,
      1940), 50-51, cited in Spafford, Building a Curriculum for General Education, 12.
19.   Atlantic Monthly, 14 (October 1929): 947-56.
20.   Characteristics of Excellence in Higher Education: Standards for Accreditation,
      1994 ed., (Philadelphia: Commission on Higher Education Middle States Associa-
      tion, 1994), 13.
21.   Francis Wayland, A Memoir of the Life and Labors of Francis Wayland, vol. 2,
      edited by F. Wayland and H. L. Wayland (New York: Sheldon and Co., 1867), 106.
      As Jacques Maritain put it in 1941, "In reality, the democratic way of life demands
      primarily liberal education for all and a general humanistic development throughout
      society." (Maritain, 1943 [1978]: 20).
22.   See note 43 at the end of this chapter.

23. AALE emphasizes that (standard one) the "mission statement reflects the impor-
     tance and centrality of liberal education and states the institution's purposes and
     goals in a manner that corresponds to the way in which its curriculum is actually
     organized and taught." Standards two and three require that the "importance of
     teaching [be] featured, supported, and rewarded in the life of the institution or
     program" and that "liberty of thought and freedom of speech [be] supported and
     protected, bound only by such rules of civility and order as to facilitate intellectual
     inquiry and the search for truth." American Academy for Liberal Education, "The
     Academy's Education Standards" <http://www.aale.org/edstand.htm> (October 23,
     2001).
         AACU standards focus more on process and articulation than on content, pro-
     viding in part that "strong general education programs explicitly answer the ques-
     tion, 'What is the point of general education?' (Principle 1)" and "embody institu-
     tional mission" (2). Such programs "continually strive for educational coherence"
     (3) and "are self-consciously value-based and teach social responsibility" (4). They
     "attend carefully to student experience" (5), "are consciously designed so that they
     will continue to evolve" (6), and "require and foster academic community" (7). Jerry
     G. Graff, Twelve Principles for Effective General Education Programs (Washing-
     ton, D.C.: American Association of Colleges and Universities, 1994).
24. Rector and Visitors, University of Virginia, Petition to the United States Congress.
     "Petition to Abolish Tariff on Scientific Books Imported from Abroad." File draft,
     November 30, 1821. Printed: Central Gazette, 4 January 1822. (Mss # 3734, Tho-
     mas Jefferson Papers, The Albert and Shirley Small Special Collections Library,
     University of Virginia Library; quoted with permission).
25. Report of the Commissioners for the University of Virginia, Assembled at Rock-
     Fish Gap, in the County of Augusta, August 1, 1818 (Charlottesville: C. P. McKennie,
     1824), 5.
26. Ibid., 5-6.
27. "It is only for the professions or executive positions in business that it is necessary
     to be able to reason logically from cause to effect and to possess special training
     such as colleges are best able to give. Unless a young person has the ability to think,
     and not merely to memorize and empirically to apply rules, as well as a special
     aptitude for the callings just mentioned, he should not be allowed to attend a public-
     supported college or university." Butler in Hodgson, The Reference Shelf, 75.
28. Ronald Barnett, Higher Education: A Critical Busines (Bristol, PA: SRHE and
     Open University Press, 1997).
29. Martha Nussbaum, Cultivating Humanity (Cambridge, MA: Harvard University
     Press, 1997), chapter 2, "Citizens of the World."
30. For a different view of the issue of breadth versus depth, see Malcolm L. Peel and
     Leo L. Nussbaum, "The Core Course Redivivus," Liberal Education 60 (December
     1974): 478-88.
31. Barnett, 5.
32. Ibid., 28.
33. Michael Oakeshott, Rationalism in Politics (Indianapolis, IN: Liberty Fund, Inc.,
     1991), 192.
34. N. Machiavelli, "The Administrator: Notes on the Academic Manna Game," Liberal
     Education 60 (December 1974): 500.
35. Barnett, 39.
36. Ibid., 29. "Why is the postmodern view so determined to drive out all belief in
     anything that smacks of the universal? At bottom, there is a fear of terror. The view
     is that any attempt to identify elements of human action or thinking—whether in the
     form of knowledge, bodies of thought, ethical principles, modes of language and

communication, or forms of life—amounts, ultimately, to totalitarianism. My suggesting that you should assent to this view of the world or these moral principles because they have some kind of objectivity or general applicability to them amounts to a form of dictatorship. It is tantamount to my saying: really, you have no choice in the matter. This is the way the world is. You can't even take it or leave it: you have to take it. You might not see the world the way I do or readily assent to these moral principles. Nevertheless, because I am more insightful than you, or because I have considered these matters more carefully, it so happen that the picture of the world I am putting before you is not just my view—it has universal validity."

37.   Maritain, 3.
38.   Ibid., 55.
39.   Advancing the System of Higher Education in Virginia: 1999 Virginia Plan for Higher Education (Richmond: State Council of Higher Education for Virginia, 1999), <http://www.schev.edu/html/reports/99vaplanfinal.pdf> (March 18, 2001).
40.   This well-established fact has been reported for several years through the surveys reported by the Higher Education Research Institute at UCLA.
41.   Report of the Commissioners for the University of Virginia, 5.
42.   Ibid., 5-6. Here we may usefully compare the continuing AALE standards with the models we employ. "The general education requirement ensures a basic knowledge of mathematics and the physical and biological sciences, including laboratory experience, intermediate knowledge of at least one foreign language, and the study of literature and literary classics, the political, philosophical and cultural history of Western civilization, and the foundations and principles of American society. Variations from this norm are allowable in cases where the outstanding character of other elements of the general education program assures substantial compliance with these standards" (standard four).

   "The curriculum's prerequisite structure, as defined and enforced, insures an orderly progression from elementary to advanced levels of knowledge, and the course definitions in the catalogue distinguish clearly among those considered fundamental (either to a general education or to mastery of a major), those less so, and those that belong to specialized subjects" (standard five).

   The remaining AALE standards provide that the "baccalaureate requirements in the liberal arts and sciences call for not less than a third of the student's course work to be taken within the general education requirement" (6), that "the institution defines and enforces academic entrance requirements that prepare students to take the required college-level general education courses" (7), and that "a student writes substantial essays during every stage of progress as an undergraduate, and thereby demonstrates a proficiency in written English" (8). Moreover, "the institution evaluates student progress in learning the elements of general education taught under Standard Four, and ascertains how well it meets the educational goals it has set for itself, either by means of a general examination or some academic equivalent" (9).

   General education courses are taught by "regular faculty members, including senior ones," and they "are regularly engaged in academic counseling" (10). "Class size is appropriate to subject matter, level of instruction, and need for class discussion" (11), and "the library and other information resources are adequate to the demands of its programs" (12). American Academy for Liberal Education, "The Academy's Education Standards" <http://www.aale.org/edstand.htm> (October 23, 2001).

43.   See, for reviews of current curricula, the following:
   •   Stephen H. Balch and Rita Clara Zurcher, *The Dissolution of General Education, 1914-1993* (Princeton: National Association of Scholars, 1996).

- Robert W. Kenny, *Reinventing Undergraduate Education: A Blueprint for America's Research Universities* (New York: The Boyer Commission on Educating Undergraduates in the Research University, 1998).
- Jerry G. Gaff, *General Education: The Changing Agenda* (Washington, D.C.: Association of American Colleges and Universities, 1999).
- Marianne M. Jennings, *The Dissolution of General Education: A Review of Arizona's Three State Universities' Programs of Study and Degree Requirements* (n.p.: Arizona Association of Scholars, 2000).
- Jerry L. Martin and Anne D. Neal, *The Shakespeare File: What English Majors Are Really Studying: A Report* (Washington, D.C.: The Forum, 1996).
- Anne D. Neal and Jerry L. Martin, *Losing America's Memory: Historical Illiteracy in the 21st Century* (Washington, D. C.: American Council of Trustees and Alumni, 2000). <http://www.goacta.org> (August 13, 2001).
- New York Association of Scholars and Empire Foundation for Policy Research, *SUNY's Core Curricula: The Failure to Set Consistent High Academic Standards* (New York: The Association, July 1996).
- Colleen Sheehan, *The Core Curriculum of Pennsylvania's State System and State-Related Universities: Are Pennsylvania's Students Receiving the Fundamentals of a College Education?* (Harrisburg, PA: The Commonwealth Foundation for Public Policy Initiatives, September 1998).

3

Access to Higher Education

A shared vision of post-secondary education offering every citizen in the Common-wealth full opportunity to attain a baccalaureate credential is at the center of the system of higher education in Virginia. It is the fulcrum on which we move to construct the entire edifice of higher education.—Advancing the System of Higher Education in Virginia

A public policy approach governing access to higher education and designed to sustain the fusionist concepts laid out above must include the following elements:

- A realistic and stable approach to funding—one that can withstand the ups and downs of the economic cycle;

- A mix of tuition, tax-payer, and charitable support;

- A "high-tuition/high-aid" policy, which requires that those who are able to pay do so and focuses public support on need;

- Incentives to encourage responsible investment in postsecondary education by entrepreneurs; and,

- Strategic deployment of public funds to stimulate meritorious performance both by students and by institutions.

The next three chapters explore the principal circumstances affecting the potentiality to realize goals such as these. Chapter 3 focuses on access, while chapter 4 emphasizes using assessment to maintain excellence. In chapter 5, we use our experience in Virginia as an example of specific policies aimed at expanding access while also enhancing quality.

Access

Excellence is not the enemy of access to higher education. In chapter 1, we underscored that the very idea of the university today must embrace both access and excellence as noble goals, which are not only compatible but also essential. Our insistence that access and excellence be paired goals does not pretend that there is no tension between them; nevertheless, the need to preserve excellence as the aim of the university need not be an obstacle to access. We accept but do not regard as dispositive the principle asserted by Clark Kerr: "The great university is of necessity elitist—the elite of merit— but it operates in an environment dedicated to egalitarian philoso- phy. How may the contributions of the elite be made clear to the egalitarians, and how may an aristocracy of intellect justify itself to a democracy of all men?"[1] This forerunner to Allan Bloom faltered on the same shoals that grounded Bloom, imagining that, because only a very few can be *fully* educated, formal education addresses the needs of that few. Formal education aims for the excellence of which most or nearly all are capable. That is why barriers to access must fall and as such are wholly incompatible with excellence.

Barriers to access do exist, and we discuss them in this chapter. These barriers include academic readiness for collegiate study, the cost of a college education, and the availability of "seats" (whether physical or virtual) within the academy. During the 1990s, it be- came painfully evident that American higher education is caught between diverging trends—demand increased at the same time that a college education became less and less affordable. We first place this demand within an historical context before turning to a discus- sion of the chief barriers to meeting the demand.

Why Access?

The central plot of the story of higher education in the twentieth century—particularly in the United States, but not limited to this nation—was that of ever-widening access. From the start of this ex- pansion, there was doubt whether the high ideal of "an education which" "equip[s] a man to derive more satisfaction out of nature and people and books and events"[2] could meet the challenge of numbers. But, from this early moment the challenge was recognized. Henry Sloan Coffin spoke in a world described by J. B. Johnston:

Between the years 1900 and 1923 the number of collegiate and technological students in the country increased from 93,000 to 370,000. . . . Between 1900 and 1910 the population of the country increased 21 per cent, while the collegiate enrollment in- creased [in the south 34 per cent, in the north and west 109 per cent, and] in the country as a whole 85 per cent. From 1910 to 1920, while the population increased 14.9 per cent, collegiate enrollment increased [in the south 80 per cent, in the north and west 100 per cent, and] in the United States 96 per cent. Collegiate enrollment therefore has increased in the last two decades from four times to six and one-half times as fast as the population.[3]

The questions raised by this dramatic growth in higher education tracked the previous spurt in high school education, a spurt that led some to question whether "too many children were in the high schools who ought not to be there."[4] Not only was the ultimate answer to the high school boom the "open door," but eventually the most adventurous souls urged that "education beyond high school. . .is part of the public school system. We recommend that the colleges stop sniveling over the unfitness of youth and address themselves to fitting it."[5]

It was an era of great aspiration that led not only to universal high school education, but to a general expectation that no limits need be placed on attendance at university. The context of higher education from the beginning of the twentieth century has been the context of democratic expansion. At no point has that goal been checked, at no point even vigorously resisted.

Even Ortega y Gasset, holding out for standards of selection in Europe, nevertheless still declared that "the university consists, primarily and basically, of the higher education which the ordinary man should receive."[6]

Triumph of Democracy in Higher Education

In the twentieth century democracy triumphed, and it is too late at the dawn of the twenty-first century to devote too much attention to the question of whether higher education ought to be for the many or the few.[7] As Alvin Kernan reminds us, ". . .history never runs backward, and to reverse the democratization of American higher education is neither desirable nor possible."[8] The real question, we shall see at length, is whether in the context of democratic higher education, there is any prospect for a still higher education. For now, and already by 1930:

> The change of college from a winnowing machine, from a self-constituted educational caste-committee, to a part of the national system for the service of all the children of all the people is so consequent to what has happened to the rest of our educational order that even the affection we all have for the personal charm of the typical college professor cannot much longer delay the overturn.[9]

The context in which we must consider the components of academic leadership and the problems of higher education must begin with democratization, but it will also include the character of college life and study.

The United States has led the world in the "massification" of higher education—the process by which increasingly large percentages of adult populations are expected to obtain a college degree. An implication of massification is that more and more people should qualify for college study. But, do they in fact qualify? Other countries are dealing with this issue by introducing "tuition" as a necessary dimension of funding higher education.[10] In the past these nations essentially paid the entire cost of higher education with tax dollars, while educating only a privileged elite. It is ironic, then, that as higher education becomes more democratic (in China, for example), these governments find it necessary to emphasize individual responsibility rather than taxpayer responsibility.

In the United States we democratized mainly through a gradual expansion of the role of taxpayer responsibility. Only California meaningfully attempted to fund higher education with comprehensive taxpayer support from the outset. We now begin to doubt the wisdom of offering blank checks, endorsed by the taxpayer, for whatever colleges and universities choose to do for however long students may need to do it.[11] The United States has also always had the example of independent or private institutions of higher education, not only as competition but also as illustrations of other ways to provide higher education. Accordingly, our present need is different from that under discussion in the People's Republic of China. They want to make sure that students appreciate the opportunity they are being afforded, while we want to assure that students are qualified in the first place.[12]

In every decade since the 1960s the chorus of the 1920s has been re-sung with increasing *fortissimo*: "Education today is in the midst of a great boom":

> Higher education has been expanding most spectacularly. College enrollments have grown from 1.4 million in 1939-40 to nearly 5 million last year; two out of five persons of college age (eighteen to twenty-one years) were enrolled last year compared with only one out of seven in 1939-40. By the mid-seventies, enrollments are expected to exceed 8 million, with more than half of all eighteen-to-twenty-one-year-olds going to college.[13]

Herbert Hoover in 1931 declared that "there should be no child in America who does not have full opportunity for education from kindergarten to university."[14] By 1966, Lineberry reported the mission virtually accomplished:

> Whereas high school had been a standard of attainment for earlier generations, it is clear that college is now becoming a common goal. Employers have raised their educational standards. Parents know that their children will need more and more schooling to enter and succeed in occupations and professions that offer better incomes and higher status.[15]

Despite this enormous consistency of experience and interpretation, however, only twenty years later Horowitz was able to write, "Differences between present and past are immense. In the 1980s over 7 million young people attend college or university full time."[16]

It may be that the focus on the pace of change operates to blind observers to the underlying elements of the context of higher education that affect most meaningfully the opportunities for academic leadership. Lineberry had quoted Benjamin Franklin: "'An investment in knowledge pays the best interest.'"[17] Though generations of Americans have acted on this belief in getting an education, they have done so without precise knowledge of the likely payoff. But for decades Americans have had the benefit of Gary Becker's modern analysis showing an "average rate of return in the form of increased earnings" of "more than 12 per cent."[18]

Horowitz, meanwhile and in her search to capture the ethos of the university campus, observed the average rate of return with a different eye:

> As I conversed with a quiet, graceful junior biology major hoping to become a doctor like her parents, I found it difficult to get her to talk about anything other than courses and studying. I kept straining to find a common ground on which we could discuss her roommates, social life, extracurricular activities, or intellectual interests, but there seemed to be none. At one point, I decided that she stuck to academic matters because she was shy. Only later did I realize that she had focused on class preparations, labs, lectures, and examinations because they were essentially all that mattered to her. It was a profoundly disturbing realization, but one that I would have repeatedly.

The student's narrowed focus on the average rate of return "disturbed" Horowitz, but all of her observations up to this awakening pointed clearly in this direction. Thus, despite Horowitz's viewing with wonder the rate of increase in college attendance between 1960 and 1980, she later clearly observed that something like a geometrical progression had been underway since 1880.[19] Moreover, she had observed the shift from private to public institutions, and the emergence of higher education as *the* path into the professions, in contrast with earlier practice. When she concluded, therefore, that today's students encounter a "college [that] moves them along to a job or a career, but for most it no longer serves to liberate their souls," she had already provided the response to her question, "What is the cause?"

> Are contemporary students less villains than victims, caught by economic forces beyond their control? Perhaps; but other generations of students confronted in college the harsh challenges of an unfriendly future and yet allowed themselves the pleasures and the pains of an intense college world.[20]

The temptation in the United States is to repeat in higher education what we did so successfully and to such bad effect with pre-collegiate education—to reduce it all to a common level. We in higher education have some advantages that enable us to resist this temptation toward homogenization, and the most important is *non-compulsory* attendance.

Our institutions of higher learning (public and private) must compete for students; they do not get them automatically. Public policy that undercuts the need for competition will contribute to a harmful homogenization in colleges and universities. Academic leaders (presidents and provosts) who fail to articulate strong grounds of competition, boasting of what distinguishes their institutions from others, risk losing credible grounds for defending public support. It is well known that all of higher education suffers from the "Lake Wobegone" effect: everybody's above average. At this point in history, however, it is critically important to give the lie to that delusion. We can afford to increase the numbers receiving college education only if we assure that we do not lower the standards under the guise of responding to public demands.

'Tis a bargain ill made that would secure Socrates from execution at the cost of surrendering control of Socrates's curriculum to his accusers. While we should be happy to bargain for his life at the cost of committing ourselves to pay due heed to the public interest, we had far rather kiss him good-bye than pretend that the public interest suffices to direct higher education. Insistence upon high standards is the right thing to do, even where we are in error about how to apply those standards.

The late Ernest Boyer betrayed a shallowness of judgment in the case of his public comment upon William Allen's nomination to the National Council on the Humanities by President Reagan, but he spoke sensibly about standards of accomplishment in higher education. He attacked Reagan's appointments with the uninformed broadside that the position should require knowledge of foreign languages, something all of the appointees supposedly lacked. He did so, however, at the very moment that Allen was engaged in intensive study of Spanish (his sixth language) in Salamanca, Spain. Boyer was very wrong to speak so ignorantly and to prostrate himself to merely partisan goals. At the same time, he took his stand on principles themselves not unworthy of our most serious consideration. And, we shall see shortly, therefore, that his strictures regarding academic leadership are of continuing value.

To provide higher education for more and more citizens we must state clearly what students accomplish in proceeding through a course of study. That means, among other things, refuting the U. S. Department of Education's attempts in the 1990s to discredit all standardized testing as "racist." Although different groups may perform differentially on certain tests (an often mis-labeled achievement gap, which we discuss later in this chapter), it remains true that those diagnostic instruments are vital for identifying the kinds of preparation that ready students for college study as well as for professional careers. Academic leadership should speak up loudly about this, rather than engaging in quiet negotiations with the Department.

Academic leadership is the point of emphasis here, because failures in leadership heretofore have led to an inappropriate politicization of higher education. Where college leaders make excuses for failing to give students a solid general education, blame parents or home backgrounds for ill-disciplined or unsafe school environments, and defend endless cost increases without providing adequate accountability, they invite a skeptical public and skeptical public officers to supply what is missing, namely, a mandate for change.

If not fully heeded as a mandate, nevertheless, a cry for change has roared forth, not only in Virginia but also in a growing number of states. We can fruitfully analyze the dimensions of this call for reform by considering these questions, which paraphrase and expand those raised by the Carnegie Commission on Higher Education in 1973: Who enters our colleges and universities? Who exits? What must a college education cost? Who pays? How we, as a society, respond to these questions will—in large measure—define and measure our commitment to access to higher education, testing whether we can overcome the barriers of readiness, cost, and capacity.

Who Enters? Who Exits?

Today, over 60 percent of all high school graduates within the United States enter college within twelve months after receiving their high school diploma.[21] This is a staggering number, especially in contrast to the 4 percent of eighteen to twenty-four year olds who attended college in 1900,[22] and is rightfully considered one of the major accomplishments of the century. Stephen Moore lauds this "steep and nearly uninterrupted increase in the educational attainment of the American people" as one of the greatest trends of the twentieth century, pointing out that "Today, the percentage of Americans graduating from college is higher than the percentage graduating from high school 100 years ago."[23]

Once the domain only of the few, the privileged and the wealthy, college campuses are now the intellectual home—for at least a brief interval—of individuals from every social and economic sector. Yet the accomplishment is not complete, for the hard reality is that a young person from a family with an annual income of $75,000 or more has an 82 percent chance of attending college by age 24, while someone whose family earns less than $10,000 per year has only a 25 percent chance of doing so.[24] Further, while nearly two-thirds of high school graduates enter college, only about one-half of those entering complete the baccalaureate degree within five years[25]—although studies by Clifford Adelman suggest that higher percentages do complete the degree eventually (as high as seven of eight, by age thirty).[26] And, as the headlines of national newspapers as well as the *Chronicle of Higher Education* remind us annually, there remains a "Persistent Racial Gap in SAT Scores."

The story published by the *Chronicle* under that headline in 1998 cited a 200-point disparity between black and white verbal and math scores that has persisted almost unchangeably for the past twenty years.[27] True, there was a period in the 1980s in which the gap seemed to be narrowing fairly significantly. But starting in 1988 it returned to pre-1980s' patterns and remains there today.

That gap was as large as 260 points in 1976, when the College Board, which administers the SAT, *started keeping track of scores by race.* It fell below 200 points in 1988, and has since hovered around 200.

Ever since we first took official notice of the achievement gap (though it is not often referred to by that proper name), we have recognized it as a problem. We have varied widely, however, in naming the problem. Some have regarded it as a reflection of the effects of discrimination, while others have reviewed it as reflecting differences in background, culture, and schooling. Still others have mused that it reflects native, unbridgeable differences. Almost everyone, however, has looked at it as a problem of race rather than as a problem of achievement, giving rise to the familiar syndrome of blaming either the victims or society in general.[28] Our task is to persuade the reader that the problem is an achievement problem, rather than a race problem; while race serves as an effective forensic tool to isolate the specific geography and demographics of the achievement problem, it does not begin to define or diagnose the problem. For that purpose, we need rather to consult patterns and evidences of achievement other than either gene pools or histories of discrimination.

Don't Blame the Victims

To begin with, let us remind ourselves that the same gap appears in every form of standardized testing that we use. The ACT and the NAEP (National Assessment of Educational Progress) no less than the SAT reflect such a gap. Moreover, all reflect similar background facts—most notably the relatively smaller percentage of SAT and ACT test takers among black high school graduates compared with white high school graduates and the still smaller percentages of black AP test takers in comparison with white AP test takers (a fact that will be especially relevant later). In Virginia for example, the first-year college class in 1996 contained black students at the level of 17.3 percent, while blacks constituted 21.7 percent of all eighteen to twenty-four year old Virginians. At the same time, 5.5 percent of black high school graduates took the ACT exam, while black high school graduates made up 21.4 percent of all graduates (this compares reasonably closely with white test takers and graduates but conceals significant differences in the make-up of the two pools).

At a still greater level of detail, the numbers of black and white ACT test takers who also follow a core high school curriculum reflect a disturbing trend: for black test takers, the numbers following a "less than core" curriculum are consistently roughly equal to the numbers following a core curriculum (the higher concentration in the lower income group entails this result). For white test takers, on the other hand, the numbers following a core curriculum are consistently greater than (and by a very large number) the numbers following a "less than core curriculum." This trend is illustrated in Table 3.1 from ACT, which shows this discrepancy in the national data as well as in the data for Virginia.

Because the testing gap remains within the categories thus distinguished, some observers question whether the differences in curriculum are explanatory. They neglect to observe, however, that *within* each category similar dynamics appear—that is, numbers of students taking Advanced Placement courses, and the specific courses taken vary sharply. Thus, the attempt to associate the achievement gap with race still faces the challenge to find an actual common ground on which to measure the gap in such a way as to discount the influence of background and especially the courses of

Table 3.1

Average ACT Composite Scores—by Level of High School Coursework, Racial/ Ethnic Group, and Family Income, 1998[29]

National Reference Group	Less than $18,000		$18,000-$35,999		$36,000 or more	
	N	Composite	N	Composite	N	Composite
All Graduates						
Total group	92562	18.5	217121	20.0	530981	22.0
Core	48614	19.5	126593	21.0	354544	22.8
Less than Core	42584	17.3	88368	18.5	172714	20.2
African-American/Black						
Total Group	25328	16.2	32779	16.9	27521	18.3
Core	13353	16.9	18804	17.6	17582	19.0
Less than Core	11708	15.4	13653	15.9	9683	17.0
American Indian/Alaskan Native						
Total Group	1979	17.6	3385	18.5	4256	20.3
Core	831	19.1	1688	19.8	2481	21.4
Less than Core	1034	16.6	1589	17.4	1693	18.8
Caucasian-American/White						
Total Group	41771	20.2	140537	20.9	432125	22.2
Core	21842	21.4	82195	22.0	289468	23.1
Less than Core	19561	18.7	57388	19.3	140216	20.5
Mexican-American/Chicano						
Total Group	7616	17.1	11198	18.2	11589	20.0
Core	3881	18.1	6132	19.1	7228	20.8
Less than Core	3685	16.1	4995	17.0	4304	18.5
Asian-American/ Pacific Islander						
Total Group	4578	18.9	7656	20.6	14798	23.5
Core	3026	19.6	5431	21.3	11270	24.0
Less than Core	1472	17.3	2083	19.0	3332	21.8
Puerto Rican/ Cuban/Other Hispanic						
Total Group	2923	17.6	5009	19.0	7169	21.1
Core	1527	18.7	3030	19.9	4977	21.9
Less than Core	1248	16.4	1847	17.5	2069	19.2

studies followed. By the time measures of the numbers of black students who have taken pre-calculus are performed, therefore, observers are dealing with decreasingly significant populations. To a much higher degree, the reference population of white test takers who have taken pre-calculus exceeds (in relation to its own base) the population of black test takers who have taken pre-calculus by several factors.

Similarly, we have identified measures that can impact the gap, of which perhaps none is more important than course-taking patterns:

> Compared to White students, African-American and Hispanic students took fewer mathematics, science, and foreign language courses. This pattern was not affected by the availability of advanced courses or by the schools' graduation requirements. However, minority students in general, and African-American students in particular, appeared to have gained an advantage in course-taking by attending a private school or a suburban public school (in contrast to a large-city public school).[30]

What remains, therefore, is to respond with specifics to the situation rather than with generalizations about race and class.

The point of these observations is not to explain away the achievement gap. Indeed, the very name, "achievement gap," establishes it as real, substantial, and pervasive. However, our aim is to suggest that we look elsewhere for a diagnosis so as to advance the likelihood of a remedy. Where reports such as the Southern Education Foundation's *Miles to Go: A Report on Black Students and Postsecondary Education in the South* have focused on participation rates, economic disparities, and statewide remedial efforts, we would suggest that we can look closer to home for the answer. In closing the achievement gap, moreover, we believe that we move most surely toward eliminating the participation gap.

We tell a story of failed education rather than of students failing. In reply to the question, "where do we go from here," our response would be, "education by any means necessary." Not only do we not blame the students themselves; we are confident that they can do whatever we will ask them to do.

The Evidence of Developmental Analysis

We buttress this position with reference to the findings of the National Assessment of Educational Progress, which has employed a "developmental" analysis to assess school and student performance in comparative perspective. The following series of tables, as well as excerpts of the text, come from the Educational Testing Service's 1998 report, *Growth in School: Achievement Gains from the Fourth to the Eighth Grade*:

There has been an explosion in standardized testing over the last 20 years or so, both to measure individual student progress and to monitor achievement at the school, district, state, or national levels. Students are almost always grouped by grade level, and the traditional focus is on tracking how students in those grade levels compare over time. Policy makers ask such questions as, "How do today's fourth-graders compare to fourth graders 10 years ago in mathematics?"[31]

A broad response to that question can be found in Table 3.2, which reflects trends in cohort growth for science, mathematics, reading and writing.

We submit that a developmental analysis is the specific response to the persistent achievement gap. Through it we may compare not only how students perform compared with one another, but also how they perform compared with themselves in relation to specific courses. By measuring "trends in cohort growth" we are able to identify specific points of difficulty and, therefore, of intervention.

Cohort growth can also be examined by race, for White and Black students. . . . *Only one of the cohort growth differences shown is statistically significant:* [emphasis added] the drop in math score gain between age 9 and 13 for White students. Of course, when viewed in terms of average age- or grade-based NAEP scores, achievement levels differ considerably by race and ethnicity.[32]

Table 3.2
Trends in NAEP Cohort Growth[33]

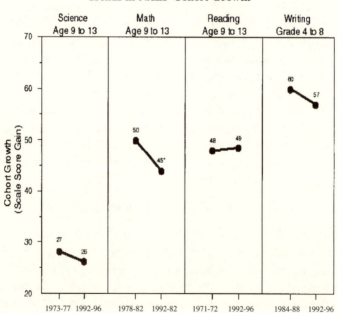

*Statistically significant difference

Table 3.3 displays the analysis of cohort growth trends by race.

Following this approach the NAEP succeeded in identifying differences in white and black students, beginning in fourth grade, and continuing throughout schooling, but showing up especially in relation to math scores. The most intriguing element of its findings, however, was that there was virtually no variation in "cohort growth." That is, black students and white students experienced like cohort growth and, after grade eight, like declines relative to international comparison groups. Tables 3.4, 3.5, and 3.6 illustrate this point, which is also discussed by Barton and Coley below:

> For Black students, the score improvement of 50 points brought them to a point in the eighth grade where they were only slightly above the average for fourth-grade White students. The gain is similar, but the level is very different, and the examples give some palpability to what the numbers mean in terms of achievement comparisons. . . . What is striking in addition to the differences among student subgroups is how close eighth-grade Black students are to fourth grade White students and how the "advanced level" for the fourth grade is considerably higher than the "basic level" for the eighth grade.[35]

Table 3.3
Trends in NAEP Cohort Growth, by Race[34]

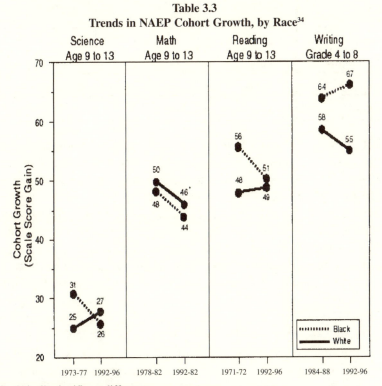

*Statistically significant difference

Table 3.4
Trends in Cohort Growth Compared to Average Score Trends
for 9- and 13-Year-Olds[36]

	COHORT GROWTH AGE 9 TO 13	AVERAGE SCORE TREND, AGE 9	AVERAGE SCORE TREND, AGE 13
Science	Level	Up	Up
Mathematics	Down	Up	Up
Reading	Level	Up	Up
Writing	Level	Level	Level

Table 3.5
Trends in Cohort Growth compared to Average Score Trends
for Black 9- and 13-Year-Olds[37]

	COHORT GROWTH AGE 9 TO 13	AVERAGE SCORE TREND, AGE 9	AVERAGE SCORE TREND, AGE 13
Science	Level	Up	Up
Mathematics	Level	Up	Up
Reading	Level	Up	Up
Writing	Level	Level	Level

Let us be very clear about the meaning of these findings. Where critics heretofore have been swift to label the differences between blacks and whites as a racial gap (and implicitly "natural"), when confronted with the identical performance distinctions between American students and students in Japan or Germany, they instinctively labeled the latter an achievement gap. We submit either that both are achievement gaps and that neither is a racial gap, or the gap between American and Japanese students, for example must also be considered a racial gap. Typically, we follow the findings regarding international disparities with a focus on the courses of study followed, the length of the school day, the length of the school year, and the rigor of studies—that is with specific attention to dimensions and conditions of achievement. Since the differences in educational practices to which most black students and most white students are subject differ as significantly, if not by the same magnitude, as the differences between American and Japanese students, then there is no credible reason to look anywhere else to explain the so-called racial gap than to the criteria of achievement we otherwise employ to explain the international gap. The time has come to redirect our attention.

Table 3.6
Cohort Growth in Mathematics
from the Fourth to the Eighth Grade, 1992 to 1996[38]

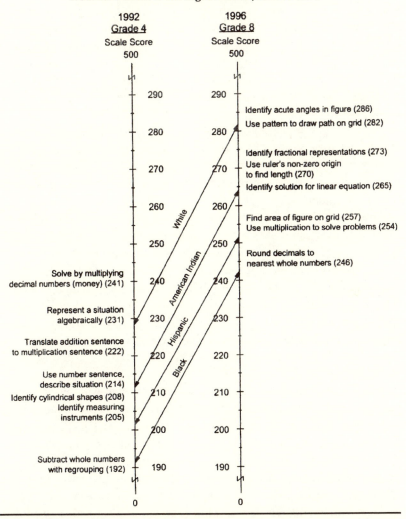

Source: National Assessment of Educational Progress data analyzed by the ETS Policy Information Center. See http://nces.ed.gov/naep

Fixing the Problem

These vitally important findings not only reinforce the suggestion made by the Southern Education Foundation that attention needs to be paid to the courses of study followed by black students. They more importantly also pinpoint a moment of intervention.

What is called for now is a focused analysis of the curricula black students follow in grades kindergarten through four. We are well aware that, at these ages particularly, many factors affect student learning, including parental education levels and parenting practices. But it would be unwise to leave it as a matter of assumption that nothing else is going on. Without a specific plan for the actual schooling experiences of black youngsters, school by school and course by course, we will be unable to isolate and respond to the achievement gap. Moreover, we know already that black student achievement improves, even if the gap is not closed, in proportion as the curriculum pursued toughens up. As we often like to say, even a black student who fails calculus will perform better on standardized tests than a black student who never takes calculus. We now require an immediate and dramatic ratcheting up of academic expectations for black students at every level.

This analysis, of course, points to the reduction of the achievement gap by means of intervention in pre-collegiate education. By definition, that is a long-term strategy (though not very long term!) rather than a fix for the immediate victims of past educational failures. For those students for whom long-term advantage is not the answer, we must be content to continue to deal with piecemeal fixes, including support for remedial education in our community colleges. What is apparent is that the point of systemic intervention is clearly at the pre-collegiate level, with respect to the achievement gap.

Additionally, the time has come to identify new ways to conceive performance measurements in the retention area—an undertaking that was initiated in Virginia during our tenure at SCHEV. A new and more productive approach to assessing retention would emphasize who the students are and where they come from—a value-added perspective—that would produce incentives for our institutions to show more attention to developing the students who arrive at university with identified needs. This new approach to measuring retention, and the overall issue of managing institutional performance, is described in some depth in chapter 4, "Evaluating Higher Education," and chapter 5, "Managing Higher Education."

Our discussion of "Who enters?" and "Who exits" our colleges and universities has, thus far, focused on one essential aspect of access to higher education—the academic preparedness of the students. In recent years, concerned individuals in many different sectors have recognized that the uneven performance of elementary and secondary schools across the nation means that students do *not* have equal access to collegiate study, since they are not given an equal opportunity to the necessary pre-collegiate academic preparation. While it is heartening to see that this obstacle has made it onto the radar screen of public concern,[39] greater attention and a substantial commitment to academic reform at all levels will be needed in order to obliterate a barrier that has barricaded the road to education for too many and for too long.

We turn now to another important determinant of access to higher education—cost. As the following section indicates, this issue has been the focus of overwhelming attention for the past decade and longer. The question before us now is whether this attention has yet resulted in appropriate public policies at the institutional, state, and national level.

What Must College Cost?

Demand has increased seven-fold since World War II and is expected to continue to grow over the next two decades. At the same time, operating costs have escalated and public-sector financial support has flattened. As a result, many colleges and universities have had to sharply increase tuition and fees and look for ways to control costs in order to avoid financial disaster. . . . At a time when the level of education needed for productive employment is increasing, the opportunity to go to college will be denied to millions of Americans unless sweeping changes are made to control costs, halt sharp increases in tuition, and increase other sources of revenue.[40]

While one would need a fine ear to hear a single, predominant note among the cacophony of concerns about higher education that have been voiced in recent years, one could nevertheless make a strong case that the issue that most worries the typical American family is the cost of putting its children through college. This concern reached a fever pitch in the early 1990s, when tuition costs at state-funded and private institutions alike spiked sharply upward. Surprisingly, however, even as the rates of tuition increases slowed somewhat and family incomes rose in the latter part of the decade, cost remained and remains a prominent concern, especially now that the impact of the latest recession has hit state pocketbooks.[41]

Prior to and during our tenure at SCHEV, cost was one of the foremost concerns for the Governor, General Assembly, and members of the Council—as well as for many families and students. The concern is a valid one and deserves attention. For example, over the fifteen-year period from 1983 to 1998, per student expenditures for educational and general programs in Virginia's colleges and universities increased from $3,754 to $8,134, or by about 32 percent more than inflation. While the overall cost of higher education shot up 32 percent more than inflation, per student state appropriations in Virginia rose from $2,542 to $4,858, about 17 percent more than inflation. In other words, the cost of higher education increased at twice the rate the public was able to subsidize.

Students, families, legislators, and the general public are right to urge academic leaders to keep college affordable. Yet, too often the real issues that affect the cost of education are obscured by political gamesmanship. The following discussion of Virginia politics will illustrate how selective truth-telling is used as a ploy in this game.

The Virginia Business Higher Education Council centered their pitch for an increase in state funding of higher education on a report that per student public support for higher education was $729 less in real terms in 1998 than in 1990. Given that information, a reasonable individual might assume that public support of higher education in Virginia had declined. But, that was not true at all.

In fact, the Center for Higher Education at Illinois State University cited Virginia for posting the fourth highest increase in support for higher education in the nation that year. Why the discrepancy? Because 1990 was the peak funding year before the recessions of the early 1990s. Moreover, it preceded a major restructuring effort in Virginia, in which colleges and universities brought down their costs, and thereby their funding needs, by streamlining their operations.

A more even-handed analysis of state support of higher education in Virginia would look at a longer, more representative time frame. For example, the Virginia Department of Planning and Budget determined that from 1974 to 2000, per student public support for higher education in Virginia increased by 90 percent in real terms.

Moreover, a more comprehensive analysis of state support would include measures beyond general fund appropriations. For example, the standard calculation of state support ignores the unusually high level of charitable (and other) contributions provided to Virginia's public colleges and universities. Because those endowments are publicly supported through favorable tax treatment, they are a vital part of the public contribution to the cost of higher education in public and private institutions. Indeed, only five other states surpassed Virginia in the level of such "other" contributions to the revenues of public institutions of higher education, and every other southern state was much lower.[42] Lastly, Virginia's generous support of private colleges through the Tuition Assistance Grant, or TAG, program should also be included in any analysis of public support for higher education and would substantially increase the overall level of contribution.

While it is useful to expose such attempts to sway the public through misuse of numbers, this is not our primary concern. For it is pointless to haggle over the cost of education without first understanding its value. We remain convinced that the primary concern of those who lead and those who fund our colleges and universities should be with the value—the worth—of the education that is being purchased, rather than its cost. For if we do not have a clear, and shared, conception of value, how can we begin to agree on a fair price? In chapter 1 we assessed the value of liberal education in a manner that should help policymakers and the public gain a better sense of its worth. We turn to the next question.

Who Pays?

For policymakers and legislators, as well as for students and families, the question of who pays for the cost of a college education is every bit as important as the question of what the education costs. In the United States, a varied and complex set of answers to that question has emerged, but nearly every variation of the response involves a mix of taxpayer, tuition, and charitable support. Only a handful of institutions throughout the country, such as Hillsdale College (in Hillsdale, Michigan) and Grove City College (in Grove City, Pennsylvania) refuse most taxpayer support, including the acceptance of financial aid supplied through national and state tax dollars.

The combined approach to funding reflects our belief as a nation that some of the benefits from a college education accrue directly to the individual while other benefits accrue to society at large. More specifically, we recognize that without public support, too few individuals might choose to attend college to generate the overall benefits to society that we seek from having a well-educated populace.

There has been substantial debate—in Virginia as well as nationally—over the appropriate proportion of the cost that ought to be borne respectively by the student and by the taxpayer. Various states have taken different approaches to this debate. Until the 1990s, California attempted to fund the cost almost entirely with taxpayer support, holding tuition to the lowest possible cost in each segment of its three-tiered system. Virginia, on the other hand, had traditionally been known as a "high tuition/high aid" state—setting tuition and fees at a relatively high rate for most of its four-year institutions, but offsetting that cost for lower-income students with generous infusions of state dollars into the financial aid programs available at the institutions.

What interests and concerns us is less the question of whether there exists some ideal ratio for tuition and tax support, but more so whether academic and governmental leaders can offer students and taxpayers understandable responses to these questions: What are the public policy objectives that drive tuition and financial aid policies? How well do these policies reward and stimulate students' academic performance?

At a minimum, policy must now clarify the ambiguities and confusions surrounding issues of access and cost. A prime example of this cloudy thinking appeared in the 1999 American Association of State Colleges and Universities "policy agenda." They called at one and the same time for "access to higher education for as many. . . citizens as possible," and also for using "state appropriations. . .to keep tuition as low as possible."[43] This consensus document failed to detect the inconsistency, in which public subsidies for the wealthy operate to exclude access for the poor. Thus, when they go on to insist that "affordable tuition" and "need-based *federal* [emphasis added] aid are the two requisite ingredients" to assure that "no American should be denied access," they neglect the necessary amendment that would require tuition to be high enough to make room for financial aid—that is, to reduce the claimants sufficiently to focus aid on the genuinely needy. Otherwise, *federal* aid serves only to facilitate (marginally to make up for) *state* subsidies for the wealthy. Buchanan and Devletoglu got it right:

> The resident in Watts, in short, subsidizes the residents in Beverly Hills to attend the University of California. To advance a subsidy to students and not require repayment is to grant students a gift of wealth at the expense of those who do not attend college or who attend tuition-colleges and pay for themselves.[44]

In short, the formula of low-tuition/high-aid is a cost-shifting formula, shifting the cost from the rich to the poor, and the benefits in the reverse direction. The only sure formula for access is high-tuition/high-aid, focusing the public grant on those in need and thus providing incentive for them to use it. The same would not occur in a no-tuition environment, for then the incentives would not offset the advantages of the well-to-do.

What Do Students Actually Pay?

The proportion of the cost of a college education paid by the student and his family compared to the portion paid by the taxpayer (or funded through the generosity of donors) varies substantially along several dimensions. Among other factors, it varies depending upon state or region; it varies depending upon whether the student attends a public or a private college; and, perhaps surprisingly, it varies depending upon the degree to which a student is seen as "desirable" by one or more institutions.[45] It also turns out that, on average, students attending colleges with very high tuitions pay a smaller percentage of the total cost of that education than do students at institutions with lower tuitions. Consider these findings:

- Gordon Winston and Ivan Yen calculate that, on average, students and their families pay only about 29 percent of the total cost of a college education. In 1991, "the average school in the US. . .gave its students an education that cost $10,653 for which it charged $3,101. The resulting subsidy of $7,551. . .was divided into $6,063 of general aid and $1,488 of individually targeted aid."[46]

- Winston and Yen also show that students at the most expensive schools have a much greater proportion of their educational costs subsidized through some form of aid or through the institution's donative[47] resources than do students at the least expensive schools. They show that "The student in an average school in the top decile is paying a bit more than 18 cents for a dollar's worth of education: the student in an average school in the bottom decile is paying 78 cents."[48]

- A significant portion of the subsidies described above is given to all students regardless of financial need, through the policy for setting tuition. Winston and Yen report that ". . .schools in the public and private sectors differ in how they distribute subsidies: more than 90% of public subsidies are in general aid set by low sticker prices while less than 70% of private subsidies are distributed that way. So 30% of private and 10% of public subsidies are distributed as individually targeted student aid."[49]

- About 61 percent of all students receive some form of financial aid, either in the form of grants or loans.[50]

- The National Commission on the Cost of Higher Education found that "Between 1987 and 1996, the instruction cost per student [at public four-year colleges and universities] increased from $7,922, on average, to $12,416, an increase of 57 percent. During this same time, the sticker price increased considerably faster, 132 percent, from an average of $1,688 to $3,918. The general subsidy, which averaged $6,234 in 1987, increased 36 percent, to approximately $8,500 in 1996. Thus, the sticker price, or tuition, increased much faster than either instructional costs or subsidy." Tuition also increased faster than cost per student at public two-year and private four-year institutions, according to the Commission's review.[51]

It is important to note, however, that few students actually pay the sticker price, particularly in private institutions. In a survey of 147 private colleges and universities conducted in 1995, David Breneman found that

Tuition discounting has become so commonplace in small private colleges with relatively low tuition—representing one end of the continuum—that at a third of these institutions, 10 percent (or fewer) of the freshmen paid the published tuition price. Of all the institutions surveyed, fewer than half of the students paid the published tuition price.[52]

The practice of tuition discounting continues to increase and the discounts are becoming steeper. The National Association of College and University Business Officers has surveyed tuition discounting practices among independent colleges and universities since 1991. Their 2000 survey found that 78 percent of students at the 211 participating institutions received some form of institutional aid, compared to 65.5 per cent who received such aid in 1991. The average award amounted to 49 percent of the cost of tuition and fees.[53] Gordon Winston and David Zimmerman interpret the trends in tuition discounting as a shift from "price competition for warm bodies to price competition for student quality," and predict that "Negative tuition will likely appear at the wealthiest colleges and universities. . .as price competition forces them to *pay stipends* to attract the best students [original emphasis]."[54]

Tuition continues to increase at a rate that exceeds inflation. The College Board reports that in 2000-01 the average cost to attend a public four-year college or university was $3,510—up 4.4 percent from the previous year. The Board also indicates that since 1980-81, tuition at both public and private institutions increased, on average, more than 115 percent above inflation.[55] Increases in tuition have had a particularly sharp impact on low-income families. Surveying tuition and income data from 1971 to 1997, Donald Heller finds that "For families in the two poorest groupings, the proportion of income required to pay for one year's tuition at a public four-year institution more than doubled over the twenty-six years." The impact for high-income families was much less severe, as during that same interval the proportion of income required to pay for one year's tuition increased by only 44 percent.[56]

In contemplating these reports on the cost of education actually paid by students and their families—and the impact of that cost—it is important to bear in mind that the real cost of a college education is not easily calculated. Few colleges and universities are able to document the full cost of educating students. The vagaries of how higher education accounts—or more to the point, fails to account—for the cost of the physical campus (land, buildings, libraries, equipment) seriously understate the actual cost of educating the students on these campuses.[57]

Confusion and gaps in full information pertain not only to the cost accounting operations of higher education, but also to its pricing practices.[58] In its influential report, *Straight Talk About College Costs and Prices*, the National Commission on the Cost of Higher Education voiced concern that the nation's colleges and universities have "permitted a veil of obscurity to settle over their basic financial operations." Much of the report was taken up with an in-depth discussion of just what is meant within higher education by such terms as cost, price and subsidy, based on the realization that "Despite their obvious differences, these different concepts are often discussed as if they were the same thing." The Commission strenuously urged higher education leaders to "strive continuously to clarify and communicate [these concepts] clearly and candidly."[59]

Some efforts have been initiated to respond to the Commission's recommendations.[60] We must hope that they will succeed in lifting the veil of obscurity, enabling students, parents, legislators, and others to gain meaningful answers to the questions about the effects of pricing a college education in the twenty-first century.

What Are the Public Policy Objectives?

Even more opaque than the veil that obscures information about the costs of undergraduate education is the mantle that shrouds the public policy objectives, which ought to be served by higher education funding policy and which do affect those costs. This opacity surely derives, in part, from the fact that public policy is pulled simultaneously in many different—sometimes conflicting—directions by the warps and wefts of public opinion and fiscal constraint.

Some might say that it is difficult to discern the public policy guiding higher education because it simply does not exist. Breneman suggests that this is true with regard to federal policy, noting that "over the years many observers of the Washington education scene" have reached this conclusion. He cites Alice Rivlin on this subject, who wrote in 1961 that "The most important fact about federal policy toward higher education is that there never has been a clearly defined policy. . . . Legislation affecting higher education has been a by-product of some other well-established federal concern, such as agriculture or public health or the disposal of public lands or military needs."[61]

Although we might debate whether the public policies (including taxation policies) that affect higher education are developed intentionally or by happenstance, we are able to detect implicit if not explicit public policy directions. During the past decade, numerous analysts of higher education have perceived a substantial change in this policy area.[62]

To give an account of these policy shifts, it is useful to review the major transitions that have taken place within the twentieth century.

At the start of this chapter we described the "triumph of democracy" in higher education and "a gradual expansion of the role of taxpayer responsibility." This process reached a particular peak in recommendations of the 1947 President's Commission on Higher Education, which maintained that:

> It is the responsibility of the community at the local, State, and National levels, to guarantee that financial barriers do not prevent any able and otherwise qualified young person from receiving the opportunity for higher education. There must be developed in this country the widespread realization that money expended for education is the wisest and soundest of investments in the national interest. The democratic community cannot tolerate a society based upon education for the well-to-do alone. If college opportunities are restricted to those in the higher income brackets, the way is open to the creation and perpetuation of a class society which has no place in the American way of life.[63]

Although the federal government began investing substantially in financial aid beginning with the G. I. Bill in the 1940s and continued with passage of the Higher Education Act of 1965, most of the work of keeping college affordable is done by the states. Arthur Hauptman notes that the states traditionally kept college affordable through a policy of low-tuition (or in some cases, no tuition) at public colleges and universities and through a general subsidy allocated to public institutions, often on the basis of enrollment-driven formulae. In 1973, two influential reports (one by the Carnegie Commission on Higher Education and the other by the Committee on Economic Development) recommended that "states should move away from a policy of low tuition to one based more on the notion of cost sharing between the states and the students and their families, such that tuition should eventually reflect one-third of the education costs." The recommendation derived from the notion that private benefits in the form of higher income accrue to individuals who attend college, but it bore heavily on the observation already made that the public subsidy itself was favoring those of higher income.[64] The recommendation garnered attention but not support during the 1970s, according to Hauptman, who points out that public sector tuition only began to "climb substantially in real terms" in the early 1980s— more in response to economic factors than as a consequence of policy analysis. The rate of tuition increase slowed in the latter part of the decade, only to accelerate at the beginning of the 1990s and to slow again toward the end of that decade.

In their discussion of the "public and private value of going to college," the leaders of the New Millennium Project on Higher Education Costs, Pricing, and Productivity argue that current "conversations tend to focus on the narrow topic of the private economic benefits that result from going to college, such as higher salaries and better jobs," rather than the value of higher education.[65] This trend reinforces the commentary on the financing of higher education, published during the 1990s and even within the past two years, that, whether by design or by drift, current national and state finance policies increasingly look to the wallets of students and families to cover the cost of a college degree.[66] Policymakers and analysts debate whether increased financial responsibility for families does not discourage the trend toward broadened participation in postsecondary education, especially affecting students from disadvantaged families.[67]

As a consequence of these changes in funding policies, many question whether access to higher education is still viewed as a shared, national goal. Based on an in-depth analysis of the funding policies for higher education in five states, as well as overall national trends, Breneman observes that "Some have argued that the underlying message of the structural changes in higher education finance during the 1990s is that access has slipped as a priority for many states."[68] However, Michael McPherson and Morton Schapiro conclude that "On the plus side, the combination of state institutional subsidies and federal aid support makes *some* form of postsecondary education financially accessible to a very wide range of Americans"[original emphasis]. But they do observe that ". . .the existing financing system may be much less successful in providing a *suitable* postsecondary experience for many disadvantaged students. The range of alternatives available to students is quite sharply constrained by their incomes under existing arrangements" [original emphasis].[69]

Still, increasing numbers of students from low-income families are enrolling in postsecondary education, at a rate of increase matching the overall increases in enrollment. Moreover, the percentage of students from the lowest income quartile who enroll in college is about 50 percent, compared with an enrollment rate of 85 percent for students from families in the top income quartile.[70] McPherson and Schapiro conclude their review of pricing, aid, access and choice with a prediction that "the group most likely to be placed at risk by the shifting environment in American higher education is the group of low-income students who do not have the strong qualifications needed for admission to selective private colleges."[71] That market segment, though, has not accounted for the dramatic increases in college enrollment since the nineteenth century. Further, it has become increasingly evident that much of middle America, crowded out of selective public institutions by the well-to-do, gains access to "better" postsecondary education mainly through the private market. As for the poor, they mainly participate in the less selective public market, and here there are legitimate concerns about the sufficiency of financial aid. The Advisory Committee on Student Financial Assistance discerns that "this shift in public policy objectives away from access at all levels has caused a steep rise in the unmet need of low-income students. . . . On average, the very lowest income students face $3,200 of unmet need at two-year institutions and $3,800 at four-year public institutions."[72]

How to Reward and Stimulate Academic Performance?

In a talk titled, "The Student Aid Game: It's Not Just the Numbers That Count," we challenged financial aid administrators from public and private Virginia colleges to re-examine the underlying assumptions that shaped their work everyday. We asked them to step back from the typical concerns of lobbying for increased financial aid funds and of laboring through a bureaucratic maze of regulations that ascertain eligibility for and compliance with financial aid programs, and to consider one important question: whether our colleges and universities achieve the intended results through our financial aid policies. We might also have inquired whether the intentions aim at the right "good."

Some policy analysts have described the financial aid programs of this country as the great engine fueling the American meritocracy. The long-standing, fundamental purposes of financial aid in the U.S. have been to support both access and choice by meeting need and rewarding talent. After decades of progress in advancing these purposes, our complex amalgam of financial aid policies and practices may no longer be so clearly focused on those aims. Many observers believe, as suggested earlier in this chapter, that our institutions have eroded the earlier commitment to ensure that qualified students would be able to attend college (regardless of their ability to pay) and that these students would have a reasonable ability to choose the colleges that best met their needs.

We believe the cost-shift described in the previous section, in combination with other factors, has distorted some of our approaches to financial aid. Over the course of the past two decades, many colleges moved from viewing financial aid as a sort of charitable investment to seeing it as a critical component of enrollment management plans. In their book, *The Student Aid Game*, McPherson and Schapiro report that private colleges, in particular, now use financial aid as a "key strategic weapon both in recruiting students and in maximizing institutional resources."[73] The statistics cited earlier in this chapter on the practice of tuition discounting demonstrate how pervasive this practice has become.

Some policy analysts now assert that the practice of tuition discounting has reached its limits and threatens the financial viability of the institutions that use it most aggressively. A recent report, *Discounting Toward Disaster: Tuition Discounting, College Finances, and Enrollments of Low-Income Undergraduates,* found that those institutions that offer the steepest discounts tended to experience lower enrollment, received less revenue from tuition, and consequently were able to invest less in core budget areas such as instruction and student services.[74] Even more widespread is the criticism that tuition discounting "obscures" the original purposes of financial aid and a concern that "the cumulative effect of this practice shifts the language and philosophy of financial aid in higher education."[75] Some worry that "the process of price competition. . .will eventually cause parents to consider it naïve and even irrational to willingly pay a tuition that might support a poorer student."[76] Yet, despite these concerns, there is no indication that tuition discounting will be discontinued anytime soon; rather, its use seems to be increasing and to be taken up by public institutions for some of the same enrollment management uses practiced by their private counterparts.

State-based merit scholarships and state and national tax credits for college tuition have also drawn fire from many critics. States seem to be investing tax dollars in new scholarship programs modeled on the Georgia HOPE program, which they might previously have invested in need-based financial aid programs. The early results from the states that have set up such programs indicate that the funds are awarded disproportionately to children from high-income families. *The Chronicle of Higher Education* reports, for example, that "In New Mexico. . .64 percent of the scholarship funds go to students whose families make $50,000 a year or more; only 15 percent of the money goes to those earning $20,000 or less."[77] However, because such programs have become extremely popular with both the public and politicians, they are likely to increase in coming years. Moreover, the reviews to date fail to produce a net analysis, in which one accounts for additional funds otherwise not likely to be provided and also for differential numbers in the eligible pool of students. In short, the alarmist statistics are not convincing.

We agree with critics of recent trends that it is important to invest public funds in order to remove financial barriers that bar students from low-income families from collegiate study. We agree, also, that we have not yet achieved this goal, on the state or the national level. At the same time, we must challenge these critics and ask whether they have fallen blindly into acceptance of a false dichotomy between the two goals of "meeting need" and "rewarding talent." Our observation suggests that this is so. Higher education too often operates on the unstated assumption that students with the most need are those with the least talent. Likewise, higher education tends also to imply the reverse—that the students with the most talent have the least need.

We want to challenge the implied assumption that there are no bright, poor kids in our applicant pools—or that there are too few such cases to need attention. If students from low-income families receive only aid that is based on "need" and do not also—or instead—receive scholarships awarded on the basis of "merit," we should pause to consider the message we convey.

Let's make this personal. When the young William Allen left for college there was little aid available to assist his efforts, despite his youthful belief that excellence would be rewarded with scholarships. Accordingly, he mainly had to work his own way through, but was able to do so and with a minimum of loans. By the time his own children began college, he learned that still less scholarship aid rewarded accomplishment, at the same time that his not quite six-figure income rendered the family ineligible for need-based aid. The rhetoric of the "lingering effects of slavery" takes on a very different meaning in that context.

We want, also, to challenge the conventional wisdom about the impact of merit-based aid on encouraging student performance. McPherson and Shapiro state that high school students will work hard for top grades in order to improve their chances of admission at highly selective institutions, but that these students will not be motivated by the chance for their work to be recognized and rewarded by a merit scholarship. That distinction makes no sense at all. Our own experience suggests instead that students do work toward the goal of such support and recognition. And the shame is that that has become a nearly empty myth in our society. Nor does the recent trend toward state-based "merit" scholarships serve this purpose, for the level of achievement required to qualify is typically quite low, and widespread grade inflation has eroded the ability of a particular high school grade point average to signal true merit.

Previous efforts to overhaul the complex puzzle of financial aid policies have been fruitless. We challenge academic leaders, policymakers, and legislators to consider whether some adjustments within the crazy quilt pattern of financial aid may make the whole picture clearer. By holding a mirror to this picture, we can see whether or not it accurately reflects our intentions.

P. F. Kluge holds such a mirror up to the financial aid policies at Kenyon College in his book, *Alma Mater*. The resulting image is unsettling. "Once," Kluge writes, "scholarships went to smart kids from poor backgrounds." He reviews Kenyon's transition to need-based scholarship in the 1970s, which he describes as "giving aid to students who qualified for admission, period." The next step in this progression was the adoption of "need-blind" scholarships. Kluge compares this form of aid to "buying talent the same way that deep-pocketed baseball owners try to purchase a World Series on the free-agent market." Of course, the first step was not "need blind scholarships" but "need blind admissions," which should have focused a spotlight on merit. But that practice was perverted when tied to aid on the basis of calculated need, in a context in which college budgets weighed more heavily than student accomplishment.

But the permutation of financial aid policies at Kenyon did not stop there. In response to complaints from students, Kenyon lowered its GPA requirement for merit scholarship recipients from 3.5 to 3.0. Next, in response to complaints from students receiving need-based aid, the requirement for those students was lowered from 2.67 to 2.0. These policy changes were made so that Kenyon would remain competitive with its peers.

Reflecting on these mutations, Kluge asks himself and the reader, "A funny competition, no, that goes lower rather than higher?"[78] As we urge our students to aim high, we believe we might take a fresh look at the possible role of scholarships that are truly based on a significant demonstration of merit.

A standard objection to earmarking some financial aid funds for merit is the argument that such a move reduces the aid available for support based on need, as reflected in some of the references cited above. We offer these two rebuttals. First, this objection rests on the false notion that those with need lack merit. Second, this objection implies a "zero-sum" game, in which carving some portion of the financial aid pie to reward talent (and hard work) reduces the amount available to meet need. We say instead we need a bigger pie and, more importantly, we need to reorder our priorities. Indeed, a bigger slice of public support for higher education and a reordered set of priorities will be essential if we are to meet the challenge posed by the anticipated growth in the college-age population over the next decade.

A Ticking Time Bomb

While the barriers of cost and academic qualifications have garnered attention from the public, policy analysts, and legislators, the third barrier to access—physical capacity—has received far too little attention in recent years. In part, this inattention results from a sense that during the expansion years of the sixties, seventies, and eighties, our system of higher education was overbuilt. In fact, there have been intervals when campus capacity has exceeded demand at enough locations to become a matter of concern to funding agencies and legislatures.[79] This phenomenon had especially strong impact on policymakers and analysts in Virginia, and the scars of earlier battles had not yet healed by the time the director attempted to turn the Council's attention to the need to plan for looming demographic growth.

During the 1970s and 1980s, many states, including Virginia, relied on funding formulae, which were driven predominantly by enrollment growth. This approach to funding offered fertile ground at least for allegations, and perhaps even the actual practice, of "padding" enrollment projections as the readiest means for increasing institutional budgets. After a number of years in which actual enrollment levels were significantly below projected levels, state planners and budget analysts fell into the habit of viewing all projections for growth through a lens of suspicion.

Yet, there is real and compelling evidence that demographic and other factors will result in a substantial increase in the number of students "knocking at the doors" of our nation's colleges and universities over the course of this decade. The Council for Aid to Education sounded one of the earliest—and, to date, still one of the most urgent—alarms of the impending surge in demand with their insightful 1995 report, *Breaking the Social Contract*:

> Will America's higher education sector be equipped to meet the needs of future students? By the year 2015, the nation must be prepared to educate over 4 million more students than it educated in 1995—simply because of population growth. If the proportion of the population that wants to attend college also increases, as we think it should, then the number will be even higher.[80]

We do not believe that the Council's warning of a potential "calamitous shortage of resources" and a dramatic reduction in access to higher education has received nearly the attention it deserves. There have been only a handful of serious efforts since 1995 to estimate the probable demand, to measure capacity in a meaningful way, or to plan to close the gap between the two.

The Western Interstate Commission on Higher Education (WICHE) and the College Board made a serious effort at estimating demand, with the results published in the 1998 document, *Knocking on the College Door*. Their projection that the size of the traditional-age high school graduating class will reach an all-time high of 3.2 million in 2007-08 is straightforward and difficult to dismiss or ignore.[81] What is more problematic is the calculus needed to translate the unambiguous, expected demographic growth into projected demand for postsecondary education.

Adelman explores three possible scenarios for estimating this growth in demand. In his first scenario, he assumes "no increase in the combined rate of immediate plus delayed-entry high school graduates (75 percent)" and applies this assumption to the WICHE estimate of 3.2 million high school graduates in 2007-08. This scenario results in an "increase of 23 percent over current enrollments—450,000 more students from age-cohort population growth alone." His second scenario assumes that current efforts to increase the academic and financial readiness of students from low-income families to attend college will yield a modest 10 percent increase in the college-going rate. In this scenario, he calculates an "increase of 31 percent over current first-time enrollments—about 600,000 more students from the combination of population growth and better preparation/higher application rates." His third and final scenario "assumes no increase in the initial 'access rate' but improvement in retention and degree completion"—also both possible results of efforts already underway at the college and pre-college levels. He suggests than even a 10 percent increase in the average college completion rate would swell the college population by 240,000 students.[82]

As Adelman points out, there are many factors that will affect the demand for higher education. He emphasizes several of these factors including: (1) the increasing number of individuals who enroll in college when they have already passed the "traditional" age for doing so (ages 18 to 24); (2) the growing demand for non-credit instruction, especially at community colleges; (3) the growing proportion of students who attend college part-time, and are thus enrolled for much longer than four or five years; and, (4) the probable growth in the number of "remote" students enrolling in distance education courses, including students from outside the United States.[83]

In addition to these factors, the economic benefits of college are likely to continue to motivate an ever-widening percentage of students to aim for postsecondary study. We do not believe that the steep ascent in the college-going rate, described in the opening pages of this chapter, has yet reached its apex. The National Center for

Education Statistics (NCES) reports that the percentage of high school graduates enrolling in college in the fall following graduation rose from 49 percent in 1972 to just under 63 percent in 1999.[84] Former President Clinton sought to make it a national goal for 80 percent of youth to complete at least two years of college. We think the proper goal should be 100 percent, despite the nay-sayers who question both the appropriateness and the realism of such a goal.

It is surprising that even within the walls of the ivory tower, there are many who do not believe that a college degree is a desirable or realizable goal for every high school graduate. Consider, for example, the following excerpts from several recent books on higher education, all written by experts from within the academy:

- "It is possible to structure an argument that says that everyone in the United States must have a college degree. Clearly that is not true. High-school graduates and technical school graduates will have very important roles to play in the new economy. Yet high-school counselors and parents feel incredible pressure to urge all students to immediately pursue baccalaureate education. This is a disservice and results in many students in our classrooms who are ill-prepared for college work"[85]

- "Not even in the United States are 'all the women strong, all the men good looking, and all the children above average.' Attending college no longer ensures an 'above average' future, and a four-year degree may not be the most appropriate goal for every American seeking a postsecondary education."[86]

- "Phrased bluntly, not everyone should be encouraged to attend college for a full four years."[87]

- "We insist that college is not for everyone, and certainly not for everyone who has just turned eighteen. . . . If among proportions of eligible high school graduates who go on to college, 10 per cent of the high school graduates represent too low a figure, then what shall we guess is too high? Surely 100 per cent, perhaps 50 per cent—experience suggests a third is about right."[88]

Nor are these opinions limited to those within the academy. The National Center for Public Policy and Higher Education worked through Public Agenda to poll leaders within business and government, as well as higher education, regarding a number of issues of concern. Along with many other findings, they reported, "Nearly nine in ten (89%) want to make trade and technical school a more appealing option for high school graduates who are not qualified for college."[89] This finding is reported within the context of concern that too many students today graduate from high school without the skills and knowledge needed to succeed in college. We wonder why trade and technical schools are seen as a desirable option by these leaders, rather than the reform of our country's pre-collegiate systems of education in such a way as to prepare *all* of America's youth for college.

In the closing section of this chapter, we expound what we see as the principled response to those who would argue against setting a national goal to make the college degree in the twenty-first century what the high school diploma was in the twentieth—that is, an universal goal. Here, we will do no more than turn to Patrick Callan to remind the reader about the economic imperative for this course of action:

> In contrast [to an earlier time, when the industrial sector offered a path to economic and social success], education is now the only road to opportunity for most people. Education beyond high school is now a virtual necessity for those aspiring to maintain or achieve employment that provides a middle-class standard of living. It has become a necessary, though not sufficient, condition for the employment to which most people aspire, employment that provides economic self-sufficiency and the conditions correlated with civic, community, and cultural life. If opportunity is broadly defined as the chance to participate fully in society, higher education has become the only road to opportunity for most Americans.[90]

What steps are policymakers and legislators across the nation taking to keep this road to opportunity open for the numbers of American who will want to travel it within the next ten years? It is difficult to find much evidence that adequate measures are even being contemplated, much less put into motion. In recent years, the states have concentrated most of their higher education reform initiatives in two areas: (1) keeping college affordable and (2) holding colleges accountable for outcomes. Affordability and accountability seem to have overshadowed access as statewide priorities. Some might argue that keeping college affordable does address the goal of access; however, there seems to be reasonable evidence that efforts aimed at affordability (such as merit scholarships, holding the line on tuition, and establishing college savings plans) serve, operating in tandem, only to make college less costly for families who would find a way to afford college even without these measures. This approach does not adequately respond to the needs of low-income students. Nor does it assure adequate physical capacity to serve the expected demand.

There are good reasons that we lack expert consensus on the impending growth in demand. One of those good reasons is the hyperbolic tendency too often characteristic of policy operatives. Everyone experienced in bureaucratic operations knows how dire prognostications for the long term serve to justify desirable policy objectives in the short term. In that context human nature is too weak to resist the temptation to fudge and to lie. We witnessed this process in Virginia, where a Governor's Commission of the Twenty-First Century and the State Council used projections that were challenged by a citizens' nongovernmental organization.[91] The subsequent report demonstrated that such projections were wildly inaccurate and cultivated the suspicion that they were deliberately so for the sake of driving state budgets. The Council director's response to the citizens' report was non-specific and effectively conceded the inaccuracy of the projections. It does not follow, however, that a rigorous analysis of capacity is unnecessary simply because one attempt was an abuse.

While no one has yet undertaken the systematic analysis that would be needed in order to assess whether substantial expansion of the physical campus is needed to meet demand in areas where large growth is expected, some experts do predict, at least by using current assumptions about the use of facilities, there will not be sufficient capacity without costly construction.[92] Adelman hypothesizes that if a rigorous national review of capacity were carried out, we might find adequate capacity, but in the wrong location (e.g., "in Boise and Bismarck, but not in Brooklyn"), of uneven quality, and poorly matched to the probable demand.[93]

When the Council for Aid to Education conducted its far-reaching review of higher education, what it found was "a time bomb ticking under the nation's social and economic foundations."[94] It is ticking still.

The Legacy

At a recent, national gathering of faculty who are concerned about liberal education, one speaker offered this as an alternative title for his remarks: "Less Access: An Idea Whose Time Has Not Come." The content of his remarks made it clear that he thought that reduced access to higher education was an idea whose time was long overdue. He suggested one specific and one general way to improve the academic performance of today's college students. His specific recommendation is not unreasonable; he urged that financial aid should be dependent upon academic performance. His general recommendation, however, runs contrary to the last century of higher education, and to all prevailing indicators of what lies ahead in the next one hundred years. His vision for restoring excellence to higher education is to limit access drastically.

But to whom would he deny access to a college education? Certainly not to his own son or daughter. Every parent today rightly envisions a college education as part of his child's future. Nor is this a new phenomenon. Writing in 1925, J. B. Johnston described the widespread desire among parents to see their sons and daughters attend college, regardless of the youths' academic accomplishments or potential.[95] One reason this is so is that parents hope and pray for the economic success of their children. But we believe there is a more fundamental prayer being voiced—one that is consciously or unconsciously influenced by an inchoate awareness that a college education nurtures proficient humanity. What parents would wish for less than this gift for their child? Parents recognize that they are the past, and our children are the future. We, as the past, care about the future, and we have something vital to offer it.

Historically, human imagination has fixed on the material inheritance the rising generation received from the passing generation and could immediately set to use. There were always other legacies, of course, some more valuable than money or property. Morality, religion, and law have been the first of these greater legacies. But they have been closely followed by science, music, and art. In fact, when we use an expression such as Western civilization, what we really convey—whether we know it or not—is that these are legacies that endure. Though it may be common enough to see families go from rags to riches to rags in three generations, it takes a far longer time to squander the capital of moral and intellectual progress. By the same token the slogan, "Dark Ages," gives profound evidence of how hard and long it is to recover from such squanderings.

In the United States at least and perhaps throughout the West, the inheritance of money and property has almost ceased to be of meaningful consequence to the immediately succeeding generations. The fact is, we now all live so very long, and our offspring enter into productive lives so far ahead of our declining years—on average— that the worldly inheritances we might give are usually more relevant to our grand and great-grand children than to our own children.

This is a sea change. It may be less noticeable in the cases in which the parents, still living, are able to assist their progeny in starting productive careers and families. Perhaps they will pay down payments on mortgages, capitalize businesses, or, not insignificantly, help to pay for professional training. But it remains true that today's youth will reach their professional peak—on average—while their parents yet live and therefore without inheritance.

No more, then, can the imagination fix on the inheritance—whether large or small—as life's lottery. What this means practically is that the rising generation is required to give thought to its mature adulthood—what it will make of its lives—without calculating on stepping into the shoes and paths of its forebears.

In this situation nothing is more important than urging our offspring to pay close attention to the moral and intellectual inheritance left by one's parents and their parents before them and so on to a time when memory no longer rouses. For the beauty of this inheritance is that the past need not have died before the future can enjoy full and undivided use of the inheritance. It is every bit as rich and fruitful in the hands of our children as in our hands, even while we still possess it.

The way to cultivate a moral and intellectual bequest to the growth of compound interest is through education, including higher education. In a moral society, all youth are our offspring, and we all share the responsibility to teach the young how to cultivate a worthy inheritance.

We must each ask ourselves, what differences we are making in the lives of the rising generation. What increment of value do we add to their self-understanding, their career prospects, and even their lifetime earnings? How do we help set them on a path toward proficient humanity? Educators, in particular, must ask these questions of themselves. These are the most meaningful questions we can ask, as became evident to one of us a long time ago, when he awakened to the realization that he had settled into a career of teaching geniuses—the brightest students in the country—and then taking credit for their accomplishments. But what did he really, except to give them a road map?

Since those days we have been inspired by the land-grant vision to assure the sufficient intellect full opportunity to flower into genius by dint of effort and careful cultivation. That is the true meaning of the nation's efforts to guarantee access to higher education.

That is the reason for our insistence that access and excellence are not in tension. That is why we challenge rather simplistic, uninformative statistics like graduation rates that measure nothing but nominal progress without attention to the pacing—the changes in velocity—that do or do not occur to students arriving at our college gates. If one student drives up to the gate in a four-cylinder, and remains in that mode, he is not going to get through faster than his eight-cylinder neighbor will. If, on the other hand, he does get through just as fast, that means he acquired an additional four cylinders along the way, while his eight-cylinder neighbor went through unchanged. That is what we mean by value added—a concept developed further in chapters 4 and 5.

The tax-paying public and the tuition-paying students and parents are paying for the added value, not merely the name and certainly not the custodial care. The change over time is profit from the investment in education, and that is what the past is interested in giving to the future.

If we, the present generation, perform our work well, our posterity will perpetuate the way of life we know, not because they will have inherited it from us but because they will see and embrace its virtue. Accordingly, this very abstract account of the reason we care about education is, in fact, the most concrete way we have to remind ourselves of what we seek in building schools, faculties, education partners, and communities in which the young see themselves as both cared for and directed. In effect, we hereby explain why we speak to the young as we do when we encourage them to study and learn. The cultivation of good habits of decision on sound moral and religious grounds is the single most important gift that education conveys. Insofar as we are able to offer such a gift, we have a moral duty to do so. The best schools, the best education, provide exactly such a gift.

That best education, as we have emphasized in earlier chapters, provides a power that enables us to see with clarity our own circumstances, our own understandings—if we mean by education liberation from all prejudice. We seem sometimes to think that it suffices just to convey prejudices and otherwise to leave people à la Jean Jacques Rousseau, to follow their natures. To leave people without discipline is a terrible mistake. An era of good feelings, or preachings about harmony, or preachings about respect, are poor substitutes for hard earned respect through diligent effort and demonstrated merit.

Our education will fail, if we are not called upon to demonstrate merit in any way that is tied to our relationship with our fellows. We may be asked often to demonstrate merit, often given hard tasks, but if insulated from any connection between our accomplishments and our relationships with our fellows it amounts to an incomplete education.

Thomas Jefferson thought that human nature could not avoid the eminence of merit once it had demonstrated itself. Bring us all together and have us all do the work and take whatever exams or challenges apply; then we would look around and see among us those who shine and pay true deference and respect to them. The great impulse today often appears quite the opposite. While there is respect of one sort for those who shine, there is likely to be more envy than deference, or, worse still, there are likely to be greater attempts to define away the shining. For example, we use race norming and other forms of invalidating testing procedures, or we attack the idea of testing itself. Any challenge that produces distinction, insofar as the distinction is socially visible, comes under attack in the age in which we now live. That amounts to an abandonment of the gift of education.

We think, then, that we have a great responsibility as individuals and also as educators. That responsibility is to try to free ourselves from prejudices inconsistent with education. Our first responsibility is to try to give ourselves what we alone can give ourselves, and that is a true education, bearing in mind that we know that it is a lifelong process. As educators, as parents, as responsible citizens, we bear an added and noble responsibility to bestow this gift upon the rising generation in the best way we can. To do so will add a value to our lives, and to theirs, which cannot be diminished.

We say that if a nation wants more excellence, wants a world in which proficient humanity is a goal pursued by all, its goal must be not less access, but more. We, as a nation, must make real and explicit the long-standing promise of opportunity that America holds out to all. Has this nation truly meant that word, "all"? That is the question before us. We embrace the answer to that question succinctly phrased by W. E. B. DuBois. He asked, "Who shall go to college?" and presaged our response, "Everybody."[96]

Three Responses

Yet, we still must face the reality that the cost of higher education cannot continue to increase at rates that outpace inflation year after year. What is the answer? We must do three things.

First, skip the polemics and statistical sophistry, and engage in an honest dialogue. We owe it to students and citizens to move beyond the empty rhetoric of more money/less waste—more taste/less filling—and toward a real discussion of where we are and where we need to go. We need serious, creative deliberation about purpose and public policy rather than partisanship and polarization.

Second, build on the track record of excellence. State systems of higher education in Virginia and elsewhere need to free their public colleges and universities from the perverse incentives and micromanagement of the current funding system so that they can do an even better job of producing a high quality education at a reasonable cost in the future. There is no reason to believe that bureaucratic central planning can do any better there than it has in every other part of the world.

Third, hold public colleges and universities truly accountable for the results they achieve with the taxpayer dollars entrusted to them. Public colleges and universities ought to be subjected to the kind of fiscal discipline that the private sector faces every day. Those that perform their missions well should be financially encouraged and rewarded. Those that do not perform their missions well should be financially disciplined.

Notes

1.   Kerr, 121.
2.   Henry Sloan Coffin, "Timeless Elements in Education," in Henry Pratt Fairchild, ed., The Obligations of Universities to the Social Order (New York: New York University Press, 1933), 457.
3.   J. B. Johnston, "How Shall the College Discharge Its Obligation to Society?" in The Reference Shelf 7, edited by James G. Hodgson (New York: H. W. Wilson Company, 1931), 97.
4.   Ernest Vancourt Vaughn, "The Origins and Early Development of Universities," in The Reference Shelf 7, edited by James G. Hodgson (New York: H. W. Wilson Company, 1931), 134.
5.   Ibid., 135.
6.   Ortega y Gasset, 59.
7.   We say this despite the insistence of some, such as William Henry, who insist that college ought to remain the domain of the few. Henry argues that, "At its present size, the American style of mass higher education probably ought to be judged a mistake—and one based on a giant lie." William Henry, In Defense of Elitism (New York: Doubleday, 1994), 64.
8.   Alvin Kernan, In Plato's Cave (New Haven, CT: Yale University Press, 1999), 299.
9.   William McAndrew, "Doubting the Deans," in The Reference Shelf 7, edited by James G. Hodgson (New York: H. W. Wilson Company, 1931), 146.
10.   "The number of countries in Europe where some form of tuition is charged to students of higher education is increasing, and the debate about introducing tuition

in those countries that do not yet have fees is heating up." Hans N. Weiler, "States, Markets and University Funding: New Paradigms for the Reform of Higher Education in Europe," Compare (October 2000): 335.

11. The Republic of Germany is also learning this lesson, to judge from a recent news report: "The right to study on and on at taxpayers' expense took a blow when a court upheld a state's right to charge tuition from students who overstay their welcome. . . . The German Federal Administrative Court said the state was justified. On average, a German student spends 13.5 semesters at college and finally leaves at age 32." New York Times (26 July 2001), A6.

12. It is hard to resist Armour's brief note on "tuition" in this context: "The opposite of the Tuition is the Intuition. Unlike the Tuition, the Intuition is free. It comes as standard equipment with the brain, and is not an extra. Intuition is knowing something immediately, without being taught, and if it were more prevalent would mean a drastic change in Academe: Professors would no longer be necessary. Nor, in fact, would Academe. Also, since everything would be seen with the mind's eye, on which it would be difficult to fit glasses, ophthalmologists, optometrists, and opticians would be unnecessary. Until Intuition becomes more evident, it is probably unnecessary to say that the Tuition is necessary.* [*Except in a State Institution. There is no Tuition in an Insane Asylum.] Tuition is essential in Academe, the land of the Fee." Richard Armour, The Academic Bestiary (New York: William Morrow & Company, Inc., 1974), 152.

13. "During the past year, some 53 million people—or roughly 28 percent of all Americans—were enrolled in school. Total cash outlays for public and private schools amounted to an estimated $36 billion, up more than tenfold from $3.4 billion in 1940. Nearly 2.25 million persons were employed as teachers, instructors and professors. It is manifest from such figures that education is one of our greatest industries." "Education: Investment in Human Capital," First National City Bank of New York Monthly Economic Letter (August 1965) in William P. Lineberry, ed., Colleges at the Crossroads (New York: The H. W. Wilson Company, 1966), 168.

14. McAndrew, 138.

15. "Education: Investment in Human Capital," 168-169.

16. "Differences between present and past are immense. In the 1980s over 7 million young people attend college or university full-time. This constitutes roughly half of American youth between the ages of eighteen and twenty-one, in contrast to an estimated 2 percent in the early 1800s who went to college. The college population of 1800 was white and male and largely of British descent; today slightly more women than men attend college, and the ethnic mix on campus mirrors, with the significant distortion of the under representation of blacks and Hispanics, that of the population. College has always served disproportionately the privileged, but the field of privilege has widened to include greater reaches of the middle and working classes." Helen Lefkowitz Horowitz, Campus Life: Undergraduate Cultures from the End of the Eighteenth Century to the Present (New York: Alfred A. Knopf, 1987), xi.

17. "Education: Investment in Human Capital," 173

18. Ibid., 173.

19. Horowitz, 5.

20. Ibid., 4.

21. National Center for Education Statistics, "College Enrollment Rates of High-School Graduates," Table #185 in Digest of Education Statistics (Washington, D.C.: NCES, 2001), <http://nces.ed.gov/pubs2001/digest/dt185.html> (May 13, 2001).

22. Laurence Veysey, The Emergence of the American University (Chicago: University of Chicago Press, 1965), 2.

23. Stephen Moore and Julian Simon, It's Getting Better All the Time (Washington, D.C.: The Cato Institute, 2000), 159.

24. Thomas G. Mortenson, "Postsecondary Participation of Students from Low Income Families," Tables presented to the Round Table Meeting of Advisory Committee on Student Financial Assistance, Boston University, April 12, 2000. <http://www.ed.gov/offices/AC/ACSFA/mortenson.pdf> (August 13, 2001), 6.

25. "More First-year College Students Return for Second Year; Fewer Students Graduate in Five Years," ACT Newsroom (April 26, 2001), <http://www.act.org/news/releases/2001/04-26-01.html> (June 7, 2001).

26. Clifford Adelman, "What Proportion of College Students Earn a Degree?" AAHE Bulletin 51 (October 1998): 8.

27. Douglas Lederman, "Persistent Racial Gap in SAT Scores Fuels Affirmative-Action Debate," Chronicle of Higher Education 45 (October 30, 1998): A36-37.

28. Adelman is a notable exception, who already in 1998 was pointing to the different experiences of black students, based on course of study: ". . .if we look just at black students who completed trigonometry, precalculus, or calculus in high school. . .72 percent had earned bachelor's degrees by 1993," a number far higher than the raw race norm. Clifford Adelman, "To Help Minority Students Raise Their Graduation Rates," Chronicle of Higher Education 45 (September 4, 1998): B8.

29. Table prepared using ACT scores data distributed to SCHEV, 1998.

30. Jeremy D. Finn, "Opportunity Offered—Opportunity Taken: Course-Taking in American High Schools," ETS Policy Notes 9 (Spring 1999): 7.

31. Paul E. Barton and Richard J. Coley, Growth in Schools: Achievement Gains from the Fourth to the Eighth Grade (Princeton, NJ: Educational Testing Service, 1998), 23.

32. Ibid., 6.

33. Ibid., 6. Reprinted with permission.

34. Ibid., 7. Reprinted with permission.

35. Ibid., 12.

36. Ibid. Reprinted with permission.

37. Ibid. Reprinted with permission.

38. Ibid., 13. Reprinted with permission.

39. Note, for example, recent efforts by the National Association for the Advancement of Colored People (NAACP) and People for the American Way to stress high academic expectations as a way to close the achievement gap. New York Times (22 August 2001): A19.

40. Council for Aid to Education. Commission on National Investment in Higher Education, Breaking the Social Contract: The Fiscal Crisis in Higher Education (N.p.: Rand Corporation, 1997), 2.

41. For example, the American Council on Education reports the following result from a recent poll: "Paying for college remains a major concern. . .[although] Americans are less worried about financing a college education than they were in January 1998." They added also that ". . .the public continues to believe that colleges do not keep tuition at an affordable level, and almost three-quarters of Americans think colleges can reduce the cost of tuition without lowering the quality of education the students receive." Stanley O. Ikenberry and Terry W. Hartle, Taking Stock: How Americans Judge Quality, Affordability, and Leadership at U.S. Colleges and Universities (Washington, D.C.: American Council on Education, 2000), <http://www.acenet.edu/bookstore/pdf/taking_stock.pdf> (July 5, 2001). Likewise, Public Agenda Online reports that 53 percent of Americans worry "a great deal" that a good college education is becoming too expensive, citing a poll conducted by The Washington Post in October 1999. Public Agenda Online: The Issues-Education, "People's Chief Concerns." <http://www.publicagenda.org issues_pcc_detail.cfm?issue_type=education&list=13> (August 6, 2001).

42. Higher Education: Tuition Increasing Faster Than Household Income and Public Colleges' Cost, 43-44.

43. American Association of State Colleges and Universities, The 1999 Public Policy Agenda (New York: AASC&U, 1999), 5.

44. James M. Buchanan and Nicos E. Devletoglu, "Students: Consumers Who Do Not Buy," in Academia in Anarchy (New York: Basic Books, 1970), 33, quoting Armen A. Alchian and William R. Allen, "What Price Zero Tuition?" Michigan Quarterly Review (October 1968).

45. "Awarding scholarships to students with high grade point averages and test scores, irrespective of family income, could mean that many colleges begin bidding for superior students in much the same fashion as athletic departments have been buying 'blue chip' athletes. . . . Indeed, the Wall Street Journal recently ran an article on merit scholarships in which it described them, using typical business terms, as 'the academic world's answer to the old-fashioned price war'. . ." Ronald Isetti, "The Future of Liberal Arts Colleges: Commercialization or Integrity?" Liberal Education 60 (December 1974), 544. In short, it was not rooted in economic science. Thirty-six years later that error would not be made: "Princeton has just given its undergraduates who receive financial aid what amounts to a significant price discount. . . . The latest price reduction, offered through the switch from loans to grants, really sweetens the deal." Gordon C. Winston, "Is Princeton Acting Like a Church or a Car Dealer?" Chronicle of Higher Education 47 (February 23, 2001): B24.

46. Gordon C. Winston and Ivan C. Yen, Costs, Prices, Subsidies, and Aid in U.S. Higher Education, Discussion Paper-32 (Williamston, MA: Williams Project on the Economics of Higher Education, 1995), 11. <http://www.williams.edu/wpehe/abstracts.html#dp-32> (June 13, 2001).

47. Winston and Yen use the term "donative resources" to describe charitable contributions made to colleges and universities and other sources of revenue obtained through means other than the sale of its services.

48. Winston, Costs, Prices, Subsidies and Aid in U.S. Higher Education, 15.

49. Ibid.,15.

50. Donald E. Heller, The States and Public Higher Education Policy: Affordability, Access and Accountability (Baltimore: Johns Hopkins University Press, 2001), 15-16.

51. National Commission on the Cost of Higher Education, Straight Talk About College Costs and Prices (Phoenix, AZ: Oryx Press, 1998), 10-11. <http://www.acenet.edu/programs/DGR/costreport.HTML> (May 20, 2001).

52. David W. Breneman and Joni E. Finney, "The Changing Landscape: Higher Education Finance in the 1990s" in Patrick M. Callan et al., eds., Public and Private Financing of Higher Education: Shaping Public Policy for the Future (Phoenix, AZ: American Council on Education and Oryx Press, 1997), 38.

53. Lucie Lapovsky and Loren Loomis Hubbel, "An Uncertain Future," Business Officer (February 2001): 25-31. <http://www.nacubo.org> (July 1, 2001).

54. Gordon C. Winston and David J. Zimmerman, Where is Aggressive Price Competition Taking Higher Education? Discussion paper-56 (Williamston, MA: Williams Project on the Economics of Higher Education, 2000), 2-3. <http://www.williams.edu/wpehe/abstracts.html#dp-56> (May 21, 2001).

55. The College Board, Trends in Pricing, 2000/01 (New York: The College Board, 2000), 3. <http://www.collegeboard.org/press/cost00/html/Trendsin Pricing2K.pdf> (June 23, 2001).

56. Donald E. Heller, "Trends in the Affordability of Public Colleges and Universities: The Contradiction of Increasing Prices and Increasing Enrollment," in The States and Public Higher Education Policy: Affordability, Access, and Accountability, 18-19.

57.   Gordon C. Winston, A Guide to Measuring College Costs, Discussion paper-46 (Williamston, MA: Williams Project on the Economics of Higher Education, 1998), 1. Winston estimates, for example, that the cost of using buildings, equipment and land may constitute anywhere from 25 to 40 percent of the total educational cost, yet that cost is seldom fully or accurately reported. <http://www.williams.edu/wpehe/abstracts.html#dp-46> (June 13, 2001). Likewise, the National Commission on the Cost of Higher Education "found that the traditional disregard of capital assets in discussions of educational expenditures is a major barrier to understanding the true costs of higher education." NCCHE, Straight Talk About College Costs and Prices, 9.

58.   Two other major obstacles to full and accurate accounting of the cost of a college degree, according to Winston, are: (1) determining whether financial aid is a cost or a price discount, and (2) allocating costs among the many activities of colleges and universities. In addition, there are substantial gaps in the calculation of the amount of tax-payer support that colleges and universities receive. For example, the value that institutions receive from their tax-exempt status is seldom taken into account when calculating the amount of tax support. Winston, A Guide to Measuring College Costs, 1.

59.   NCCHE, Straight Talk About College Costs and Prices, 5, 7, 18. Efforts are now underway to develop more comprehensive, accurate, and uniform reporting of the costs of postsecondary education. For example, in a direct response to the report of the National Commission on the Cost of Higher Education, the National Association of College and University Business Officers initiated its "Cost of College Project" in 1998, with the primary goal to "develop a common methodology for calculating the cost of an undergraduate education at the full range of colleges and universities around the country." National Association of College and University Business Officers, "Interim Report of the Ad Hoc Committee on College Costs" (Washington, D.C.: NACUBO, February 2001), 2.<http://www.nacubo.org/public_policy/cost_of_college/> (July 1, 2001).

60.   Examples include the "Cost of College Project," initiated by the National Association of College and University Business Officers in 1998; the directive given to the Commissioner of Education Statistics as part of the 1998 Higher Education Act (HEA) reauthorization to convene forums nationally for the purpose of developing nationally consistent methodologies for reporting costs incurred by postsecondary institutions in providing postsecondary education; and the charge to the Commissioner to develop a "higher education basket" in coordination with the Bureau of Labor Statistics.

61.   David W. Breneman, "Is There a Federal Policy Toward Higher Education?" in The Uneasy Public Policy Triangle in Higher Education: Quality, Diversity and Budgetary Efficiency, David Finifter et al., eds. (New York: American Council on Education and Macmillan Publishing Company, 1991), 19 [quotation from Rivlin is from The Role of the Federal Government in Financing Higher Education (Washington, D.C.: Brookings Institution, 1961), 118].

62.   See, for example, Patrick M. Callan and Joni E. Finney, Public and Private Financing of Higher Education: Shaping Public Policy for the Future (Phoenix, AZ: Oryx Press for the American Council on Higher Education, 1997), xi-xii.

63.   President's Commission on Higher Education, Higher Education for American Democracy (Washington, D.C.: GPO, 1947) v.2, p. 23, quoted in the introduction to Donald E. Heller, ed. The States and Public Higher Education Policy: Affordability, Access, and Accountability (Baltimore: Johns Hopkins University Press, 2001), 1.

64.   Arthur M. Hauptman, "Reforming the Ways in Which States Finance Higher Education," in The States and Public Higher Education Policy: Affordability, Access,

and Accountability, 69. Economists such as Hautpman stress that low-tuition po-
lices are "inefficient in that large subsidies are provided to middle- and upper-
income students who could afford to pay more" and that a "preferable strategy from
the viewpoint of efficiency would be to reduce the subsidies provided to all public
sector students by raising tuition levels somewhat and to reallocate some of these
resources in the form of more funding for grants to low-income students. . ." Arthur
M. Hauptman, "Trends in the Federal and State Financial Commitment to Higher
Education," in The Uneasy Public Policy Triangle in Higher Education: Quality,
Diversity and Budgetary Efficiency, 124.

65. New Millennium Project on Higher Education Costs, Pricing, and Productivity,
Reaping the Benefits: Defining the Public and Private Value of Going to College
(Washington, D.C.: The Institute for Higher Education Policy, March 1998), 8. This
contrasts strongly with the description in Cheryl D. Lovell, "Past and Future Pres-
sures," in Joseph Losco and Brian L. Fife, eds. Higher Education in Transition: The
Challenges of the New Millennium (Westport, CT: Bergin & Garvey, 2000), 124.

66. And such a shift did take place, although some of the effect was offset in the past
couple of years. Note, for example, the finding of the State Higher Education
Executive Officers association, SHEEO, that, ". . . appropriations per FTE [i.e.,
Full-Time Equivalent] student (in constant dollars) continue to increase, but have
not returned to the high levels of 1986 through 1988. Since 1993, state appropriations per full-time equivalent student have increased in constant dollars. . . . In the
years between 1988 and 1993, state appropriations per FTE student fell by more
than 15 percent, but have now recovered to 1984 levels." Mary P. McKeown-
Moak, Financing Higher Education in the New Century: The Third Annual Report
from the States (Denver, CO: State Higher Education Executive Officers, June
2001), 5.<http://www.sheeo.org/finance/fin–01–report.pdf> (August 13, 2001)].

67. Three major policy changes during the 1990s added to the cost burden for students
and their families: ". . . a shift of responsibility away from public and governmental
sources to students, families and institutions; a shift from grants to loans as the
predominant form of student financial assistance; and an increasing reliance on
allocated tuition fees as a source of student financial assistance for students in
private and public colleges and universities (Heller, xi).

68. Breneman, "The Changing Landscape: Higher Education Finance in the 1990s," in
Patrick M. Callan et al., eds., Public and Private Financing of Higher Education:
Shaping Public Policy for the Future (Phoenix, AZ: American Council on Education
and Oryx Press, 1997), 52.

60. Michael S. McPherson and Morton Owen Schapiro, The Student Finance System
for Undergraduate Education: How Well Does It Work? Discussion paper-11
(Williamston, MA: Williams Project on the Economics of Higher Education, 2000),
2-3. <http://www.williams.edu/wpehe/abstracts.html#dp-11> (June 13, 2001).

70. Joseph Losco and Brian L. Fife, "Higher Education Spending: Assessing Policy
Priorities," in Higher Education in Transition: The Challenges of the New Millennium, 57.

71. "The accompanying purpose of the higher education system that is at risk of being
shortchanged is that of providing educational opportunities to qualified students of
all backgrounds." Michael S. McPherson and Morton Owen Schapiro, "Financing
Undergraduate Education: Designing National Policies," National Tax Journal 50
(September 1997): 569.

72. United States Department of Education. Advisory Committee on Student Financial
Assistance. Access Denied: Restoring the Nation's Commitment to Equal Educational Opportunity (Washington, D. C.: Department of Education, February 2001),v.
<http://www.ed.gov/offices/AC/ACSFA/access_denied. pdf> (August 13, 2001).

73.   Michael S. McPherson and Morton Owen Schapiro, The Student Aid Game: Meeting Need and Rewarding Talent in American Higher Education (Princeton, NJ: Princeton University Press, 1998), 1.

74.   Kenneth E. Redd, Discounting Toward Disaster: Tuition Discounting, College Finances, and Enrollments of Low-Income Undergraduates (Indianapolis, IN: USA Group Foundation, 2000).

75.   "Discounting and Its Discontents: The Cost of Maintaining Enrollment," Change 26 (July-August 1994): 34.

76.   Gordon C. Winston and David Zimmerman. "Where is Aggressive Price Competition Taking Higher Education?" Change 32 (July-August 2000): 17.

77.   Jeffrey Selingo, "Questioning the Merit of Merit Scholarships," The Chronicle of Higher Education 47 (January 19, 2001): A20-22.

78.   P. F. Kluge, Alma Mater: A College Homecoming (Reading, MA: Addison-Wesley Publishing Co., 1993), 192-3.

79.   The Western Interstate Commission for Higher Education and The College Board aptly describe enrollment trends and high-school graduating class size from the 1960s to the 1990s as a "rollercoaster," noting the peak in the late 1970s followed by the steady decline after 1977 and the bottoming-out in the mid-1990s. They forecast "another steep rise into the 21st century." Western Interstate Commission for Higher Education and The College Board (WICHE), Knocking at the College Door, 5.

80.   Council for Aid to Education, 9.

81.   WICHE, 1.

82.   Clifford Adelman, "Crosscurrents and Riptides," Change 31 (January/February 1999): 20-27.

83.   Ibid.

84.   National Center for Education Statistics. Condition of Education, 2001 (Washington, DC: NCES, 2001), 75.

85.   Richard L. Pattenaude, "Administering the Modern University," in Higher Education in Transition, 166.

86.   Robert Zemsky and Gregory R. Wegner, "Shaping the Future," in Public and Private Financing of Higher Education, 70.

87.   Lucas, 44.

88.   Neusner and Neusner, 112-13.

89.   John Immerwahr, Taking Responsibility: Leaders' Expectations of Higher Education (San Jose, CA: National Center for Public Policy and Higher Education, 1999), 10.

90.   Patrick M. Callan, "Reframing Access and Opportunity: Problematic State and Federal Higher Education Policy in the 1990s," in The States and Public Higher Education Policy, 85.

91.   The Commonwealth Foundation of Virginia, "Assessment of Higher Education Enrollment Estimates in the Commonwealth of Virginia" (February 1, 1995).

92.   William Zumeta, "Public Policy and Accountability in Higher Education: Lessons from the Past and Present for the New Millennium," in The States and Public Higher Education Policy, 159.

93.   Adelman, "Crosscurrents and Riptides," 26-27.

94.   Council for Aid to Education, 2.

95.   Johnston, 101.

96.   W. E. B. DuBois, Darkwater: Voices from Within the Veil (New York: Schocken Books, 1972), 216-17.

4

Evaluating Higher Education:
Waiting for Change

Know thyself.

A recurring theme in the previous chapter—sometimes implicit, sometimes explicit—is that the trust that the American public places in our systems of education, including higher education, has diminished during past decades. We are all too familiar with the factors that have contributed to this fraying of the public trust. They include, but are not limited to:

- Skyrocketing tuition inflation;

- Cost increases that continue to outpace the Consumer Price Index;

- Political correctness and issues of civic/moral misbehavior;

- Tuition discounting utilized as a strategic enrollment tool;

- A small, but widely publicized, number of instances of questionable institutional practices, such as the Stanford indirect cost accounting extravagances[1] and the overlap group's calculations that precipitated an investigation by the Justice Department;[2] and,

- Concern within and outside the academy about large class size, use of graduate student instructors, and perceived imbalance between research and teaching in faculty merit systems.[3]

Overall, however, we think that the problem that most damages the public's trust in higher education is a perception of declining quality. The decline in the quality of the K-12 educational opportunities for many of the children in our country was well documented by the *Nation at Risk* report in 1983, and dismaying accounts continue to this day. Since that time, concerned public officials at the local, city, state, and national level have proffered countless speeches, numerous plans, and a significant amount of funding aimed at rectifying these problems. During much of this interval, these same officials have sought comfort in the thought that while there were gaping holes in the quality of primary and secondary education available at many school districts in America, at least our system of higher education is regarded as the best in the world. Nevertheless, there are indications that the quality of the education offered at many colleges and universities has declined, or at least that they are not graduating students equipped with the level of knowledge and skills that informed observers expect them to have. Evidence of the decline can be found in a number of publications,[4] as well as by talking with those who hire our graduates. Evidence may also be gleaned through conversations with faculty and administrators at colleges and universities.

But the information available from our colleges and universities with regard to the quality of their inventory of wares and their "output" is a mixed bag. On one hand, retired administrators acknowledge the problem in their memoirs and some of the faculty own up to it in conversation with friends and colleagues. On the other hand, the academic leadership and even many of the faculty of the majority of colleges and universities often deny staunchly that a problem exists. Rather than acknowledging that persistent upward creep of the GPA is due to grade inflation, they suggest that students are performing better than ever. Rather than admitting that poor performance on tests might result from poor learning—or poor teaching—they challenge the ability of such tests to assess learning. Rather than persist in the effort to teach grammar, spelling, and syntax, they denounce the rules of composition as rigidly authoritarian and encourage students to emphasize feelings over articulate expressiveness.

It is indeed ironic that institutions, which still occasionally offer students the opportunity to read Herodotus and Plato, do not themselves heed the Delphic oracle's advice: *Know thyself.* Too often, those who lead America's colleges and universities advance the myth of incomparability[5] rather than visible efforts to evaluate the quality of the education they offer. They settle for measuring what is easy to measure, such as simplistic graduation rates, rather than measuring what is most important. They fall back on reputational rating scales, as measured by *U.S. News & World Report* or *Kiplinger's*, rather than providing students and families with a more in-depth and more honest way of evaluating how an institution will best fit a student's needs and educational goals. Generally, the colleges and universities, particularly the large research universities, rely on growth in numbers—inertial growth—to tell their stories. Yet, the only accurate way to evaluate progress on the central mission of teaching is through dynamic growth.

Parker Palmer well captured the sense of dynamic growth in teaching in a 1997 article:

> We need to open a new frontier in our exploration of good teaching: the inner landscape of a teacher's life. To chart that landscape fully, three important paths must be taken—intellectual, emotional, and spiritual—and none can be ignored. Reduce teaching to intellect and it becomes a cold abstraction; reduce it to the spiritual and it loses its anchor to the world. Intellect, emotion, and spirit depend on each other for wholeness. They are interwoven in the human self and in education at its best, and we need to interweave them in our pedagogical discourse as well.[6]

Evaluation or assessment in the best sense communicates accomplishments across these dimensions, reflecting the interactions and mutual influences that constitute the dynamism of an institution. "The aim of education. . .is to guide man in the evolving dynamism through which he shapes himself as a human person—armed with knowledge, strength of judgment, and moral virtues—while at the same time conveying to him the spiritual heritage of the nation and the civilization in which he is involved."[7] Thus, effective assessment conduces toward proficient humanity.

What Can We Learn from Graduation Rates?

One of our priorities at the State Council of Higher Education in Virginia was an initiative to change the overall approach to evaluating the performance of the Commonwealth's colleges and universities. The performance-funding proposal, which the Council endorsed during our tenure, consisted of several closely interwoven strategies (including a performance funding initiative which is described in some detail in chapter 5), centered on a new metric for measuring institutional performance. The proposal provided a new approach to understanding and measuring graduation rates, and it was developed gradually over a period of several months. The approach we urged, and an explanation for choosing a new approach, built upon an invitation to dream up new ideas about a relatively old topic—graduation rates. The question is "What can we learn from graduation rates?" Implied within that question is this specific focus—"what *new* can we learn from graduation rates?" As Earl Weaver once said, "It's what you learn after you know it all that counts."

What do we already know about graduation rates? One thing that we know is that only about four out of every ten students graduate within five years of entering a four-year public college as first-year students. Within Virginia, we know that 55 percent of the students who entered senior, public colleges and universities in 1990 graduated within five years and 60 percent did so within six years. We know that graduation rates vary substantially from one institution to another. And, we know from many studies, that "the most important factors explaining the differences in institutional graduation rates are the pre-college academic backgrounds students bring with them when they enroll in college."[8]

Once we know these things, however, what have we really learned? A winning coach of one of Virginia's athletic teams admits that 90 percent of success in coaching depends on success in recruiting. For admissions officers, one goal is to recruit students who have a good chance of being successful at their institutions. If a winning record—as measured by the number of students who graduate within a set number of years—were our primary purpose, then we might settle for a strategy of recruiting bright students and aim to make sure they leave college at least as bright and perhaps a bit brighter. Our motto might be "do no harm."

But our purpose is not simply to churn out diplomas. Our concern is to contribute—in significant and measurable ways—to the cognitive, intellectual, and psychosocial growth and development of our students. Our aim is to make a difference in their lives. One might argue (and, indeed, we would argue) that our potential to make a difference in the lives of our students is greatest where the need is also great. We want to do more than to make a difference; we further persist in asking ourselves, "How can we tell if we made a difference?" Graduation rates, in isolation, tell us very little about either of these matters.

When we begin to look at graduation rates with fresh eyes, and consider them in combination with other information, we gain insight about the real impact of a college education.

Can Colleges Affect Graduation Rates?

Building on research done by Sandy Astin, Thomas Mortenson has published a study that compares the *actual* versus *predicted* graduation rates for 1,100 colleges and universities. He suggests that by studying those institutions whose actual rates exceed their predicted rates, we can learn about factors that "foster. . .the rate at which admitted freshmen complete their bachelor's studies within six years of matriculation."[9]

Mortenson not only compared these rates for individual institutions; he also compiled the data in order to rank states. His calculations ranked Virginia sixteenth in the nation, with a state average residual of 1.2—that is, the difference between actual and predicted graduation rates, weighted based on enrollment. Based on that measure and the fact that 55 percent of Virginia's students graduate within five years compared to 43 percent nationally, we may reasonably conclude that Virginia is doing something right, although it still has room for improvement.

The challenge is to study those institutions whose actual graduation rates exceed those predicted in order to learn, in detail, just what it is that they are doing right. The collective responsibility, of course, is then to share that knowledge in ways that allow all institutions to increase the value that they add to students' lives through their collegiate experience. An added challenge is to replace a simplistic measure like graduation rate with a more meaningful way to evaluate the performance of public institutions in adding value to students' lives.

We may look to existing studies for guidance on where best to direct our attention as we seek to understand why some institutions graduate students at a rate greater than their predicted rate. There are two main areas where we ought to focus—student characteristics and institutional practices.

Student Characteristics

Within the area of student characteristics, fresh efforts might yet be guided most productively by Vincent Tinto's 1975 model of student persistence and the numerous studies that have attempted to validate his model. Much of Tinto's research focused on the concept of "person-environment fit." One way that we might put this research into practice, at the same time that we seek to enrich the research knowledge base, is to work closely with high school guidance counselors to develop in-depth profiles that would help students choose a college based on probable "fit" with regard to educational outcomes.

Another important area of research and potential practice under the umbrella of student characteristics involves students' preparation for college during high school.

Laura Horn and Xianglei Chen recently studied factors that are associated with the successful transition to college and with college persistence for "at-risk" students. They asked about these resilient students: "How are these students different from their less success-ful at-risk counterparts?"[10] What they found is that "resilient stu-dents had more positive attitudes about school, had more cohesive families, had parents who were more supportive of their schooling, and had peers more engaged in school" than their less successful counterparts. They further found that various types of college prepa-ration activities increased the odds of moderate- to high-risk stu-dents attending college and their chances of persisting in college. Examples include talking to at least two people about financial aid, getting help preparing for entrance exams, and getting help in the college application process.

What can we learn from this study? Colleges can significantly improve the educational outcomes of college students by instituting active outreach programs to high school students. Nothing adds more to chances for success in college than a challenging pre-collegiate course of study. Another focus of such outreach programs ought to be on activities that involve students in thinking about, talking about, and applying for college and for financial aid.

More importantly, though, collegiate outreach programs to high school students should focus on academics. Adelman's research underscores that "the strongest pre-college predictor of whether a student will succeed in earning a bachelor's degree is the academic intensity of the student's high-school courses."[11] Adelman urges col-leges to increase significantly the number of high-school-to-college bridge programs and to start those programs earlier, between the junior and senior year of high school, if not as early as middle school. He points out that only 35 percent of the 1,800 four-year colleges in the country had such programs in 1995, the most recent year for which data were available. He further recommends adoption of a rolling admissions schedule, with an aim of keeping students en-gaged longer with their high school studies and allowing more time to prepare for college admissions tests. And, he stresses the need to switch from a focus on social skill development—the emphasis of many of the existing programs—to academic preparation.[12]

Many Virginia colleges and universities have outreach programs. With regard to such programs, we must acquire renewed respect for failure—that is, the more challenging courses students take, even if they do not succeed, the better are their chances for college success. We readily acknowledge that we learn from failure in sports, but somehow forget that wisdom in other areas of endeavor. We might better keep in mind Baseball Hall of Famer Christy Mathewson's advice, "You can learn a little from victory. You can learn everything from defeat."

We add another to Adelman's list of ways the academy can affect the readiness of high school graduates for college-level work. We must acknowledge the impact of college admissions requirements on the high school curriculum. We complain readily enough about its "dumbing down." But, what are we doing to reverse the process? SHEEO (the professional organization for State Higher Education Executive Officers) conducted a major study of state strategies that support successful transition of students from secondary to postsecondary institutions. According to that survey, thirty-one states have taken steps to strengthen the academic rigor of the high school curriculum by establishing required high school coursework units for college admission.[13] Virginia made a start in strengthening the academic rigor of the high school curriculum with the adoption of its Standards of Learning. Now, it needs to assess their impact. Moreover, the time has come to augment "standards of learning" with "standards of exposure." The National Assessment of Educational Progress has made abundantly clear that what sets the achievement levels of American students apart from many students in other countries is far more their studies than their abilities.

Institutional Practices

In addition to trying to influence student characteristics that are associated with success in college, we can also study institutional practices. Many have done so, but there remains a need for more study. In some cases, the research findings to date are inconclusive. We need industry standards here as much as we do in automobile safety. "Institutions should develop guidelines and procedures for assessing their overall effectiveness as well as student learning outcomes."[14] Accrediting agencies, thus, must go beyond urging autochthonous guidelines and procedures, and aim for meaningful inter-communicability. There are usually multiple factors operating simultaneously that seem to foster or impede students' academic progress, so that it becomes difficult to determine which factors have the greatest impact and to determine which factors have direct impact and which are indirect.

Even so, the research findings to date about institutional characteristics point to areas where higher education leaders might most productively concentrate their efforts. We all know that institutional quality, as gauged by selectivity, has the most influence—right? Wrong! Once we control for pre-collegiate academic student characteristics, we find that, "net of other factors, measures of college selectivity and prestige account on the average for no more than one or two percent of the total variance in educational aspirations, persistence, bachelor's degree attainment, and educational attainment generally," according to Ernest Pascarella and Patrick Terenzini.[15]

In their extensive 1991 summary of the research on *How College Affects Students,* Pascarella and Terenzini point us toward the areas where we may have the most opportunity to improve student success by how we shape institutional practices. The following types of programs and organizational characteristics appear to be strongly associated with student success:

- Strong orientation and advising programs, particularly those with an academic focus and those that extend throughout the entering semester;

- A solid institutional emphasis on teaching critical problem-solving through general education;

- A high level of personal involvement with and concern for the individual student, manifested by faculty and staff throughout the institution, including significant levels of student-faculty interactions beyond the formal classroom setting; and,

- Encouraging students to live on campus, and perhaps designing residential settings that encourage student involvement—although the research on the impact of specialized residential arrangements shows mixed findings.[16]

Opportunities for Future Progress

We add to this list of institutional characteristics that can influence student success the following overarching goal: Our aim should be to foster habits of mind—an organizational culture—that communicate high expectations to the students, while providing academic and co-curricular programs that combine high challenge and high support.

We see then that there are a number of activities that we in higher education can undertake to change graduation rates. But, if we are going to *learn from* graduation rates, there is another set of activities we must undertake. As Margaret Miller (then president of the American Association for Higher Education) said at a SHEEO conference in February 1998, statewide systems of education tend to be "program rich but system poor."[17] We think rather that we tend to be data rich but information poor.

If we are to learn what we need to know from graduation rates, we must do two things about our data. We need to rethink which data we collect and we need to use the data we have more creatively. For research, evaluation, and the improvement of institutional practices, we would ideally want a database that would support cross-institution tracking of students from high school, through college, and might even support assessment of post-college outcomes. For we know that

> . . .student-based assessment, as opposed to institutional and program assessments, generally provide data that cannot easily be glossed over or dismissed. What has the student learned. . .? What does that person lack in college level skills, knowledge, and comprehension? Can a graduate identify important figures and events in history, write a coherent essay, discuss intelligently the ideas in literary and philosophical texts, . . . demonstrate mathematical ability and scientific thinking?[18]

At the same time, we would need to weigh the feasibility of such a database against desires to minimize the reporting burden for institutions. We also must be mindful of student privacy requirements.

Not less important is the need to devise a means to identify institutions in relation to the students they actually serve. An institution whose mission is primarily to serve at-risk students doubtless accomplishes much—and perhaps far more than a selective admissions institution—when it graduates a significant number of them in as few as five or six years. An accurate measure of graduation rates would reward such an institution for its relatively superior performance. Teaching the students we receive is both more difficult and more valuable than teaching the students we select.

Virginia's performance-funding model, discussed in the next chapter, was precisely designed to reward this sort of superior performance.

Are We Making a Difference?[19]

The not-so-hidden agenda of the new "Program Approval" policy developed during our tenure at SCHEV (described in chapter 5) was to lead a shift toward full integration of routine assessment and program innovation, driven *within* the institution rather than from without.[20] Adopting an approach such as this to measuring the performance of colleges and universities has a necessary corollary—the adoption of a new, and enhanced, approach to assessing student learning. And, this new approach starts when the faculty and academic leaders of an institution ask themselves, "Are we making a difference?"

This is the question that Charles McClain and Darryl Krueger, pioneers in making systematic assessments of education performance, regularly asked each other as they began their effort to improve the educational experiences of students at Truman State University (in Kirksville, Missouri). There is ample evidence that they made a huge difference in the quality of the educational experience via their use of systematic evidence to inform their decision-making on campus. Experts who have examined the assessment structure at Truman State have concluded that it causes the campus community to think more clearly about the desired outcomes of a college degree and as a result to analyze which methods, processes, and curricula are most likely to achieve the desired results.

Ralph Wolff, director of the Western Association of Schools and Colleges, speaks of the need to develop a "culture of evidence" on campus. By this, he means that discussion, debates, and decision-making on campus must come from valid evidence—not tradition, prejudice, or power plays.

Nevertheless, if scholars were to look closely at the decision-making processes on most campuses, they would find that evidence in the form of solidly collected and analyzed information is rarely the driving force. In the classroom, faculty demand supported argumentation from students, but they rarely practice the same discipline in their own meetings.

Assessment Programs: Thin Veneer or Core Activity?

In the September/October 1998 issue of *Change*, Ted Marchese concluded that assessment activities at most institutions "remain a thin veneer."[21] Likewise, the dean of a prominent school of education was once heard to say that assessment has not had much impact on college teaching. Contrast those statements with the above-mentioned experience of Truman State University, where assessment is so deeply embedded in the institution's culture that their 1997 recruitment for a new president explicitly sought candidates with "strong, demonstrable commitment to. . .the proactive use of assessment data for the improvement of teaching and learning."

What accounts for the different experiences and conclusions exemplified in these statements? There are three primary factors that determine the effectiveness of an institution's assessment program:

- First, clarity about purpose. Is there a shared understanding of why assessment is being done? Does the purpose meet a compelling, internal, and widely perceived need?

- Second, faculty involvement. It is impossible for an assessment program to have significant impact without extensive faculty engagement. Further, leadership from deans can make a real difference, as the senior author discovered while Dean of James Madison College, where he highlighted the role of assessment in advancing teaching and learning at the College.

- Third, assessment activities should be systematic and integrated into the academic and student development programs of the campus, not sporadic and isolated.

Sandy Astin, Tom Angelo, and others describe assessment as a powerful tool to assist the academy in its important work of talent development. In his 1991 book, *Assessment for Excellence*, Astin argues persuasively that the effectiveness of a college or university should be judged by how much and how well it contributes to the cognitive and affective development of students, rather than on the basis of reputation or resource acquisition.

Clarity of Purpose

Throughout our tenure at SCHEV, we challenged the use of simplistic, uninformative statistics such as graduation rates that measure nothing but nominal progress without attention to the pacing—the changes in velocity—that do or do not occur within students. We need measures that focus on value added, such as the measures included in the Virginia performance-funding model and the revised process for program approval. Though unrelated to concepts of "profit," the "value-added" idea holds here the same operational meaning it held for economists and management theorists early in the twentieth century:

> [Economic Value-Added] shows us what we need to find out and whether we need to take remedial action. EVA should also be used to find out what works. It does show which product, service, operation, or activity has unusually high productivity and unusually high value. Then we should ask ourselves, what can we learn from those successes.[22]

This concept may by analogy be applied to higher education, although the rule of profit above cost of capital—including taxation—

cannot be applied. As a driver of assessment it will highlight useful change/ growth and problematic performance.[23]

The superior measure of success is an institution's capacity for dynamic change—the constant refinement of procedures, resources, and facilities that is the only true path to excellence. Quality of academic life, rather than quantity of academic life, ought to be our paramount concern. In chapter 5, we describe how the Council of Higher Education endorsed a new approach to the review of new academic programs at Virginia's public institutions. Central to the revised program approval procedure was a significant reform of the state's relationship to assessment processes at the campuses. Under the revised approach, the Council's main role was to ensure that each institution put in place procedures for continuous quality improvement and that the procedures were integral to institutional planning. It was then up to each institution to devise the most appropriate means to implement this state policy.

Faculty Involvement

The second factor that determines the impact of an institution's assessment program is faculty involvement. To foster change from within, we need to ensure that we assess core activities, not those that are peripheral. Student learning must be at the center of our assessment programs. This means, of course, that faculty engagement must also be at the heart of the enterprise. It is the faculty who must consider what questions to ask and what evidence to gather. There is little point in gathering information about student learning if that information is not used to improve teaching.

Most faculty want to be reflective practitioners, who take the time to observe the impact of their teaching on student learning and who use these observations to improve the practice of their craft. There are, however, two potent forces that hinder this inclination—the tradition of faculty autonomy and the fact that research trumps teaching in the merit system at many campuses. There is some evidence, however, of change taking place in connection with both of these factors—change generated from within the academy and change stimulated from without.

Assessment can aid not only in developing student talent, but also that of the faculty. Increasing numbers of faculty see collaboration and peer review as valuable means to improve classroom performance, but on some campuses these approaches meet strong opposition. Faculty evaluation and development are, however, complex areas and deserve thoughtful consideration.

The chief criticism of peer review in teaching is the claim that it mainly involves retailing hearsay. That is an odd criticism for two reasons. First, it is usually the case that so-called hearsay emerges only in contexts in which faculties stubbornly resist classroom visitation as a routine. It hardly seems fair to blame hearsay when direct evidence is deliberately withheld. Secondly, and far more importantly, what is casually called "hearsay" is, in fact, the meat and potatoes of academic life, *namely, deliberate, self-conscious discussion about teaching among colleagues.*

Dean Allen reminded his colleagues at James Madison College that teaching at the highest levels and with the most reliable results sets institutions apart in the field of higher education. Because this results from the purpose, rather than an accident, of the institution's existence, we constantly bear the obligation to speak knowledgeably about the goals and methods of education.

The first question to engage our attention when we speak of the evaluation of faculty ought to be the question of whether and in what way they may constitute models for others who would seek like success. Do they contribute meaningfully to the foundations of knowledge regarding undergraduate instruction? What other institutions perform comparably or better in this regard? How might they assess their own performance in this regard, by which we mean to ask, are they able to articulate standards by which they are willing to be judged in a court not of their own making? Upon becoming a dean, Allen attempted through a questionnaire distributed to the faculty to gauge this dimension of the College. Too few faculty responded to permit any reasonable conclusion about the faculty as a whole, but the few who did respond indicated some ambiguity concerning consciousness of the relative value of the College's contribution. Might that ambiguity reflect hesitation to engage such a judgment?

Because we value teaching—undergraduate teaching—above all other dimensions of performance within higher education, the question of how we might phrase relative contributions within this arena is a necessary prelude to questions regarding internal consistency in the application of standards of evaluation. We need to know, for example, whether we regard the least acceptable level of accomplishment in any given institution as comparable to the least acceptable level of accomplishment elsewhere. Or, is that least the average elsewhere? The best? What does it mean to say that a faculty member demonstrates sustained excellence in teaching, when compared with teaching in institutions one would regard as comparable or nearly so?

It would be easy to mistake questions of comparability as a fruitless exercise in filling out bureaucratic scorecards in place of *self-conscious* integrity regarding a faculty's program and its intrinsic requisites. We submit, however, that the case is precisely the reverse; namely, mistaking one's own sincerity of purpose as sufficient justification before disinterested observers. The fact that one's mission is unique does not require that it be wrapped in preciosity. It is time to discard the myth of incomparability.

An example: some institutions quite plausibly claim to educate undergraduates rather by virtue of the specific discipline they require of the students, no matter what native gifts the students bring with them. By the discipline required of students, we mean theoretical sophistication, familiarity with canonical interpretations and intelligent challenges to them, and carefully integrated study across a general range of concerns, systematically developed through increasing levels of difficulty and, therefore, a coherent curriculum which uses the humanities to vector its content. These institutions may plausibly compete with institutions that prefer to work only with the most gifted students and in the mode of narrow specialization as the preferred method of undergraduate education. Comparisons between these two types of institutions ought not to be avoided because of the supposed gap between the elite and other institutions. If institutions that educate by virtue of required discipline succeed as well as they think they do, then it is well time to inquire—or, better, to state—why they do so.

Every discussion of assessment contains at least implicitly a discussion of faculty evaluation. The conception we now offer suggests an approach to faculty evaluation. Because we begin from self-consciousness of a particular approach, is it not reasonable first to judge faculty, not by student reaction, but by their respective abilities to articulate this approach both in their teaching materials and in their own evaluative commentaries on their teaching? Moreover, would not this requirement produce in turn, as direct evidence of teaching ability, reasonable reliance on a faculty member's capacity to persuade colleagues that the faculty member understands and can appropriately relate the conditions of success of the curriculum as a whole?

In these questions we do not aim to depreciate the value of student evaluations, on which we rely in their proper role (which is a second-order role).[24] Perhaps we need to be more explicit about the role of student evaluations. Is it not true that, while we do not regard them as definitive evidence of good or excellent teaching, we do consider them as highly probative—that is, as having diagnostic value rather than interpretive value—with respect to bad teaching? In such a case, a faculty member's student evaluations would have most value when indicating symptoms that may require medication, much as blood pressure or body temperature serve when abnormal to indicate a regime but offer scant assurance of health when normal.[25]

At the center of the evaluation of faculty teaching, accordingly, ought to stand the reality that we value teaching to the point of making excellence—not mere acceptability—a sine qua non for faculty advancement. Does this mean, as it implies, that an excellent researcher but mediocre teacher ought not reasonably to rely upon promotion?

We may appreciate faculty scholarly contributions—not defined narrowly—on the conviction that scholarly growth is a necessary complement to teaching excellence. Accordingly, we may encourage faculty to engage in continuous intellectual development, not only through means of course preparation but also through independent and collaborative research and creative endeavors. Clearly, assessment of research contributions must be mission dependent. In the research university, one may rightfully be mindful to adapt teaching requirements to the criteria that characterize membership in that larger faculty. Nor should an understandable preoccupation with teaching obscure, in faculty evaluations, the obligations that descend from that research university status.

The questions to pose, however, are whether it is possible, given the research mission, that an excellent teacher with no research accomplishment might yet rely upon promotion? Should we make an allowance for teaching not only unchallengeably excellent but also beyond the research university norm? The Boyer Commission thought so:

> What is needed now is a new model of undergraduate education at research universities that makes the baccalaureate experience an inseparable part of an integrated whole. Universities need to take advantage of the immense resources of the graduate and research programs to strengthen the quality of undergraduate education, rather than striving to replicate the special environment of the liberal arts college.[26]

Concede that mediocre teaching cannot rescue a record of excellent research; is it also true that it requires the value added of excellent research (or at least a teaching load beyond the norm) to attain the highest merit recognition within the research university?

We will not speak of the equally interesting question, how we evaluate research excellence. Research excellence is intrinsic but secondary to our topic here, namely, the levels of intelligible inter-communication among colleagues that we demand in teaching. Insofar as research accomplishments inform classroom instruction, they are relevant to this conversation. For one could scarcely credit a claim to impart to undergraduates what cannot with greater effect be communicated to informed, if lay, colleagues.

Pervasive and Systematic Assessment

To have a real impact on student development, assessment must be systematic and thoroughly integrated into the student's classroom and co-curricular experiences. We know from examples like Truman State University and Alverno College (in Milwaukee, Wisconsin) that it is possible to build and use such assessment programs. We do not lack the technical expertise to put such assessment programs in place at every campus.

What benefits result from systematic assessment? Count at least these:

1. Assessment creates an attitude of excellence and accountability;
2. Assessment gives the ability to measure outcomes and creativity;
3. Assessment points out how to achieve outcomes that are meaningful; and
4. Assessment practices provide information to interested university partners and build confidence in faculty decision making.

American higher education does not lack the technical tools needed to improve the quality of its product and outcomes, and to regain the trust of the public. The art of assessment has progressed sufficiently that one may now earn a doctoral degree in Assessment and Measurement at James Madison University in Harrisonburg, Virginia. Nor, we think, can any reasonable case be made (although some academic leaders do proffer this as an explanation) that our colleges and universities lack adequate funds to make the needed improvements. What then might explain the fact that so few institutions have begun to make such improvements, or have made so little progress if they have initiated an attempt?

The Role of Public Dialog

Dialog that engages the full educational enterprise is particularly needed today. Many individuals within and outside the enterprise have described the 1990s as a decade in which educational reform has been near the top of national and state agendas. While a good start has been made in some areas, much remains to be done if we are to achieve the scope of reform urged in *A Nation at Risk* and other major studies.

One critical task that has not yet been fully accomplished is the engagement of a sustained, honest, and purposeful public discourse both about the reasons why reform is needed and the goals it is intended to achieve. There has been no lack of rhetoric and reports. All of them remind us of the truth conveyed by the fabulist, Jean de la Fontaine, in his brief tale called "Education." There the opposite fates of the twins, Caesar and Laridon, remind us that intellect *and* character are the goals we seek and, moreover, that we can achieve the best of both only as a result of deliberate effort. What has been lacking is real engagement among the stakeholders within and outside the academy in a setting that promotes listening as well as speaking, moving from finger-pointing or hand-wringing to constructive development of solutions, and evaluating frankly what we have and have not done.

It would be a shame and a waste if in this hour we did not move beyond the platitudes of "more money," on the one side, and "more savings," on the other. Every informed observer must know that the path to better education is rather a conversation about what makes education a public good and not just a useful tool. Thus, we should begin right now to rescue our conversation about education from the green eyeshades. It is no more true that public support for education is declining than it is true that we can reasonably expect legislators to move into a period of economic downturn[27] with a focus on raising tuitions at our public institutions. We can ask for commitments to guarantee our campuses appropriation increases at the level of inflation plus an increment for merit. But we can do so only if we provide a conversation that unites around the good of education rather than divides around supposed supporters and opponents.

We know that, in a democratic society, major policy changes result either from a long period of consensus building or from a perceived crisis. The adoption of managed health care exemplifies a massive policy change that resulted from a perceived crisis. We are not yet at a full crisis in education—although there are parts of the overall education system that are in crisis, particularly the elementary and secondary institutions in certain urban school districts. Overall, however, there is still potential for educators, policymakers, and legislators to create change through consensus building.

The Health Care Crisis as Warning

We can, moreover, learn much about the nature of the change we must fashion by studying the factors that led to the imposition of managed health care and tracking its development and results.

In the *Wall Street Journal*, Richard Vedder posed this question, "What sector of the American economy has faced rapidly rising costs for several decades, with third parties, including government, paying most of the bills?" He responds, "Health care? Sure, but also higher education. And the economics of rising costs are likely to force radical changes at many of our colleges and universities."[28]

The relentless increase in the cost of higher education, which has consistently outpaced the Consumer Price Index year after year, is certainly the most obvious parallel to the agent of health care reform. But there are issues underlying the cost increases, which we must also understand.

One issue that Vedder addresses is productivity. He has hard words for us on this topic. "Most of us today teach the same way Socrates did more than 2,300 years ago, albeit not as well. What other profession has had absolutely no productivity advance in 2,300 years?"[29] Now, we happen to believe that the dialectic approach to teaching advanced by Socrates remains the most effective teaching approach ever devised. It is hard to envision a more fruitful approach if we measure productivity in terms of student enlightenment. A professor himself, Vedder may be engaging in the hyperbole that President Tim Sullivan, of the College of William and Mary, once called "an honest and noble tradition" in academia. He knows, surely, that the goal of teaching is to elicit independent production from students and not to produce standardized widgets.

Still, Vedder has accurately pinpointed one of the key issues that we in the academy must address—faculty productivity.[30] We need to address productivity at two levels. At one level, we have a public relations problem. Despite the efforts of the faculty over the past several years to dispel a negative public image, many outside the academy still view teaching as a relaxed profession—to put it mildly. Is not this a perfectly understandable confusion? After all, the Latin term, *schola*, yields our name, "scholars," but originally means, "leisure." The fact is, useful learning is the highest and best use of leisure. We should rather exert ourselves to inculcate appreciation of leisure well used in high callings than defer to the colloquial impression of leisure as a surcease of labor. But we cannot afford to consider faculty productivity exclusively a PR issue. We must also find ways to increase faculty productivity. At Michigan State University, President Peter McPherson led a productivity revolution that emphasized increasing faculty contact with students. Faculty workload reviews are a legitimate response to the concerns that have been expressed.

A second, critical issue hidden within the cost increases in health care and higher education is a mindset of growth. A 1995 article on "The Health Care Mess: A Bit of History" (from *JAMA: The Journal of the American Medical Association*) makes this important point. Much of the mess that the health care industry experienced in the 1980s and 1990s can be attributed directly to earlier successes of the industry. Following World War II, the United States faced major deficits in health care personnel and acute care hospital beds. The authors of this article, Julius Richmond and Rashi Fein, observe that the problems they cite "...were corrected, indeed overcorrected. Furthermore, our various health care efforts worked not only to increase resource inputs, availability of care, and access, but to improve health outcomes." The difficulty that Richmond and Fein astutely critique is that

> Policymakers, health care professionals, hospital administrators, and the public had no experience with adequacy of resources. We behaved as though we still had deficits. The United States was growing; incomes were expanding. It was easy and natural to assume further growth and to plan within an ethos of expansion that had come to be considered synonymous with progress.[31]

Most will readily agree that by substituting a word here or a phrase there, these quotations could refer directly to higher education. No one has missed the relentless prophecies of cohort growth over the next decade and the increasing likelihood of over-building on campuses. The successes of our colleges and universities in responding to the demand for higher education, which was fostered by the GI

Bill and which led to our own post-World War II expansion, have left us equally shackled with a mindset of growth. Open-ended, infinitely expanding enrollment is the very soul of the large, research university, and particularly the public university. There, productivity is far more routinely measured by growth in numbers—matriculants and dollars—than by any other factor. The broad administrative challenge that we in higher education must ponder is how to privilege dynamic approaches to learning over inertial growth.

A closely related problem to the mindset of growth—for both health care and education—is that most of the growth has been evolutionary rather than revolutionary. Both professions have lacked a unifying vision that might shape growth and policies. While the pluralism of higher education as a system is one of its strengths, disjointed incrementalism is not the healthiest method for growing an individual institution.

Given these and other similarities in the problems faced by the health care industry and the academy, must our fates also be the same? The physicians tried to ignore the fact that economic realities no longer could leave their god-like status unchallenged. Managed care filled the vacuum and imposed reform on them.[32]

Richmond and Fein conclude that the health care providers did not move quickly enough, saying, "It has been surprising that the control of medical care moved out of the hands of health care professionals so rapidly and with so little resistance."[33]

It is up to those within the academy—particularly the faculty—to demonstrate to a concerned public that we can effectively control our own fate. But we cannot control our fate from within the Ivory Tower.[34] An active, sustained conversation with the public that we serve must be at the heart of our restructuring efforts. There is good news and bad news in this. The good news is that the public still waits for us to do something on our own, and the bad news is that they are *still* waiting.

America's colleges and universities have the tools and the resources they need to restore the quality of higher education and public trust in it. What is questionable is whether they have the will to do so.

Notes

1.   See, for example, "Controversy over Charges by Stanford Prompts Critical Review of Entire Indirect-Cost System," *Chronicle of Higher Education* 37 (April 3, 1991): A22.
2.   Described in Thao P. Matlock, "The Overlap Group: A Study of Nonprofit Competition," *Journal of Law and Education* 23 (Fall 1994): 523-47.

3.   But compare this list with the similar list produced by Clark Kerr a generation earlier (1963): "What are the current concerns? There are: problems related to costs. . .problems related to accommodating the vast numbers. . .problems related to public service. . .problems related to the supply of trained personnel for industry and the public. . .questions about the quality and availability of research. . .problems related to the exploitation of new discoveries. . . . Additionally there is a general public concern with 'morality' on the campus" (Kerr, 1982: 106).

4.   We cite, as representative, the following:
    • Stephen Trachtenberg, president of George Washington University, writes that executives of major corporations who not long ago eagerly sought out college graduates, now lament "the extent to which they've been let down by American educators at every level from kindergarten to graduate school, the extent to which they can no longer take for granted that possession of an undergraduate degree or graduate degree means *anything at all* in terms of actual knowledge and usable skills acquired" (original emphasis). Stephen Joel Trachtenberg, *Speaking His Mind* (Phoenix, AZ: American Council on Education and The Oryx Press, 1994), 46.
    • Christopher Lucas tells us that ". . .employers are reportedly being forced to do what they once relied on colleges for, namely, to sort out large numbers of college graduates whose verbal and quantitative skills are unequal to the challenges of the workplace. Estimates vary, though it has been alleged that upward of sixteen out of every hundred graduates may be considered academically deficient" (Lucas, 111).
    • The Rand Corporation found in a 1993 survey that, "Over one-half of a national sample of college upper class students were unable to perform cognitive tasks at a high-school level; three-quarters of the faculty surveyed in a recent poll felt that their students did not meet minimum preparation standards." Roger Benjamin et al., "The Redesign of Governance in Higher Education" (N.p.: Rand Corporation, February 1993), 9.
    • Chester Finn and Bruno Manno cite similar results in their critique of the American university: "A 1993 federal survey found that few graduates of four-year campuses reached the highest level of literacy—which involved such things as interpreting a substantial news article. Only about half were capable of writing a brief letter explaining an error made on a credit card bill." Chester E. Finn and Bruno V. Manno, "What's Wrong with the American University?" *Wilson Quarterly* 20 (Winter 1996): 47.

5.   There is in Virginia and other public systems a frenzied fear of intra-system comparisons, tending to foster the use of inconsequential performance indicators.

6.   Parker Palmer, "The Heart of a Teacher," *Change* 29 (November/December 1997): 15.

7.   Maritain, 10.

8.   "Actual Versus Predicted Institutional Graduation Rates for 1100 Colleges and Universities," *Postsecondary Education Opportunity* no. 58 (April 1997): 1.

9.   Ibid., 2.

10.   Laura J. Horn and Xianglei Chen, *Toward Resiliency: At-Risk Students Who Make It to College* (Washington, D.C.: U.S. Department of Education, 1998), 5.

11.   Adelman, "To Help Minority Students, Raise Their Graduation Rates," B8.

12.   Clifford Adelman, "Diversity: Walk the Walk, and Drop the Talk." *Change* 29 (July/August 1997): 34-46. Interestingly, the *New York Times* reports in 2001 that the NAACP and People for the American Way Foundation have jointly launched a three-year campaign focused on the academic backgrounds of black and Latino students as a means to address the "achievement gap." This is a very important and welcome—if none too soon—change of focus. *New York Times* (22 August 2001): A19.

13.   State Higher Education Executive Officers, "State Strategies that Support Successful Student Transition from Secondary to Postsecondary Education: Symposium and Briefing," February 17-19, 1998.

14.   *Characteristics of Excellence in Higher Education*, 16.

15.   Ernest T. Pascarella and Patrick T. Terenzini, *How College Affects Students: Findings and Insights from Twenty Years of Research* (San Francisco: Jossey-Bass Publishers, 1991).

16.   Ibid.

17.   SHEEO, "State Strategies that Support Successful Student Transition from Secondary to Postsecondary Education."

18.   Colleen Sheehan, *The Core Curriculum of Pennsylvania's State System and State-Related Universities: Are Pennsylvania's Students Receiving the Fundamentals of a College Education?* (Harrisburg, PA: The Commonwealth Foundation for Public Policy Alternatives, September 1998), 47.

19.   Many of the ideas in this section were developed jointly with Dr. Karl L. Schilling, then Associate Director for Academic Programs at SCHEV.

20.   Additional information about the SCHEV Program Approval policy is available at http://www.msu.edu/~allenwi.

21.   Ted Marchese, "Assessment and Standards," *Change* 30 (September/October 1998): 4.

22.   Peter Drucker, "The Information Executives Truly Need," *Harvard Business Review on Measuring Corporate Performance* (Cambridge: Harvard Business School Press, 1991 [1998]), 14.

23.   "Strategies to reduce the need for remediation include: (1) aligning high school requirements with college content and competency expectations; (2) early intervention and financial aid programs targeted at students at the K-12 level that link mentoring, tutoring, and academic guidance with a guarantee of college financial aid; (3) student follow-up and high school feedback systems; (4) improved teacher preparation; and (5) K-12 school reform." Ronald Phipps, *College Remediation: What It Is; What It Costs; What's at Stake?* (Washington, D. C.: Institute for Higher Education Policy, 1998), ix.

24.   However, it may fairly be said that what actually happens to students after they leave a professor would be even more probative of teaching ability than student evaluations. This form of assessment is peculiarly difficult to establish, however, and perhaps also even more subject to the interplay of chance than any of the other evaluative techniques. Who, after all, gets the credit for the Rhodes Scholar, or the Nobel Prize winner?

25.   Lederman argues that it makes sense to think of students as consumers in order to benefit from a robust diagnostic model. Marie Jean Lederman, "Consumer Evaluation of Teaching," *Liberal Education* 60 (May 1974): 242-48.

26.   Boyer Commission on Undergraduate Education, *Reinventing Undergraduate Education: A Blueprint for America's Research Universities* (Stony Brook: State University of New York, Stony Brook, 1996), 5.

27.   A downturn that was plainly visible to trained eyes if not yet publicly acknowledged in the summer of 1998.

28.   Richard Vedder, "Higher Education at Lower Cost," *Wall Street Journal* (31 August 1998): A17.

29.   Ibid., A17.

30.   "At least four conditions require colleges and universities to increase productivity:

   1.   Demands are increasing virtually all aspects of the higher education enterprise. . .

   2.   . . .the strength [or weakness] of the economy. . .

3.   . . .dramatic advances in technology. . .

4.   The public is increasingly frustrated. . .by a sense that colleges and universities are responding to internal priorities with inadequate attention to public
concerns. . ." Aims C. McGuinness and Peter T. Ewell, "Improving Productivity and Quality in Higher Education," *AGB Priorities* No. 2 (Fall 1994): 3-
4.

31.   Julius B. Richmond and Rushi Fein, "The Health Care Mess: A Bit of History,"
JAMA: Journal of the American Medical Association 273 (January 4, 1995): 69.

32.   Ten years later, the federal government feels the need to step in and to manage
managed health care.

33.   Richmond and Fein, 70. Cf., Peter A. Buxbaum, "Lower Costs, Fewer Choices,"
Transportation & Distribution 36 (December 1995): 48.

34.   "In American higher education, changes influenced by the market are accepted in a
way that reforms originating in concerns for educational policy are not" (Kerr, 169).

5

Managing Higher Education: Lessons from Virginia

> In a country like this. . .if there cannot be money found to answer the common purposes of education. . .it is evident that there is something amiss in the ruling political power.
> —George Washington to John Armstrong
> Mt. Vernon, April 25, 1788

The operational aspects of the university must perform consistently with the purpose in view. This observation derives from the first chapter in this book, but it constitutes also the guiding principle of this fifth chapter. One plans for the modern university, and for every system of higher education, far more effectively where one remains well informed of the purpose of higher education. Precisely because we never can know, whether as individuals or as institutions, what the future holds for us, we live with an uncertainty that can be relieved only by clarity regarding our mission, the future we aim to realize in place of the one we do not know.

The vision of a university is like that of Janus—looking back while contemplating, preserving, and transmitting a cultural, historical and scientific heritage and looking ahead to create new knowledge and prepare our students for their own work of shaping the future. Likewise, the vision of the university must encompass the broad view (the society, the nation, the state) and the narrow (the university, the school, the department). Useful metaphorical guidance for such range of vision was conveyed by George Washington when he wrote to his friend and fellow revolutionary, George Mason, from his camp at Middlebrook on March 27, 1779. In this correspondence, Washington emphasized the need for the states, as parts of a whole, to tend to the affairs of the nation, as well as to the affairs of each individual state. He wrote:

149

> To me it appears no unjust Simile to compare the affairs of this great continent to the Mechanism of a Clock, each State representing some one or other of the smaller parts of it, which they are endeavoring to put in fine order without considering how useless and unavailing their labour, unless the great wheel, or spring which is to set the whole in motion, is also well attended to and kept in good order.[1]

Washington's just simile suggests that the quality of planning for individual institutions must depend, in part, on effective planning for whole systems. In turn, the quality of planning for systems rests, in very great measure, upon the effective participation of individual institutions and their counterparts in the process. In the case of Virginia, one speaks of the system of higher education in the most inclusive terms, encompassing not only the thirty-nine public institutions but also the thirty-nine or so, nonprofit, private colleges and universities, as well as the thirteen or more for-profit, private, postsecondary institutions. Moreover, that particular "system" of higher education is part of a larger continuum of education in that Commonwealth—a continuum that stretches from kindergarten through secondary schools to colleges and universities and beyond.[2]

Today the public planning imperative for higher education entails conscious midwifery of higher education systems without diluting the independence of the colleges and universities within those systems. As a guide to public decision-making, it is absolutely essential to place the unique and valuable contributions of each college and university within the context of a whole. No single college or university—no matter how large, how effective, or how entrepreneurial—can be expected on its own to meet all of the higher education needs of any state or comprehensive jurisdiction. But we can expect, and ought to ensure, that each system as a whole will meet those needs and meet them well.

This chapter narrates our experience in Virginia as a model of meeting those needs in an environment of emphatic decentralization, in which great flexibility is afforded to each institution to determine how it will achieve its mission. Three major undertakings in Virginia are related here: (1) the long-term, statewide strategic plan presented in the *1999 Virginia Plan for Higher Education*, (2) a revised process for program approval, and (3) a new, performance-based model for allocating state funds to the colleges and universities. These policy changes, operating in tandem, would not only permit greater decentralization and institutional flexibility, but would do so while simultaneously encouraging continuous quality improvement and solid accountability to the state. For example, the *1999 Virginia Plan* includes a strategy to revitalize restructuring processes in a way that married state goals for planning with meaningful strategic planning processes in the institutions. The new program approval policy (which ultimately required amending the *Code of Virginia*) delegated the approval of academic programs to the institutions, where it rightfully belongs. The performance-funding model aimed to provide long-term, consistent funding in an atmosphere of heightened responsibility.

Necessarily, this blueprint for change was driven foremost by the Council's own strategic plan, which aimed to locate decision-making as close as possible to those working directly in the delivery of educational programs. The new era of decentralization was meant to couple institutional flexibility with accountability (thus avoiding the British nightmare of minutely elaborated point scales for institutional performance). The goal: replace a make-work bureaucracy of pre-approval paperwork with meaningful procedures that rely first and foremost on each institution's own assessment of its outcomes and make use of that assessment in system-wide and institutional planning for continuous assessment.

University administrators are apt frequently to repeat William Edward Deming's apothegm, "what gets measured gets better." It is important no less frequently to remind them of the correlate, that what fails to get measured gets neglected.[3] This makes it imperative that assessment focus on intrinsic and systematic performance and not merely momentary issues of heightened concern. It requires the best efforts of many persons to identify measures that can adequately convey the value that higher education adds to the lives of individuals and communities, measures that look at a wider range of benefits than simply the boost that a college degree gives to one's lifetime earnings. The greatest challenge may well be to cultivate the sensibility, the language, and the benchmarks that convey the far-reaching value of that "public good" that we call a college education—a task of educational leadership more than anything else. Here, too, we may rely upon George Washington, who counseled the young drafters of the Constitution to pursue "a conduct [that] will stamp wisdom and dignity on the proceedings, and be looked to as a luminary, which sooner or later will shed its influence."[4] Any educational policy that would do as well should no less certainly enjoy an influence like to that of the Constitution itself.

Strategic Planning: Virginia

Each generation takes on the responsibility for conveying its accumulated store of knowledge and wisdom to the rising generation,
while also keeping in mind the opportunity to progress on its own
beyond the pathways of knowledge that its forebears have traveled.
Traditionally, we summon "vision" to guide the planning of such
progress, but "habits of mind" might be a more apt expression—the
kind of habits of mind conveyed by an expectation of excellence
and an assumption of dutifulness. Such was the attitude that Rosa
Lee Allen often exhorted women to embrace in words such as these:

> In order that a man may reach the truth, two qualities are necessary. One is moral sense,
> earnestness of purpose, desire to do that which is true. The other is intellectual clear-
> ness, the ability to think straight. Man's efficiency in respect to truth is his moral
> purpose (or desire) plus his ability to think straight. Many men have the moral courage
> and desire to be true but lack the ability to understand what is the truth. Conversely,
> many know the truth but lack the moral courage to enact the same.

We approached strategic planning in Virginia with the goals of
moral sense and intellectual clarity. The Code of Virginia charges
SCHEV with the responsibility to update its strategic plan bienni-
ally. Previously SCHEV's "Indicators" series served to fulfill this
mandate in a merely token manner.[5] For the 1999 plan, we took a
different tack. The broad goals of this document included some ideas
about a new, more flexible approach to planning.

Those of us who toil in the academy surely recognize that a certain degree of "fluidity and discontinuity" has been "central to the
reality" of our institutional lives during the past decade.[6] We also
know that nothing suggests a slowing down of the pace and scope
of change in this new millennium. How then, in such an environment, might we go about constructing meaningful habits of mind to
guide higher education during the first years of that millennium? Is
not planning fundamentally incompatible with flexibility?

The planning task is further complicated by the fact that, in every
jurisdiction, there are always many separate agents who will not only
shape the plans, but even more tellingly, will have a hand in constructing the reality of higher education as it unfolds in the years
ahead. These agents are situated outside as well as within the campus, and achieve variable results through their efforts, as Clara Lovett
points out: "We [faculty] know how to hold one another accountable through processes of regional or disciplinary accreditation.
Accreditation reports, however, do not come close to providing the

data and insights that elected officials need about our institutions."[7] In Virginia the players are the governor; the General Assembly; the boards of visitors, administrations, faculties, staffs, and students of institutions; the ad hoc commissions that are appointed from time to time (most recently, the Governor's Blue Ribbon Commission and the General Assembly's Joint Legislative Committee on Higher Education Funding Policies); and the state policy organ, the Council itself. A similar array would characterize most North American jurisdictions.

The planning task is to orchestrate the efforts of such multitudes with a plan that promises harmony and balance, a plan that inspires action—not long on fulsome rhetoric while short on substance. Mary Catherine Bateson offers some guidance on this task. We might start by conceiving of a plan that more resembles a jazz improvisation than a symphony. As Bateson writes, "Jazz exemplifies artistic ability that is at once individual and communal, performance that is both repetitive and innovative, each participant sometimes providing background support and sometimes flying free."[8]

In developing the *1999 Virginia Plan for Higher Education*, we imagined something like a galvanizing jazz composition. To be more precise, we attempted an innovative rendition of an old standard, something like Marcus Roberts' recent interpretation of Duke Ellington's "How Long Has This Been Going On?" The underlying melody of the 1999 plan echoed the strains of "quality, access, and affordability," which had long been the overarching themes of earlier biennial Virginia plans. When the Council approved its own agency strategic plan in 1998, it once again ratified quality, access, and affordability as guiding principles.

Part of the excitement of jazz comes from a discordant fusion that gives it an edge. There is often an unseen tension among the broad and familiar aims of quality, access, and affordability. The goal, however, is to find a workable balance among these aims. Providing a top-quality education, even without regard for the cost, would be a challenge, but it is a far greater challenge to deliver a top-quality education at an affordable cost. Likewise, one must not permit serious efforts to keep college affordable to degrade the quality of the education. While aiming for harmony and balance in an overall system, we strive to make the inherent tension a source of creative energy in a fusionist approach.

We like the jazz metaphor for the *Virginia Plan*, in part, because one of its chief goals was to free the institutions to play their singular notes in accord with their own inspiration and in tune with the aspirations set forth in their individual missions. A hallmark strength of higher education in Virginia—as many of our state systems—is its effective combination of mission distinction and institutional autonomy within a framework of supportive coordination. Who would not soon tire of a jazz performance that offered only Artie Shaw on the clarinet, no matter the inventiveness of his lyricism? Oscar Peterson's magnificently constructed solos are made still more pleasing when the rest of the trio joins back in.

Virginia's *system* of higher education, in short, is a system of intended results attained through the orchestrated and coordinated efforts of the diverse public and private institutions that provide for identified needs. Collaboration plays a critical role in shaping comprehensiveness of coverage. No single institution's mission answers to every goal identified by the Commonwealth as the object of the system of higher education. Accordingly, the Council of Higher Education, as the system's coordinating agency, ascertains the adequacy of provisions to attain those goals across all of the institutions existing or that may be brought into being. The responsibility for making those decisions is most appropriately placed on the shoulders of the Boards, administration, and faculty who have been entrusted with the shared governance of colleges and universities.[9]

Truth in Advertising: An Open Process Toward Public Ends

Because this approach offers renewed confidence in higher education leadership as counter to the tide of distrustful accountability, academic leaders must undertake this responsibility soulfully, in an environment that mandates explicit and articulate performance before a broader public. Nothing so surely damns higher education than the familiar tendency to withdraw into baronial chambers of privilege and to address all others as so many unwashed herds. To win needed trust from the public, each college and university must shape its decisions and its contributions to the system from a planning perspective that is "at once individual and communal." The aim ought to be to achieve system-wide goals through a protean synergy. It is entirely possible to shape institutional plans, as well as statewide plans, with an understanding "that there is a large whole to which all belong."[10]

Planners must also engender the degree of support for the plan that will be needed to put it into motion. One way to engender that support is by inviting full participation throughout the process. The process we used in Virginia started by culling common themes, issues, and goals from the public institutions' own strategic plans.

The Council approached its task guided by the words of the virtuoso bassist and composer, Charlie Mingus: "Making the simple complicated is commonplace; making the complicated simple, awesomely simple, that's creativity."[11] We worked in concert with numerous advisory groups; we bent our creativity to quilting from the rich, complex patchwork of the colleges' and universities' own strategic plans a simple, yet compelling design for the system as a whole. Nor is it irrelevant that the quilting art composes out of the commonest elements, even rejects. We sought to articulate what Bateson calls "a vision worth fulfilling, not a demand for retrenchment and austerity."[12] Early in the process, the most vital component was the generation of concerns and input from interested and knowledgeable persons around the Commonwealth. We involved SCHEV's regular advisory groups[13] in the initial development of the plan and continued thereafter to seek their input and counsel. We invited a group of thirty individuals from a wide range of institutions to serve as a Strategic Planning Advisory Committee. Further, since the plan embraced the entire system of higher education in Virginia, not just the public institutions, we also invited the presidents of the private institutions to participate. Opening the web of communication still wider, we sponsored a series of regional forums to discuss a draft of the plan. This move engaged individuals from local communities, businesses, and school districts, as well as from the academy, offering their thoughts on goals and issues to include in the Plan.

Process isn't everything when it comes to strategic planning, but it is the start of everything. We hoped to challenge all participants to aim as high as Ella's pure notes, to be as boldly inventive as Miles, and to pour hearts, minds, and souls into the effort as fully and intentionally as Satchmo played his horn. We acted on a vision of continuous improvement (one we shared with principal campus administrators) by systematically setting goals and benchmarks, measuring progress, reflecting on what we learn through the assessment of progress and results, and feeding that learning into a relentless drive for improving processes and outcomes. We also shared another conviction—namely, that the policies that a state uses to appropriate general funds to the public colleges and universities should provide incentives for continuous improvement.

The 1999 Virginia Plan: Advancing the System of Higher Education in Virginia

The *1999 Virginia Plan for Higher Education: Advancing the System of Higher Education in Virginia* recommends five broad goals for reforming the higher education system in ways that build on past success, reaffirming the Commonwealth's commitment to make higher learning available to all, and offering a new approach to achieve the aims of access, quality, affordability, and accountability for the century ahead.

The following five interlocking goals reshaped the public policy framework that constitutes the public commitment to higher education and defines much of the Commonwealth's relationship to its colleges and universities—both public and private. The driving force behind these goals is the expectation that these public policy changes, if realized fully, will substantially enhance the abilities of the individual campuses to achieve system-wide results through their advancement of each institution's distinctive mission. What the system—the public commitment—accomplishes in relation to these goals shapes how the diverse institutions will act concretely to realize educational excellence.

The five goals are:

1. To improve the opportunities for strategic decision-making at all public colleges and universities by promoting decentralization within a context of continuous quality assessment.

2. To strengthen the ongoing assessment of Virginia's colleges and universities by focusing on outcomes and value-added analysis.

3. To anticipate the future needs of students, faculties, and communities through improved system-wide planning.

4. To encourage collaborative programming across institutions.

5. To evaluate capital infrastructures at public and private campuses for the purpose of assessing system capacities and options for delivering academic programs.[14]

Rather than discuss in detail here the goals themselves or the thirty-three specific recommendations for achieving these goals, it will be more useful to present the overarching themes of access, quality, affordability, and accountability, which shaped the entire strategic plan.[15]

The Vision: The Public Good of Higher Education

A shared vision of postsecondary education that offers to every citizen in the Commonwealth full opportunity to attain a baccalaureate credential is at the center of the system of higher education in Virginia. It is the fulcrum on which Virginia constructed the entire edifice of higher education. The baccalaureate is the premise of an argument that envisions a full range of educational opportunity: from the role of the two-year associate degree in support of transfer options and vocational and technical training, to the role of graduate education in support of undergraduate education at the frontiers of knowledge, through the growing role of formal education to support life-long learning. We recognized also that the vision is subject to the measure of each person's ability. We singled out the baccalaureate as the explicit goal of higher education in order to target undergraduate learning as the priority concern at this moment and to acknowledge, with former Virginia Governor Jim Gilmore, the growing necessity of education through the baccalaureate for life in the twenty-first century.

This vision supports a diverse set of institutions self-tailored to the needs and choices of specific students and communities. It also embraces the full range of educational offerings required to support effectively a comprehensive scope of programs. Those offerings include world-class research and graduate programs at appropriate institutions, bridging programs to provide for transfer into baccalaureate programs, land and sea grant extensions that penetrate the entire state, extensive opportunities to support research that sustains growth in knowledge and service to communities, and a broad array of public service engagements that expand the bases of student learning at the same time as extending to communities the fruits of scholarship in service of social and economic needs.

But the breadth and complexity of the envisioned outcomes of the system are also grounded in the complex nature of the very act of education. Education—the best education—offers far more than the simple transmission from teacher to student of knowledge and skill development. The best education fundamentally transforms the learner. Moreover, it is an act that involves as much the active participation of the learner as of the teacher. This transformational ability of education is the primary reason for our public commitment to it. For the process of educating individuals transforms not the individual alone but our entire society.

Public policy does not invent higher education. To that extent, public policy seeks to profit from an enterprise that has its own logic and purpose:

> Yet extraneous burdens superadded to the normal task of education must be accepted for the sake of the general welfare. . . . The duty of educators is obviously twofold: they have both to maintain the essentials of humanistic education and to adapt them to the present requirements of the common good. Education has its own essence and its own aims. This essence and these essential aims, which deal with the formation of man and the inner liberation of the human person, must be preserved, whatever the superimposed burdens may be.[16]

The vision of the *system* of higher education in Virginia, therefore, originates in the public commitment to profit from higher education by extending public support to higher education and creating nearly universal access to it. That commitment grows out of the broader commitment to support public education in general, reflecting especially the need for a higher education to sustain a continuing source of instruction for a pre-collegiate education. From this commitment we highlighted the "education contract" between the Commonwealth and its citizens.

Education supported by publicly appropriated funds aims to advance the common good by means of the good that education offers to individuals. The ultimate limit on the funds to be appropriated, therefore, must be the sum required to reach the goal, and in every era the public must advance as far in that direction as its means allow. This moral commitment imposes the need for a continuous balancing of multiple missions and goals. This moral commitment should be the fire in which are forged interlocking strategies to ensure access, quality, affordability, and accountability in a system of higher education. In a democratic regime, this moral commitment leads ineluctably to the promise and the realization of universal access to higher education.

The Imperative of Universal Access

Since Thomas Jefferson first articulated his dream of an aristocracy of achievement arising out of a democracy of opportunity, there has been a strong, implicit contract between the Commonwealth and its citizens. Through a combination of hard work and education, every individual aspires to achieve the American dream of prosperity, well-being, and a life of dignity. Through milestone legislation such as the Morrill Acts of 1862 and 1890, the G.I. Bill, the National Defense Student Loans, and that program's many successors, the nation, in concert with the states, has sought to guarantee that a modest income need not be a barrier to higher education. Virginia at times led and at times followed in pursuit of this dream, but it has articulated the dream in a full-throated manner for the past three decades.

What fuels the ambition for nearly universal access to higher education? Virginia citizens fundamentally believe and expect that investing in the education of individual citizens promotes the overall well-being of society. They look to education not only as the chief vehicle to promote the well being of the current generation but also as a gift and legacy that each generation offers the next. Yet, today, some fear that that far-sighted education contract, long embraced by the nation and the Commonwealth may be broken in our time.

The *1999 Virginia Plan for Higher Education* recommended a series of actions that the Commonwealth should take to reaffirm this far-sighted education contract and to guarantee that future generations of Virginians could benefit from it. All the goals and recommendations articulated in this plan are based on the conviction that earlier generations of Virginia's leaders and citizens who signed on to this contract were right. Investing in the education of individual citizens does promote the overall well being of society.

Are we willing to make that investment? Some observers suggest that society today is less willing to invest public funds in higher education. These observers point to a tendency for leaders and taxpayers to view higher education mainly as a private good—something that delivers economic benefits only to the individuals who attend college—rather than as a fundamental public good—something that delivers important economic and social benefits to the community as a whole. An underlying purpose of the *Virginia Plan for Higher Education* is to engender discussion about and raise awareness of higher education as a public good—by looking at both the cost *and* the value of that good.

Managing Enrollment Growth

To keep the doors to higher education open, policy organs should work in concert with the colleges and universities to anticipate and manage enrollment growth. Enrollment growth has been subject to constraints of available resources including faculty, staff, facilities, and funds. States and the colleges and universities can choose to increase financial support to keep pace with enrollment, to constrain enrollment growth based on resources, or to find new ways to accommodate increases in enrollment without concomitant increases in funding.

But enrollment grows in a wave pattern, imposing the need for adjustments downwards as well as upwards. Based on projections of the size of Virginia high school graduating classes through 2012, first year classes will grow from 2003 through 2007 and decline afterwards. Virginia must, therefore, accommodate the growth without building excess capacity.

As a first step, funding for enrollment growth should be targeted to identified deficiencies—matching student populations and institutional potential to accommodate growth. It is possible to accept growth without problem, if we resolve to manage growth. As a second step, the state should insist that enrollment growth be justified by new demand. Several recommendations for managing enrollment growth are offered under Goal Three of *The Virginia Plan* ("to anticipate future needs of all constituents of higher education through improved system-wide planning").

Quality: A Focus on Outcomes

How do we define quality? How do we know whether Virginia's public and private colleges are providing the high-quality teaching and the overall academic and student life environment that will help students attain their educational goals?

Determinations of quality in higher education have traditionally been based primarily on the work of the admissions office rather than the graduation office. That is to say that general perceptions of institutional quality are more often influenced by the readily available academic qualifications of admittees rather than by the accomplishments of graduates. Other traditional indicators of quality are the academic qualifications of the faculty, the amount of money spent by the institution on instruction, and the beauty of campus facilities—all commonly referred to as "input" measures.

The *1999 Virginia Plan for Higher Education* pursued a new conception of quality. This plan suggests that excellence in higher education is best evaluated not by who comes in, but rather by who leaves—as indicated by a variety of "output" measures.

This new way of defining and assessing quality in higher education shows up strongly in the strategic plans of many of Virginia's colleges and universities. Further, at every one of the meetings held to discuss the *1999 Plan*, participants spoke frequently and compellingly about why this change is necessary and appropriate. It is clear that a new attitude toward excellence in higher education is already emerging at public and private campuses throughout Virginia and that faculty and administrators have begun adapting institutional practices based on this new attitude. All the goals and recommendations in the *1999 Plan* are designed to work in an interconnected way to promote an outcome-based vision of quality and to enhance the capability of Virginia's colleges and universities to deliver excellent programs.

Affordability: Controlling Costs and a New Approach to Funding

During the latter part of the 1990s, the Council, General Assembly, and governor took a series of important short-term steps to address the issue of affordability. Since 1994, Virginia's public colleges and universities have undertaken and reported on efforts to contain costs through restructuring. The *1999 Virginia Plan* assumed the continuing need for colleges and universities to restructure, to reallocate resources internally, and to review and focus on priorities. Restructuring (the equivalent of "right-sizing" in industry) remains a permanent feature of the landscape of higher education—within Virginia and throughout the nation. Collaboration among institutions is one means that is used by Virginia's colleges and universities (both public and private) to minimize costs, while also enhancing quality and expanding access.

The old, formula-based, input-focused approach to appropriating funds proved unworkable—and largely unused—for the crisis decade just passed. The studies and debates conducted by the Blue Ribbon Commission on Higher Education (1999), the Joint Legislative Subcommittee on Higher Education Funding (1999), and SCHEV produced new models, using new approaches. Recommendations 1.1 through 1.5 of the *Virginia Plan* outline the development of a performance-funding model.

Accountability: Self-Control, Not Regulation

Virginia's statewide system of institutions of higher education is responsible to the Commonwealth in general and, as a consequence, accountable to a number of different constituencies: to the governor and the General Assembly, who appropriate taxpayers' dollars to assist public and private institutions in carrying out their missions; to students and their families, who are both consumers and the immediate beneficiaries of higher education; to businesses and other employers, who benefit from the presence of a well-educated workforce; and to private donors, both individual and corporate, who provide funds that enable the institutions to maintain a margin of excellence that would not be possible through public support and tuition revenues alone. During the discussions that led to the development of the *Virginia Plan*, presidents, provosts, chief financial officers, and faculty at Virginia's public and private colleges and universities insisted upon their strong sense of accountability to all of these constituencies.

While accountability has long been embraced as a top priority for Virginia's system of higher education, during the past decade voices from a number of quarters have called for an increased emphasis on this broad aim. Nor is Virginia alone in this experience; state governments, coordinating and governing boards, and concerned citizens throughout the country have urged colleges and universities to take steps to become more accountable to the constituents they serve. Why is this so? Highly publicized cases of mismanagement within higher education reinforced the sense that a tougher system of accountability was needed. What most observers seem to mean by accountability is that institutions, private and public, must manage their resources as a public trust within an atmosphere of distrust, restraining costs and enhancing output.

Beyond increased cost-consciousness, many observers now recognize that a *new approach* to accountability is needed.[17] All the *Virginia Plan* goals were designed to work together to make use of a new approach to strengthen accountability while simultaneously increasing access, enhancing quality, and controlling cost.

Do not confuse accountability with regulation. These two concepts are diametrically opposed. While regulation means control from an external source, accountability necessitates self-control: being answerable for results or outcomes, while maintaining autonomy and a degree of flexibility. Virginia's system of higher education has traditionally drawn strength from the autonomy of its institutions, but in a *de facto* environment of velvet-gloved regulation. We sought to reduce the burden of bureaucratic regulations and to enhance the institutions' flexibility in responding to changing circumstances. One of the messages expressed most strongly in meetings with faculty and administrators at the public colleges was the need for a paradigm shift in our thinking about how best to achieve accountability. Now is the time to switch from a system of pre-approval regulations that drain administrative time and constrain strategic planning to a system of post-audit accounting of results.

If we want our institutions to act *like* businesses then we must empower them to act *as* businesses. Allowing institutions the ability to manage their resources is paramount to their success. Further decentralization and greater flexibility is required—with this will come greater accountability and greater productivity.

Strong Institutional Governance

Institutions of higher education have traditionally maintained a system of shared governance, in which the faculty, the administration, and the governing board, respectively, have defined roles in institutional decision-making. The faculty collectively organizes—and to that extent owns—the curriculum, but this does not mean a system of exclusive or private ownership. The faculty is rather responsible to students, administrators, and board members; it must generate, sustain, *and publicly defend* its decisions concerning what is taught. The faculty carries out these responsibilities subject to review by the institution's governing board, which has final authority over all aspects of the institution's operations, subject to continuing oversight by the legislature. The faculty must be responsive to the legitimate expectations of these various bodies for educational outcomes, and assessment of student learning has long been a state-mandated means of holding the faculty and their institutions accountable in Virginia.

Because of its system of autonomous institutions of higher education, Virginia has relied substantially on the boards of visitors in its system of university governance. Higher education serves multiple societal purposes, of which the advancement of knowledge is only the most important. Governing boards are typically composed of persons from a variety of occupations and professions, and they often provide a perspective on academic matters that is more pragmatic and less academic than that of academics. It is therefore important that members of these boards have an appropriate understanding of the system of governance at the institutions on whose boards they serve and their fiduciary responsibility in relation thereto.

Accountable to Students and Families

Finally, accountability to students and their families, the consumers of higher education, is of paramount importance. In this regard, it is essential to note the distinction between academic and nonacademic aspects of students' interaction with the institution. For example, a student stands in the role of consumer when complaining about the long lines at registration or the short hours during which a computer lab is open. However, that same student does not stand in the role of a mere consumer when complaining about the difficulty of a calculus course or the tough grading practices of a history professor. This distinction points out another important difference between higher education and most business enterprises.

The system of higher education should seek to be responsive to the consumer-oriented needs and interests of students, while at the same time insisting upon challenging each individual to attain the highest degree of academic excellence of which he or she is capable. In this way, the institution and the student are accountable to each other, as well as to the society that supports both. The institution is empowered to achieve its stated mission—to provide a quality education for the student—while raising the threshold for graduates.

In summary, then, strategic planning in Virginia provided a comprehensive process and structure for strengthening both the performance and the reputation of higher education. Carrying out its state-mandated responsibility, the Council provided a plan to meet changing needs and expectations. Using transparent deliberative procedures, the Council developed five goals and thirty-three recommendations that responded to the agenda of access, quality, affordability, and accountability. Focusing more upon changing *how* the business of higher education is carried on than upon any attempt to redefine the business itself, the *Plan* eventuated in a coordinated set of strategies, policies, and funding mechanisms—all targeted to produce a system of results, framed by a shared vision to offer every citizen in Virginia full opportunity to attain a baccalaureate degree.

Program Approval and Outcome Assessment

If then, the Council of Higher Education for Virginia were serious about utilizing a new approach to accountability, what specific measures would be needed to realize this goal? Two broad policy changes were endorsed, which augured sweeping change in the methods through which institutions would be held accountable and offered new incentives for institutions to commit to a process of continuous improvement. Goal One of the *1999 Virginia Plan* ("To develop long-term, stable funding provisions") produced the Virginia performance funding model, which is described below. Goal Two of the *Plan* ("To strengthen the ongoing assessment of Virginia's colleges and universities by focusing on outcomes and value-added analysis") was partially realized in the revision to the Council's program approval process.

A strategy to revamp assessment processes built upon Virginia's strength. In the mid-1980s, Virginia was a leader in the national movement to adopt assessment practices at colleges and universities. One reason, no doubt, for assessment becoming widespread at Virginia's public colleges and universities was the fact that the Code of Virginia mandates such practice. More importantly, however, the faculty and administrators at Virginia's colleges and universities learned through first-hand experience the value of assessment for improving quality.

If assessment was alive and well, why then did we recommend strengthening it? One reason, of course, is that in a system committed to continuous assessment, the goal is always to take the "strong" and make it even stronger. More to the point, Goal Two suggests a new area of focus for the assessment programs at Virginia's colleges and universities: encouraging the institutions to build on their success in using assessment as a tool for strengthening academic programs and to expand their use of assessment as a tool to improve student learning. Most importantly, however, Goal Two served as the spur, or the launching pad, to inspire confidence in Goal One, which involved a major transformation in funding provisions for higher education. We recognized that the context in which we labored was one that made the future of higher education largely if not wholly dependent on the progress of undergraduate education.

We remain at the threshold of a substantial transformation of undergraduate education. What would it take to infuse Virginia's or any state's entire system of higher education with deliberate attention to best practices in undergraduate education? A starting point is to articulate a coherent and compelling goal of study (reflected in our report on "General Education"), coupled with dedication to sustain quality through continuous assessment.

As a practical matter, in order to provide an incentive for Virginia's public colleges and universities to strengthen their assessment practices, the Council put in place a sort of quid pro quo. In return for a streamlined procedure for the review and approval of *new* academic programs (one in which some of the responsibility would be shifted away from the Council to an intra-institutional locus), the institutions committed to develop more concrete measures for assessing the *outcomes* of programs. Thus, we proposed substituting for a make-work, bureaucratic pre-approval process a much more meaningful evaluation of results through processes that would be primarily developed and carried out within the institutions.

While the set of modifications to the program approval process that the Council finally endorsed was less extensive than what was initially envisioned, the resulting policy does move assessment in Virginia in the right direction—a move away from "bean-counting" and regulation to real accountability for results.

Paying the Piper: Fiscal Reforms

The diversely structured but consistent architecture of the *1999 Virginia Plan* touches upon every essential concern of contemporary higher education. It is not an exaggeration to say, however, that it stands and falls almost entirely upon the realization of its funding provision: the Virginia performance-funding model.

In order to engage in the meaningful strategic decision-making urged throughout the *Plan*, Virginia's public colleges and universities needed added control of their human, fiscal, and capital resources. Further, to engage in long-term strategic planning, they needed an improved ability to anticipate future funding provisions and to understand the probable impact of their planning on funding provisions—while keeping in mind that economic conditions are invariably subject to some unpredictability. Planning and budgeting needed to be more closely coordinated. Also, the overall provisions for allocating taxpayer support to public and private institutions needed to be more securely connected to the public policy purposes that originated the support.

In developing the 2000-02 budget recommendations to the governor and General Assembly, the Council intended to make such recommendations using a new approach to determine institutional appropriations. The new approach maximized autonomy for decision making at the institutional level while holding the institution accountable for the use of such funds. A fundamental aspect of this model was to recognize mission differentiation and differing staffing patterns and to account for them accordingly.

The strategic objectives were driven by the Council's vision, communicated in express terms. And the full-fledged proposal that followed fleshed out this broad architecture.[18] What the Council sought was a plan that would seek streams of revenue and streams of feedback information, flowing like rivers in opposite directions but intersecting at a point of optimal efficiency. They sought a plan that was as institution-specific as formula funding, as information-rich as performance funding, and as flexible as a block grant.

Council further sought to reward productivity, to heighten accountability, to avert lowest-common-denominator standard measures, and to balance access and quality. At the same time, they wished to rely upon the discipline of the free market and to encourage cost-containment. Finally, they sought assurance of efficiency—core knowledge as an outcome—and decentralization. A goal that was unstated, but which should have been apparent, was to fit the colleges and universities to come through the next economic downtown with minimal financial trauma. (Unfortunately, the leadership at Virginia's institutions uniformly failed to appreciate the value of such foresight while yet in the middle of dramatic prosperity.) What answered to these numerous design specifications was the performance-funding model.[19]

The key components of the funding model are:

- *Initial Assessment of Base Budget Adequacy*

- *Block Grant*—Defined as the prior year's base budget and comprising all Educational and General (E&G) appropriations (general fund and tuition and fee revenue).

- *+/- Technical Adjustments*—One-time-expenditures (e.g., Y2K), expenditures funded through other sources such as certain technology purchases, and annualizing salaries.

- *+ Inflationary Growth Factor*

- *+/- Base Budget Adequacy Adjustment*—Periodic review of base budget adequacy.

- *+/- Incentive Funding*—funding tied directly to performance.

Background of the Funding Model

From the early 1970s through the early 1990s, Virginia employed a formula funding, enrollment driven "input" model that used discipline-specific average student/faculty ratios and other mathematical indices to project future resource requirements. Appendix M, as it was called, was abandoned in the early 1990s when recession-en-gendered across-the-board funding cuts rendered its formula-driven recommendations of little use.

With the demise of Appendix M, formula funding was replaced with practices that were based on institutions' current operating budgets and ad hoc biennial recommendations regarding additional funds for salaries, enrollment growth, operations and maintenance, library materials, technology, capital outlay, and various institution-specific initiatives. Because this process does not provide for the application of consistent, stable, and comprehensive planning guidelines, it engendered a funding environment characterized by uncertainty, fragmentation, and intensified log-rolling.

Toward the end of developing a more systematic funding approach for higher education, the Council reviewed options for revising Virginia's higher education funding policies. A January 1999 Council retreat formed a consensus favoring a block grant approach. This approach would decentralize the front end of the funding process, thereby maximizing the ability of Virginia's public colleges and universities to allocate resources creatively and efficiently in pursuit of their institutional missions.

The Challenge:
Deregulation/Decentralization and the Block Grant

The challenge for state governments has been to provide higher education the tools necessary to manage their affairs while at the same time ensuring that institutions are accountable to the public for the efficient use of the resources they receive. Kenneth Shaw, chancellor of Syracuse University, in a 1996 essay entitled "Helping Public Institutions Act Like Private Ones,"[20] challenged states to volunteer to be the first to attempt true regulatory reform. Virginia was in a position to accept such a challenge.

Virginia had been discussing deregulation/decentralization, since the early 1980s. During the 1990s, under the leadership of the Secretaries of Finance and Education, much had been accomplished in providing opportunities for decentralization in areas of financial management. However, much of the conversation centered around benefits to the institutions with little focus on benefits to the state. The *Virginia Plan* proposal provides a new paradigm, discussing deregulation/decentralization not only in the context of benefits to the institution but also with regards to benefits to the state.

For organizations effectively to manage resources they must be in control. That means that they should not be so over-regulated that they cannot quickly make decisions about people to hire and the amounts to compensate them or what to buy and from whom to buy it. If every resource, whether physical, human, or fiscal is controlled by central processes, institutions cannot be fully accountable for their actions and hardly at all for failure to act. This is the premise behind deregulation and decentralization. In order to hold institutions fully accountable for results and outcomes, the institutions must first be in full control of their resources. Therefore, a system of accountability, whereby the state has key indicators by which it measures institutional success, and an effective audit process are integral to this model.[21]

Along with a base budget, provided in the form of a block grant, institutions should be deregulated from unnecessary central processes. Such deregulation in Virginia comes not in the form of exemptions from law but in the form of freedom from regulations promulgated in administering the law. The state could provide general best practice guidelines/principles, from which institutions would establish their own internal policies and procedures.

Such indicators might include graduation and retention rates, diversity, yield rate of admission offers, and overall financial performance. In addition, each institution would have a plan for evaluating student learning outcomes and presenting those findings yearly plus changes in teaching methods, etc., to improve outcomes. Audits would be used more frequently and effectively.

Constructing our own model, we expanded Shaw's guidance with some general principles that we developed collaboratively. In November of 1998, the Council adopted the following list of college and university administrative best practices:

- Careful selection and training of administrative personnel;

- Organizational structure that provides appropriate division of duties;

- Thorough and continuous monitoring, control, and reporting of operating budgets versus actual operating results;

- Well-communicated written policies and procedures;

- Annual administrative self-assessments led by the university controller; and

- An extensive internal audit function that provides both financial audit and management services functions.

These best practices should be used in conjunction with and supplemental to existing management standards and management tools. They offer a series of performance objectives that:

- Relate to the conduct of the financial and administrative operations within and throughout each fiscal year;

- Reflect commonly held views and experiences as to policies, procedures, and practices that, when applied on a consistent and thoughtful basis, help protect a college or university from unexpected financial reverses or other negative circumstances;

- Contribute over time to producing the most effective financial and administrative support for an individual institution; and

- Can be both affirmed by senior management of an institution and confirmed through appropriate review by internal audit staff and public auditors.

When an institution fails to manage its human, fiscal and capital resources in appropriate manners and as dictated by appropriate standards, it should fall into receivership. This means, under the block grant or "charter" plan, that the institution would lose its deregulated status and again become part of the state's centralized processes whereby its management would be closely scrutinized and a recovery plan required. Should the institution not take corrective action, and within a reasonable amount of time begin to demonstrate positive outcomes, the state should seriously consider closure. Like any business that fails to manage its resources effectively and efficiently and whose product suffers, it goes out of business. A truly deregulated environment brings this consequence as well.

No one would ever be surprised by a failure of these dimensions. The Council in Virginia, as policy organ, would systematically examine institutional performance on an annual basis in order to identify areas of potential concern. It should examine how well an institution performs with respect to the best practices criteria, internal controls and procedures, and state fiscal policies and standards. If after significant intervention through receivership, the institution still fails to perform to expectations, then the policy organ would have the authority to recommend closure.

Base Budget Adequacy Adjustment

Once an initial assessment of base budget adequacy is conducted and any funding inadequacies addressed, the block grant approach provides "steady state" funding for public colleges and universities by protecting their current budgets against inflationary erosion and providing them with far greater flexibility regarding the management of those budgetary resources. Although the block grant provides stable, progressive, and long-term funding, it remains true that changes in circumstances over time can require readjustment. The recurrence of incentive funding in base budgets acts as effective insurance against deficiency. Moreover, the Council decided to determine periodically whether emerging inequities, future conditions, or system objectives would necessitate reassessment of an institution's base budget adequacy.

To accomplish this goal staff must periodically review the adequacy of each institution's base budget. In relation to such reviews, pre-established "triggers" should serve to identify institutions requiring "out of cycle" review. Options for such triggers include *significant changes in institutional mission*, *programs*, *enrollments*, and *new construction*.

Devising the procedures and methods to apply base budget adequacy assessment is an involved process. In some instances, such as faculty salaries, peer group comparisons may be the appropriate method. In others, more involved assessment of program-specific unit costs or projected changes in operating and maintenance needs may be required. In addition, procedures are needed for reviewing the triggers themselves. For instance, enrollment growth should not correlate with reduced entrance standards. These methods and procedures can only be elaborated subsequent to adopting a block grant approach, but they must be adopted well ahead of the time frame in which such reviews would occur.

Incentive Funding/Performance Funding

The Virginia Council decided that a specified percentage of state higher education funding should be set aside to create a pool of monies to reward an institution's performance in relation to student outcomes and other areas as determined by the needs and interests of the Commonwealth. The focus of performance efforts was to be on outcome measures rather than input measures.

To create this incentive structure only a composite index of weighted averages across several outcome measures would suffice. The outcome measures are institution-specific performance targets or "expected" values. Such institution-specific benchmarking controls for the diversity of mission, which is characteristic of Virginia's and most states' public colleges and universities. Once a single, weighted performance metric is derived for each institution, however, relative comparisons among institutions guide the allocation of performance funds. In other words, although an institution's performance will be *measured* only against its own targets or expected values and, therefore, only in the context of its own unique mission, once measured, performance funds could be proportionately allocated across institutions by the measure of how each fared against its own expectations.

We identified six measures that can effectively support incentive funding (recognizing that others are possible): graduation rates, retention rates, scores on "exit exams," post-graduate placement, faculty productivity, and, for two-year programs, successful "transition" rates.

Lessons from Virginia

Virginia's relevance to others has everything to do with Virginia's circumstances relative to others. Few of the pressing issues in Virginia higher education would be unfamiliar to others, not only other states in the United States but other countries around the earth. Consider, for example, the issue of Virginia's status as a "high tuition/high aid" state. Would the picture look differently if viewed from the perspective of the People's Republic of China, undergoing a massive re-definition that includes intentionally introducing tuition charges in higher education and defending them not only on economic grounds but also on grounds of "responsibility" on the part of the students?

As a matter of fact, most issues that confronted Virginia in 1999 were globally recognizable. An extensive literature and periodic conferences[22] confirm, for example, a general need to respond to what is called "massification." A good working definition of "massification" would be the experience of a growth in demand driven by enhanced educational requirements beyond the general demographic variables. Thus, where education once served the few, throughout the world, it increasingly serves the many and out of all proportion to increases in population numbers. The demand for access to higher education has been driven by new political, economic, and social expectations far more than by population numbers. Politically, a general rule of inclusiveness across all classes prevails.

Economically, increasingly the minimal criteria for well being are calibrated to higher education. And socially, today nothing serves more to distinguish the putatively independent individual from the dependent subject than higher education. This last distinction, for example, lies at the heart of many a welfare-state response to need and explains why "welfare to work" is routinely mediated by enhanced education or training.

The Shanghai Municipal Education Commission illustrates the changes to which many education authorities have been subject. When the Commission managed a system of free higher education, consistent with the norms of the People's Republic of China, it matriculated approximately 14 percent of each age cohort (of which only 45 percent had even graduated from "high school"). While the 14 percent was one-third of "high school graduates," it was only a tiny fraction of the age-eligible cohort. Without giving precise details, the Commission reports the number of college-goers dramatically increased (for 1998, total enrollment in Shanghai's forty institutions was 165,000, a number comparable to Virginia's enrollment in public institutions though a comparatively smaller percentage of the age-eligible cohort). As enrollment has grown (and therefore extended the reach of higher education to more people of modest backgrounds), the Shanghai Commission has abandoned "free higher education" and its generous grants to individuals. It has embraced instead a system of tuition and financial aid.

The tuition experiment began with "contract students" in 1983; a "pay for education" system was in place by 1989 (though with only nominal fees), and only ten years later the tuition fee had increased from 100 to 3800 currency units, or 38 times! This evolution (how very like California's experience from the mid-1960s to the 1980s!) produced financially stronger institutions at the same time as generating a public "scholarship and loan funds" program. Thus, China's response to massification has been very clear: a combination of individual responsibility and public support for the needy. One offshoot: greater institutional autonomy.

Hungary, on the other hand, preserves a fairly rigidly structured, European system of advancing through higher education (with about 17 percent of the age-eligible and schooling-eligible cohort gaining admission to university). Nevertheless, in the past decade the number of first-year university students has tripled and enrollment has grown 150 percent. Because the overall age cohort has actually decreased in number, this means that much greater numbers are gaining the educational prerequisites for university admissions. Thus, relative enrollment has tripled. "Nevertheless, as higher education has remained the single most important means to further or sustain one's social position and privilege, it also remained a means of relatively sharp division" between haves and have-nots. In this context Hungary, too, introduced tuition fees, but then rescinded them in 1998—leaving in place a heightened, highly elaborate structure of quality assessment and accountability. "Students are still dominantly recruited from the highest deciles of society for whom higher education is still mostly free of tuition."[23] Reform agendas oscillate between parties/governments, reiterating concern with access, restructuring, and autonomy, but unable to deliver for any but the most privileged classes.

German analysts describe the paradox of public "under funding" of higher education coupled with a "serious lack of flexibility to generate additional funding in a largely state-dominated system." The German constitution guarantees each prospective student a "place" in the public institutions (i.e., there is to be *some* institution for everyone and therefore little or no room for the institutions to select their own students). Nevertheless, a 1996 OECD report lists Germany as serving only 30 percent of the age-eligible cohort (compared to 35 percent in the Netherlands, 40 percent in the United Kingdom, and 50 percent in the United States). More tellingly, within Germany only 7 percent of lower income groups reach university, while 72 percent of higher income groups do so. Thus, the most privileged are the beneficiaries of the no or low tuition regime in Germany as elsewhere. The system of free public higher education in Germany consumes 1 percent of GDP compared to an OECD average of 1.6 percent and a U.S. figure of 2.4 percent exclusive of the highly elaborated private market in the U.S. Such statistics (low proportionate enrollment, low public spending rate, little or no private spending) would seem to suggest that Germany has avoided the pressures of massification and the imperatives of higher education reform. In fact, however, Germany experienced a 38 percent growth in enrollments between 1977 and 1997.[24]

Consequently, in Germany, too, individuals speak of two prevailing options: increased efficiency, on the one hand, and tuition and fees on the other hand. Naturally enough, this discourse is powerfully driven by expectations of greatly increased demands for higher education in Germany. It is "crucially important for Germany's economic future that the necessity to educate as many students as possible to the highest standards possible will be better understood." "When [only] one-third or even one-half of an age group enters higher education, though, there is an obvious need to redefine basic goals." Accordingly, among the considerations that emerge is stress upon determining some "just equilibrium" between private and public responsibility for higher education.[25] To be emphatic, this discourse derives from the consistent discovery that a system of free, public higher education catering to the privileged cannot be preserved, while the less privileged are not only being admitted to but expected or demanded to participate in higher education in greater numbers.

Perhaps unsurprisingly very few strategies have emerged around the world for responding to this need (the urgency of which varies not so much with the different numbers from one country to the next but with the different pressures of democracy and equality from one country to the next). High on the list of strategies are performance funding strategies. Systems as diverse as Mexico, Denmark, and the United Kingdom have tried performance funding.

The strategies that are generally held to work, more or less, are earmarked taxes for education; special education taxes (a Nigerian example); general system reform; flexible planning to meet needs of specific areas/constituencies; defined goals for systems with a focus upon specific institutional missions; and aid directed to students rather than institutions (i.e., vouchers and other means of fostering individual responsibility and institutional accountability). Charging tuition is not added to this list (though it is typically connected with increasing student aid), because the results are uneven around the world. Several countries have introduced tuition (notably Britain), while others have had the Hungarian experience of rescinding tuition fees in the face of protests (notably Mexico). Although charging tuition in general seems to work, when coupled with high student aid, it is very much an open question whether nations and states will have the political capital and will to make significant tuition charges stick.

Unproductive strategies include strategic sector investment, formula funding methodologies, and output measures for which quality specifications are difficult to impossible to articulate. Numerous states in the United States moved through the 1990s from previous funding and management paradigms to new ones, almost all moving in the direction away from enrollment-driven funding formulas toward approximations of base budget funding coupled with performance and incentive programs. The experiences of Texas, Maryland, North Carolina, and Florida, among others, suggest that earlier strategies of driving public appropriations for colleges and universities through vaguely constituted "peer" comparisons and enrollments were unproductive when stressed by economic dislocations.

Similarly, it is easy to infer from many of the remedies proposed what the perceived defects of prior arrangements were. In Virginia, itself, the chief tout for public higher education in the state, the Virginia Business Higher Education Council, presents fairly stark criticisms of higher education, in the process of pumping for greater public funding. It called in a 1998 report for "major structural changes in internal governance systems" (including tenure) designed to overcome inefficiencies in the educational process.[26] It also declared, "we cannot afford. . .competition, or allocation of scarce resources to programs already well-established at other public institutions." Finally, this private Council declared that colleges and universities must become "customer sensitive, quality driven, and cost effective," by which it seems mainly to mean re-formulation of degree requirements and procedures and facilities for progress toward degree completion, including significantly mounting "introductory" courses in an on-line venue. The Business Higher Education Council's lack of success in its ambitious efforts would suggest that the strategies of revising or eliminating tenure, co-opting colleges and universities in a business-political establishment, and employing pseudo-market peer comparisons are no more productive than strategic investing and other such undertakings. They do not further the main work, which is to render higher education both fit for its task and also acceptable to society at large.

Work Remaining

The main work, as we see it, is to help the system of higher education recall and return to its truest and deepest purpose—the development of proficient humanity. Daniel Bonevac recommends that "the most important thing those who care about higher education can do, then, is seek to articulate a compelling and encompassing picture of what the university ought to be."[27] We seek to create our sketch of that picture in this book and in our day-to-day work at

Michigan State University. We do not suggest, as have many critics of higher education, that the academy ought to return to some former version of itself. We agree with Alvin Kernan that "we have a new, democratic kind of higher education, one that will fit the interests and values of twenty-first-century America in many fundamental and important ways."[28]

Chief among the characteristics of the twenty-first-century university is, and must be, universal access to it. We echo Kernan's sentiment that this twenty-first-century university ". . .has arrived with some very rough edges and a strident ideology, both of which need considerable smoothing against the grindstone of accumulated knowledge from the past and the real, present needs of an effective education system."[29] In other words, we can make good on the promise of the democratic university only if we develop those habits of mind that will make education its most treasured charm.

Notes

1. William B. Allen (ed.), *George Washington: A Collection* (Indianapolis, IN: Liberty Classics, 1988), 125-26.
2. Critics within Virginia doubt that there is any system at all: "Virginia's higher education system appears to be a 'system' in name only. It seems to lack many basic ingredients of a system (e.g., 'corporate' strategic direction and business plans. . .effective performance management and accountability systems, etc.). It appears to function as a loose confederation of independent fiefdoms. . ." (The Commonwealth Foundation of Virginia, 13). It will become apparent in what follows, however, that this view derives from too narrow a perspective regarding higher education.
3. "What gets measured gets attention, particularly when rewards are tied to the measures. Grafting new measurements onto an old accounting-driven performance system or making slight adjustments in existing incentives accomplishes little." Robert G. Eccles, "The Performance Measurement Manifesto," in *Harvard Business Review on Managing Corporate Performance*, 26.
4. Correspondence from Washington to James Madison, March 31, 1787, in Allen, *George Washington: A Collection,* 363.
5. ". . .each institution will provide both supporting documentation and a 600-word description. . .of the most significant ways it has used assessment to improve programs, plans, allocate resources, and track the effects of restructuring initiatives. This information will be published as part of the Indicators of Institutional Mission, which has replaced the Virginia Plan." ("Assessment in Virginia," State Council of Higher Education in Virginia, adopted May 31, 1996).
6. In her biography of five extraordinary women, *Composing a Life* (New York: Penguin Group, 1990), Mary Catherine Bateson suggests that "fluidity and discontinuity are central to the reality in which we live" (p. 13). She argues that an environment of change and unpredictability can generate a new way to understand and perhaps to guide experiences, a new means by which we might give a sense of coherence to our lives. She offers, as an example of one such means, "a book about life as an improvisatory art, about the ways we combine familiar and unfamiliar

components in response to new situations, following an underlying grammar and an evolving aesthetic" (p. 3).

7.   Clara M. Lovett, "State Government and Colleges: A Clash of Cultures," *Chronicle of Higher Education* 47 (April 27, 2001): B20.

8.   Bateson, 2-3.

9.   It has become fashionable in recent years to lambaste the shared governance model, which higher education has so long deployed. And, indeed, there are numerous instances in which either the administration or the faculty (or both) have failed to wield the leadership called for by each in this model. Nevertheless, we agree with Charles W. Smith's sense that, "What nearly all critics of this situation fail to recognize is that empowering faculty has produced a remarkably efficient system of governance, given the issues and tasks that confront higher education." (Smith, 39).

10.   Bateson, 240.

11.   Quoted in Quinn Eli, ed. *Many Strong and Beautiful Voices* (Philadelphia: Running Press, 1997), 40.

12.   Bateson, 239.

13.   These advisory groups are the General and Professional Advisory Committee (presidents and chancellors), the Instructional Programs Advisory Committee (provosts and deans), and the Finance Advisory Committee (chief financial officers).

14.   Adelman emphasizes the failure of most systems of higher education nationwide to inventory and evaluate the capacity of their physical plants to accommodate the enrollment growth, which is anticipated for the first decade of this century (as discussed in chapter 3). He concludes that ". . . in the absence of trade-offs (personal and instructional) and new investments in physical plant, technology and faculty, we do not have the capacity for 2 million new traditional students, let alone for all other populations that seek the doorways to learning" (Adelman, "Crosscurrents and Riptides," 27).

15.   A complete copy of the plan, as published, is available at http://www.msu.edu/ ~allenwi.

16.   Maritain, 19. Also, cf., Oakeshott: "A university is not a machine for achieving a particular purpose or producing a particular result; it is a manner of human activity" (Oakeshott, "The Idea of a University," 96).

17.   Consider, for example, Lucas's admonition: ". . .institution of higher learning must learn how best to respond to public demands for accountability. Simplistic formulas and cookbook recipes (what critics contemptuously and rightly refer to as 'bean-counting') will not suffice. Today's accountability movement is not apt to disappear conveniently any time soon. But only when institutions are clear as to what they are about can they frame meaningful responses about their performance, *and only at whatever level of precision and exactitude the questions posed allow* (original emphasis). At root, issues of accountability speak not only to matters of procedure or technique, but to basic intellectual purposes and goals" (Lucas, xv).

18.   Detailed information about the Virginia Performance Funding Model is available at http://www.msu.edu/~allenwi.

19.   The Council of Higher Education is tasked under *Section 23-9.9* of the *Code of Virginia* to "develop policies, formulae and guidelines for the fair and equitable distribution and use of public funds among the public institutions of higher education" and to use those policies, formulae and guidelines in making recommendations to the Governor and the General Assembly regarding the "approval or modification of each institution's [budget] request." At its regularly scheduled meeting of May 18, 1999 the Council adopted the funding resolution.

20.   Kenneth A. Shaw, "Helping Public Institutions Act Like Private Ones," in Terrence J. MacTaggart, ed., *Seeking Excellence Through Independence* (San Francisco: Jossey-Bass Publishers, 1998).

21.   In 1995, the "Legislative Study Commission on the Status of Education at the University of North Carolina" underscored this perspective with two recommendations (numbers two and five) seeking to "reward constituent institutions for performance," basing "management flexibility" for institutions on "stringent management performance requirements." Nevertheless, its 1996 "Revised Funding Model" (effectively a disguised block grant approach), which was predicated on developing "performance incentives" among other high priorities, was forced to defer incentive provisions to subsequent developments concerning funding. That is, performance elements had to be treated as add-ons. It is, therefore, perhaps unsurprising that, in 2001, North Carolina is not among the twenty-one states publishing an "accountability/benchmarks/performance report" according to the most recent report from the State Higher Education Executives Organization (SHEEO, "State Accountability Reports," <http://sheeo.org/account/act-reports.htm> [August 6, 2001]).

22.   One such conference is the 1999 conference, "Global Higher Education: Common Benefits, Common Responsibilities," held in Washington, D. C. and organized collaboratively by the Academy for Educational Development and the Institute for Higher Education Policy.

23.   Peter Darvas, Education Economist, World Bank, "Higher Education Reform in Hungary: Current Priorities and Strategies." August 19, 1999. Paper delivered at the conference on "Global Higher Education: Common Benefits, Common Responsibilities," organized by the Academy for Educational Development and the Institute for Higher Education Policy. Washington, D. C., August 19, 1999.

24.   Brita Baron, director, German-American Academic Exchange, New York Office, "Summary of the Country-Specific Issues or Concerns," August 19, 1999. Paper delivered at the conference on "Global Higher Education: Common Benefits, Common Responsibilities," organized by the Academy for Educational Development and the Institute for Higher Education Policy, Washington, D. C., August 19, 1999.

25.   Ibid.

26.   Virginia Business Higher Education Council. *Virginia First 2000—Business and Higher Education: Partners for the Learning Economy*, (no date or place of publication. Address of Council: 800 East Leigh Street, Suite 106, Richmond, Virginia 23219. Tel. 804-828-2285), 10.

27.   Bonevac, 21.

28.   Kernan, 300.

29.   Ibid., 300.

6

Epilogue: The Rhetoric of Higher Education

The characteristic problems and crises of higher education resist the formularies of administrative planning and public policymaking. Who does not know that questions of subject matter, terms of participation, and relative power, deriving from intractable "culture wars," vitiate each harmonizing attempt to fuse the intrinsic characteristics of higher education with the robust divisiveness of contemporary democracy? What rhetoric can embrace the feminist and the canonist, the ethnic chauvinist and the common heritage advocate, the technology as progress exponent and the liberal educator?

This fusionist enterprise by no means pretends to reconcile all combatants of every conceivable division within higher education. Still, we do not believe that we have failed to bring forth strong claims to distance the terms of division from the central questions of the needs for and of higher education. We believe, rather, that the foregoing chapters are unassailable in setting forth a principled basis for public support of higher education without surrendering to any precious nihilism. Moreover, we believe that we have succeeded in a manner that extends the most inclusive grounds for participation in the conversation about higher education.

The measure of every ethic, however, lies in its application to practical circumstances requiring judgment. Accordingly, we close this analysis with an illustration of several rhetorical productions conforming to the principles set forth herein and directly addressing some of the vexing and some of the not so vexing change arenas in contemporary higher education. Excerpting selected major addresses we delivered, we take up the issues of women in education, the role of the library in the technological age, the place of foreign language in the curriculum, the problem of race in higher education, education in technology, moral judgment, and education for citizenship. Here is where the reader will see the foregoing principles at work.

I. "The Library as the Center of Learning"[1]

Now, I want to acknowledge right away how commonplace talks about the future of libraries have become. I do nothing extraordinary in that regard. In fact, you could reasonably think it unimaginative of me even to attempt it. Does not everyone today anticipate a world of libraries rewired by technology to power conceptually and structurally altered realities for libraries?

On the other hand, I think it would be fair to reply that the very question, "What is the future of libraries?" is becoming an intruding anxiety by virtue of its so frequent repetition. After all, it is hardly the case that the mission of the academic library has become so opaque that we risk losing any reason to come to work if we don't rapidly reinvent the library!

In fact, this is the chief concern that has led me to trot out a challenging thesis on this occasion. I state the concern thus: Too often I hear hand-wringing lament about the urgent need to re-conceive the library in the face of rising technology. The laments sometimes seem to bear the stamp of a fear that the library itself has disappeared before our very eyes, or at least threatens to do so. What I do not understand is whether this futurism reflects a greater sense of the potential of technology to reshape humane practices or an ignorance of the fundamental mission of libraries.

My thesis, simply put is this: We can best think about the future of libraries if we can still think of them as centers of learning.

I know that the role of librarians in teaching information literacy skills to our students is a role that is prominent today and one that is likely to continue to grow in importance. But that role, in and of itself, does not begin to convey what I have in mind. Indeed, though I will forebear, I invite you in your leisure to work through the contrasting etymological implications of "bibliography" and "information literacy." You will find a sea change there, although the root of literacy is still "to read."

Thinking through the same matter metaphorically rather than analytically, may I not hold that the library's special role in the academy has something to do with the fundamental nature of the academy itself? In particular, we probably best conceive of the academy as an arena of transgenerational conversations focused on the most intense and most important human questions. While students look to faculty members to present the "thinking of the ages" as the heart of their own studies, we cannot escape the reality that, unless librarians sustain the ready availability of the conversations of the ages in the form of collections—about which I will say more later—the professors will have but little to offer students.

The reason for this, quite clearly, is that we professors, though perhaps confident of our capacities, can never escape the realization that we never do more than to approach the full fund of wisdom that age-old conversations offer us. The fact is that, even though we may know Socrates, it is the librarian who keeps Socrates ready to hand for us to get to know. In that sense the librarian must know Socrates as well. And although I might well be able to insist that I possess a much clearer, or at least more intimate, understanding of Socrates than any librarian I happen to know, it remains true that I would know nothing of Socrates at all but for librarians who serve as matchmakers.

What this metaphor means to me is that the librarian is or should be no less a member of the faculty than I. The reason for this is that it is not, in fact, a matter of random chance what intellectual marriages get made in libraries. Many things have been said and written that have in their own right no particular claim to considerate intellectual observation. To that extent, therefore, it is indeed the task of the library and the function of the librarian to distinguish, not between the good and the bad book, but among the works that are "right" to engage the conversation across the ages.

I have seen this illustrated in my own teaching, as recently as one year ago when I offered a course entitled, "Moral Fables and What They Tell." That class attained heights undreamed largely because of the collaboration with a librarian, who supervised the digitization of Michigan State University's fable collection synchronously with the class and my students' participation in mounting an exhibit of the library's fable holdings. I could more surely distinguish a fable from a fairy tale than my colleague, but I would not have been able to do so at all but for the resources made available to my review by my colleague. The librarian's eye for the conversation was the key; he did not require the exactitude of science in order to spawn a clear, scientific understanding. Because of him, I gave my students what was more valuable than a particular truth; I gave them the library of truths.

Yet another way that librarians have conceived of their changing role in this age of information is to see themselves as knowledge managers. I cannot resist mentioning an old saw, which that particular function brings to mind. Commencement in one ivied community evoked from a senior faculty member the observation that "universities are full of knowledge; the freshmen bring a little in and the seniors take away none at all, and the knowledge accumulates." Much of that knowledge accumulates in libraries.

What I have in mind, however, is the fundamental role that librarians have played for as long as we have had libraries. It has to do with the vital role that librarians who are deeply engaged with the collections they and their predecessors have built can play in assisting scholars not only in locating materials relevant to answering the questions of their research, but also in thinking through what questions to ask. Through their own active intellect and scholarship, as well as their knowledge of collections and of indexing and retrieval tools, librarians help scholars define the parameters of their research.

Emerson asks, "What is the hardest work in the world?" He answers, "Thinking." In the hurried pace of contemporary life and the press of daily business, it is easy to get sloppy in our thinking or even to try to avoid it altogether. But, thinking is the essential work of the university and I believe it is also the essential work of librarians. We need to watch out for our tendency to think of libraries as a place where librarianship is done, rather than as a place where thinking is done.

A good friend of mine recently shared with me a passage she had read by Norman Cousins, which well captures this conception of the work of the library:

> A library is not a shrine for the worship of books. It is not a temple where literary incense must be burned or where one's devotion to the bound book is expressed in ritual. A library, to modify the famous metaphor of Socrates, should be the delivery room for the birth of ideas—a place where history comes to life.[2]

I would emend Cousins to say, "where life comes to history." My central thesis, then, is that we should find it next to impossible to conceive of the university without thinking first and fundamentally of the library.

From the library we organize our forays into inquiries that are the more important because the less foreseen. I speak of the library as a center of learning because, in this respect, it is the center of the university's reason for being.

Permit me to contrast the library with the classroom. I would expect any sympathetic listener to doubt whether the classroom were not more fully the center of learning than the library. I reply quite simply, that the classroom at its best launches our searches and our conversations, but in my experience it is the library that nurtures and sustains them. Moreover, the library engages us singly, while nevertheless presenting entire communities of discourse to our disposal. To be sure, libraries have hours (schedules) no less than do classrooms. What we do with those schedules in the one and the other case, however, differs profoundly.

Let us not think of the academic library as a book depository, therefore, not only in the information age but also throughout its history. Think, rather, that it is the expression of a recurring conception of learning through repeated generations over many centuries. That recurring conception structures an expectation that one could find a center in which the pathways to inquiry have been not only marked out but also organized so as to reward inquiry.

This important work throughout history has been the work of librarians but not only librarians. And this is where the thesis I pose to you takes on its sharpest urgency. For I maintain that the librarians have indeed been partners in thought with the faculties and departments in our universities—at least wherever they have performed properly. Typically today, or at least until recently, collection development turns around close collaboration between faculties and bibliographers. But if we focus, for an instant, not on that process of building collections, but the resulting logic of the collections built, we should begin to realize that a library is not a collection of any books or information. It is always this or that collection of books or information. And the key to the business is the "this or that." The judgment that sustains the academic library is, in fact, a continuing work of active intellect (or at least should be in the best case), and that is the work that has enabled the library to become the center of learning. It is both expression and resource for the highest hopes for learning any faculties ever form.

Perhaps my notion of the library as a center of learning begins to be clear to you. I mean by it that the library's role in the university is not best understood as an administrative or support function but far rather as an academic or intellectual function. That is the reason the "collection" should always be important to the librarian; it is, in fact, the connection between the librarian and the professor that ought to create the "collection." That joint intellectual construction is so essential to the continuing work of higher learning that I do not think it possible to conceive of carrying on the work of higher education without it.

Consider, for example, the now already-familiar faculty lament that, "just because information is found on the Web, that does not mean that it is a legitimate foundation for research." You have surely heard it as often as I have. But what does it mean? It means that the extensive data storehouse that the Web has become has not been organized by a guiding conception of human inquiry. It is a mere collection, not a library.

Every library is, in fact, a "special collection," and if I were to join the futurist in attempting to foresee what would become of the so-called "traditional" library in the age of "information technology," I would suggest that you look to the arts, practices, and competencies of your "special collections" department in order to appreciate the eventual role of the library altogether. Nor would that be a restricted role; in most respects it would constitute final recognition of the enduring role of the library as a center of learning, in which the book custodian and the book consumer, to speak blithely, are united in intellectual exertion. The librarian as curator—well-informed resource—is the model of the librarian from the past and should be the model of the librarian in the future.

To reach that stage, though, universities must recognize that the role of the library, which is the foundation of the role of the librarian, must be at the center of the academic enterprise. It is not an auxiliary activity, and can no more be marginalized without harming the university than the university can be marginalized within society without harm to society. We have centers of learning to begin with, because humane practice is fostered only by advances in learning.

A final view of what I mean in all of this may be evoked from remarks I presented to the Foreign Language Association of Virginia. On that occasion, I defined a language as a store of untranslated meanings. Without developing the conception further here, I think it will be plain to you if I extend the figure to the library, as the store of meaningful human conversation. In light of the distinction adduced, I would say that the library is to the university what language is to humanity. In that light it is no less vital to the advance of humane consideration.

Gertrude Himmelfarb, in her essay, "Revolution in the Library," states that the use of information technology has enabled a ". . .revolution, not only in library services but in the very conception of the library. But—and this is a large but—all this would be to the good only if the virtues of the new library are made to complement, rather than supplant, those of the old."[3] I choose Dr. Himmelfarb's dictum as a fit close to these remarks, but only with the caveat that I think the challenge of technology has been to force us to strengthen our conception of the library as a center of learning.

II. "The Dangers of Foreign Language Study"[4]

Rather than to talk with you about the pleasures of studying foreign languages, I want to say a few words about the dangers of foreign language study.

As a way of putting this on the right footing at the outset, I am reminded of this theme because there are so many things that I have done, which are shaped by my own education, that I would not have conceived possible to do in the world. I feel somewhat sheepish coming among you, who are teachers of foreign languages and know very well how these things can be done. But so much of my own learning—apart from nothing more than a year here and a year there in one course or another—derives from my own study rather than systematic instruction.

Nevertheless, among the things that result from that study one shows up in conversations I sometimes have, as, for example, when my partner appeals to me, "Please make me a gin and tonic," and I reply without pause, "Zap, you're a gin and tonic!" Now, I submit that I would not do that if I had never learned any foreign languages. It is a dangerous thing to be prompted to untimely witticisms! We hear the colloquialisms of our English usage, but when they ape the forms of declined languages we slip bonds of familiarity to pursue dreams we recall from abroad. In the process we recommit to the rules of a periphrastic language, without having to be so pedantic as to instruct, "please make a gin and tonic for me." This is most uncivil behavior, and therefore a danger that results from foreign language study.

Whether folk understand our witticisms or sarcasms at the moment we indulge them, they reveal something important about those of us who have acquired heightened sensitivity to differences in languages. While it may prepare us to talk to others, it more importantly encourages us to understand ourselves, to understand how we use our own language. We have all heard—and probably repeated time and again—that the student who learns a foreign language learns so much more about his native tongue and how to use it well. I, at least, have certainly given that response to the student who looked at me rather wistfully—if not resistfully—and wondered "why?"

Still, dangers lurk even here. We identify the easy temptations in the case of folk who imagine they can converse unperceived because the folk around them speak a different tongue. I expect that many of you have experienced that uneasy feeling while traveling abroad: are they talking about me? And, of course, they often are! On occasion I have surprised such naïve natives, belatedly revealing myself aware of their conversation despite my alien appearance. But new linguists are no less susceptible to this danger than native-born folk. Language can be a cover for rudeness.

Embarrassments abound here, even when no harm is meant. This occurred to me once, as I entertained a young couple early on in my first stay in France. I confess: my French was rather rough and ready. I arrived there having studied French for only three of the twelve-week summer course that had been interrupted by the death of my mother and, subsequently, for only one year immediately prior to my departure on the Fulbright appointment. On the other hand, I had already become deeply steeped in my subject, Montesquieu, whose French I read with ease. That is, of course, wonderfully elegant French, French from the eighteenth century, redolent of grand ambition and things we no longer think about (to use an expression he might have used). I learned so much of my vocabulary from Montesquieu. In fact, I did not hesitate in turning to my young friends in France and inquiring as I imagined he might have done, "*Est-ce que vous avez vous enjouis à San Francisco?*" once they had told of their recent journey to America. I did not know that this trope was perhaps never used this way and far more significantly used only in a specialized and intimate colloquial sense in the twentieth century. But I did recognize the blushed scarlet that sat before me that autumn evening.

The dangers of foreign language study show up still more meaningfully in the case of Thomas Jefferson, a serious multilinguist though largely self-taught. You may well know that Jefferson was often at odds with President Washington. Indeed, Jefferson created the Democratic-Republican political party specifically to resist Washington's agenda (or at least what Jefferson thought the agenda to be). This occurred as he sat in Washington's cabinet as the Secretary of State. Jefferson had a criticism of the president that he did not dare to write or publish in English; so he published it in Italian, likening George Washington to a "Samson" in the field of battle and a "whore" in the nation's councils. Unfortunately, this screed eventually made its way across the Atlantic and out of the safe Italian into an English translation. You can readily imagine the difficulties this occasioned in the relationship between the two thereafter and for the balance of their careers. Foreign language tempts us to try to get away with things; that's a danger of foreign language study.

We think, when we acquire a foreign language, that we have an additional instrument of communication. I'd like to challenge that assumption. We are tempted to think of foreign languages as so many collections of synonyms and cognates—warehouses or repositories of words and meanings that we can match up with words and meanings in our own native warehouses or repositories. I challenge that definition of a foreign language, for it seems to me that a foreign language—or a language simply—is rather more a store of unduplicated meanings. The reason we care to study a foreign language is to gain access to those unduplicated meanings, meanings that we cannot approach through our own particular storehouses, those with which we were reared.

When we talk about multiculturalism and getting to know other people, I think it exceedingly important that we do so in a framework that encourages us to learn from them who they are rather than to learn who they are through our particular prisms. That is why I like to think of a language as a store of unduplicated meanings. This means, in turn, that we gain access to it only by entering it. We cannot do that by standing outside it.

Let me illustrate by the story of how I came to learn Italian, for it reflects exactly what I am saying. One of my areas of study has been the works of Harriet Beecher Stowe, with whom you are all familiar. As I began to look into the development of *Uncle Tom's Cabin*—but also pursued Stowe's education, her background, and all of her other writings—I came to discover many things, including her extensive facility in languages. I realized, for example, that *Uncle Tom's Cabin* grew out of her reading of Tocqueville's *Democracy in America* in the French. For the name of the ship on which Uncle Tom was shipped south, *La Belle Rivière*, was taken from Tocqueville's account of his descent from north to south along the Ohio and Mississippi Rivers.

Upon a closer look at Tocqueville's work one realizes that the entire plot of *Uncle Tom's Cabin* is structured around the dramatic motion of *Democracy in America*. Stowe's work takes on a much grander significance when placed in that context.

That study drove me deeper into Stowe's work and her large list of writings until eventually I stumbled across a work in her name called *Dio Dispone*. It is written in Italian, and there is absolutely no record of any such thing in any manuscript or note or any of the materials that Stowe left behind. I was in a bind, for I did not know Italian. I needed to know if she wrote the novel, and I could not determine it from any external evidence. The only chance I would have was to read the novel and then to determine whether it conveyed the meanings I had already come to recognize as the work of her own intellect. If I could see that the arguments, the structure, the particular concerns that were familiar to me from her work in English (the same kinds of things one would seek in my work published in Italian), then there would be some reasonable prospect of attributing the novel to Stowe.

Thus, I had to learn Italian. I got out the primers, set to work for several months, and finally read *Dio Dispone*. I came to the conclusion that this was a very fine take-off on Harriet Beecher Stowe. Someone (perhaps someone who could not so openly publish a Protestant tract in Italian) had read a great deal of Stowe and had a great deal of appreciation for her work. But it was not, in fact, Harriet Beecher Stowe's work. I could not have arrived at that conclusion without learning the Italian (a translation would have misled me, even if one had existed). Now, here is my point: had I had it translated and read it only through the store of unduplicated meanings familiar to me, I could not have made so sure a judgment about whether those expressions were likely her own. I had to see them and understand them in the language in which they were written.

And so, what is the most important danger in the study of foreign languages? Foreign languages conceal meanings. They do not conceal them absolutely; they conceal them only to the unlearned. They only conceal them to those who do not take the time to study. But they are perfectly concealed except that we are willing to venture into other realms of learning and study. That is why I suggest the study of foreign languages, its dangers notwithstanding. Moreover, it is the finest instrument human beings possess for keening the intellect. I do not know that it would have been at all possible in my development, to have pursued the areas important to me without being able to study the languages that are so intimately connected with the evolution of those historical and philosophical principles at the center of my own concerns.

I suspect that one would want to talk about foreign languages within the broader context of cultural and literary transmission. Of course, I particularly enjoy those aspects of it as well. But what interests me now is the fact that there is a direct connection between foreign language study and liberal education. What I have seen intermittently, as have so many more before me and as so many do even now—as indeed all of you—is to discover that while foreign language may be a discipline, it has a value far beyond its capacity to spawn a professional career. It is rather a disciplining of the mind than a professional discipline. It is a necessary tool, and not merely ancillary, in pursuing important questions about the human soul, about the prospects of human development.

As I look around I become somewhat frustrated, I confess, that we do not have as intuitive a response to foreign languages as what used to characterize education. When Alexander Hamilton went off to King's College from the isle of Nevis in the Caribbean and presented himself for matriculation at age thirteen or fourteen, he was sat to read and translate passages in Greek, Hebrew, and Latin. That was his entrance examination. I do not suggest that we must revert to that. We could leave off one of the three. But I am concerned to see a pattern emerging in many of our universities of, first, withdrawing required foreign language study and, secondly, trying to force it down into the kindergarten through twelve level by adopting admissions criteria for studying foreign languages that are minimal at best. Then we say to teachers at the "K through twelve level," it is now up to you to make sure that all the language anybody needs has been provided for the future of our university students.

I think we need to revisit that issue; I think we need to revisit it even as we are revisiting standards of learning and seeking to strengthen kindergarten through twelve education. I do not believe that we should remove it from "K through twelve." I think it belongs there. I wish that I had had so much more of it. When I began to study Greek I was a graduate student. And I assure you that at that advanced age I came to realize that I would have been far better off if I could have begun at age nine or ten. So, yes, I think we should have vigorous and ambitious foreign language study in grade school and in our high schools. Nevertheless, I like to remind people of what is not often mentioned when we speak of the facility with which the young can learn a foreign language. We often fail to tell parents particularly that the young forget it just as readily. They learn it quickly and they lose it quickly. The strength of foreign language study is carrying it into maturity. Its benefit comes to bear in our lives as we carry it on into maturity. Once we have gained mature command of a tongue, we never lose it. I am aware that you have had the same experience I have had. We think that if we haven't used a language for a while, and it does not come immediately to the tongue, then perhaps we have lost it. But all we have to do is to step from a plane in a foreign land and hear the sounds around us. Then we realize, yes, we still have it. We may have to learn a new cliché or two, but we still have it. That does not occur to the young that way; they need more discipline; they need more study. And they need to bring consciousness of other languages into maturity before permanent acquisition.

We need to ask whether we are making permanent acquisition of foreign languages possible for our students. We need to ask it through high school. We need to ask it still in university. We need to ask whether our general education curricula are giving due and appropriate attention to foreign language study. When the Council of Higher Education releases its report on general education I am quite certain you will find underlined the section that concerns foreign languages. For, in all candor, that area harbors more confusion about standards and practices than any other area of the curriculum. It is true that people do not know whether they desire to require history or to make it one of a long list of things. People are not exactly sure what to ask for in the way of English, whether what we really need is literature or whether just a course in composition will do. They are not altogether certain what instruction in mathematics is required, whether one ought to strain one's brain a time or two or whether "mathematics for the unfamiliar" isn't an acceptable alternative. But there is no greater confusion anywhere than in respect to the standards, criteria, and expectations for foreign language study.

In the first place it is conceived that it does not really matter what language one studies. Now here let me tread on somewhat dangerous ground. I think it does matter. There are many wonderful languages all over the face of the earth, but not every language is equally a gateway to higher reflection. Human beings do have a history.

Those histories are related in these storehouses of unduplicated meaning. In those areas in which the histories that have evolved have allowed co-tangent and interpenetrating experiences among people, we have far greater opportunities to build our awareness of the nature of human life. We can identify the languages that bear those traditions in that manner. While there would be wonderful intellectual purpose, and even moral purpose, in studying the life and language of a remote tribe, perhaps even rescuing it and reducing it to writing and grammatical rules, the acquisition of that language will not bear as importantly on one's intellectual development as the acquisition of Greek or Hebrew. That's an accident of history, not a moral judgment. That's just a reflection of who we are and where we have been. As we speak of foreign languages, we can never forget who we are and where we have been. We want to be able, through foreign languages, to gain access to stores of reflection. And that principle will tell us which languages most commend themselves to our students to study. It is not just a question of whether we live within a global society. I am all in favor of globalization. But I do not believe that the argument from utility is an argument that is strong enough to carry us through what we need to do in order to make decisions about higher education and liberal education in particular.

In fact, I am reminded of the tale of the mouse who was escorting her youngster through a house toward the mouse hole. She heard behind her the sound of an approaching cat. They began to run, but the cat drew nearer. They were not going to escape. She stopped, turned in her tracks, and said, "Bow wow!" As the cat scurried off, the mother mouse turned to her youngster and observed, "See, I told you that there is value in learning a second language." Yes, there is utilitarian value in learning a second language. There is particularly utilitarian value in a society that now boasts so many second tongues (or original tongues, I should say, in the presence of the second tongue of almost all of us, English). It helps if we can understand one another when we speak from our particular stores of unduplicated meanings. But as a practical matter we are not all going to learn the several hundreds of languages now current in the United States. We are, however, all going to learn English. And when we have all learned additional languages that can respond to standards and criteria of educational progress, and that can be reasonably and meaningfully included in general education curricula, and that we ought to be able to expect from an educated people, then we can be confident of sustaining our progress.

In 1950, fewer than 20 percent of the citizens in the Commonwealth had had any college experience. By 1980 that number was reaching beyond 50 percent, and it is growing. We can now foresee the day when virtually every citizen of Virginia will have had college experience. Pause for a moment and imagine what that means. What will we be able to say whcn that day comes, when everyone we meet in the streets we will greet as a college person? Will we have any idea of what they bring with them in that college education? Or will our standards have wandered so far afield that it will no longer mean anything more than that they live on Compton Street?

That is why standards are important. Just as we are reaching the threshold of proving the democratic promise that we can educate a whole society, that we can infuse it with all of the thoughtful reflection that is necessary to make democracy work, at that moment, I submit, we are least of all permitted to weaken our standards. At that moment, we should be most insistent on being certain we get full value for the nominal accomplishment of giving everyone a college education. Therefore, I would like to invite you to think with the Council of Higher Education and with me about ways that we can revive honest concern with demanding study of foreign languages as part of the repertoire of an educated person.

I know that this is, of course, a difficulty. In my last assignment it soon became clear to me—after long conversations with faculty from the language departments and the College of Arts and Letters—that my desire to have everyone study a foreign language had some pretty awful consequences for teachers of foreign languages. They would have to teach countless sections of first and second year foreign languages for the rest of their lives. Without the requirement, if they taught only students who were really interested in majoring in a foreign language, they would get to teach advanced courses. They would teach literature, culture, geography, and philosophy—not grammar. Well, I am a bit quirky. I love grammar! I love teaching it, studying it, repeating it. So, take what I say with something of a grain of salt, if I don't seem sympathetic. But I think beyond the ardors of teaching introductory level classes, I would offer a certain joy, a certain challenge that comes from sponsoring any student at any age in the discovery of new wonders. I acknowledge the joy of relaxing among the splendors of the things one has learned to care most about at the most advanced levels and to have fellow spirits around. They are practically colleagues—not students—at that level. But that is never so enjoyable as to sponsor the discovery of new wonders. That is what we do in those introductory courses. They may become drudgery, but then they have to be rethought. As we all move through a grand new effort to make assessment play a central role in our lives, let us give thought to benefit from assessment to make the work we do as exciting for us as we wish it to be for our students.

We at the Council will soon release the latest report on restructuring, and we will say of our colleges and universities that at some point it seems that we are in danger of seeing restructuring and the attendant assessment becoming a thin veneer, an administrative requirement carried out to satisfy the State Council, but one that does not reach far enough into the faculties and student bodies to have a meaningful impact on academic programs. We are concerned about that. We rely upon you to prevent that happening. We rely upon you to assure that the process of continuous assessment, continuous quality review, is constantly reinvigorating and, above all, is an opportunity for you to establish some standards that our institutions will uphold.

Finally, let me say a few words about the essential role of the faculty. Processes must be in place to assure that those who have most responsibility to conduct the education of our students will bear the greatest weight in determining the success of that education. I think that is important in no area so much as it is in the area of foreign language study. I urge you to carry the banner yet another leg in this race that we all must run. I want, too, to congratulate you. For when I am among teachers of foreign languages, I know that I am among those who have had to insist for a long time on being respected as a part of the curriculum rather than being shunted off onto a siding. All too often that temptation has made our educational enterprise a doubtful one. I hope now that we are in an era when we are all going to be running on the main track.

III. "Of Parable and Talents"[5]

My remarks to the graduating class will highlight the use we make of the many gifts we each are given in our lives. It will not surprise you, I think, to hear that this son of a Baptist minister turned, as I have so often before, to Scripture to prepare my remarks. Nor do I so merely because this college yet embraces its Christian heritage and values. The parables were explained by the Master as mysteries to all but them who had "eyes to see" and "ears to hear." With Scripture I invoke that power of poetic intervention that makes light and sound in the work of understanding.

In Matthew 25:14, I read these words:

> For the kingdom of heaven is as a man traveling into a far country, who called his own servants, and delivered unto them his goods. And unto one he gave five talents, to another two, and to another one; to every man according to his several ability; and straightway took his journey.

Matthew then tells us that "he who had received five talents went and traded with the same, and made them other five talents." Likewise, the man with two talents doubled his by putting them to use. But the third man—the man who had been given but one talent—hid that money in the earth.

When the time of reckoning came, the lord of these men praised the two who had multiplied their talents, saying to each of them, "Well done, thou good and faithful servant: thou hast been faithful over a few things, I will make thee ruler over many things: enter thou into the joy of thy lord." But the fellow who had hidden his lone talent was cast into darkness.

Our lessons from this parable are plain enough. I hardly need point out the aspect of the parable that encourages wise financial investment. I want, rather, to draw our attention to this message of the parable: As stewards of those talents and other gifts that have been granted to us, we each are charged with their growth and sound utilization.

The focus of our celebration today, however, is on the labors and the success of you students who are about to receive this outward certification of your attainments. You know that the person who is ultimately responsible for how your talents are increased and how they are put to use is you. It is fitting for you to reflect with pride on your accomplishments and to consider how you have developed—in mind, soul, and body—during your time at Averett.

The fact that so many of you have carried out your studies while also managing the responsibilities of work and family makes your achievements all the greater—while in no way diminishing the accomplishments of those fortunate enough to pursue collegiate or graduate studies full-time. Today we commend all of you and proclaim our pride in what you have done.

A commencement, as the name implies, is a time to look forward as well as back. And so, we not only reflect upon what you have accomplished but also look ahead with anticipation to what you will do next. Now that you have honed and increased your talents, how will you put them to work anew?

In *The Web and the Rock*, Thomas Wolfe wrote:

> If a man has a talent and cannot use it, he has failed. If he has a talent and uses only half of it, he has partly failed. If he has a talent and learns somehow to use the whole of it, he has gloriously succeeded, and won a satisfaction and a triumph few men ever know. [6]

Our hope—indeed our expectation—for you is that you will know that triumph, or, if you have known it already, that you will encounter that satisfaction again and again, in new and expanded ways throughout your lives. Our prayer for you is that you will put your talents to work not only in pursuit of economic gain but also in service to your family, friends, colleagues, community, and nation. We pray that you, remembering the many gifts that have been given to you, will repay those kind investments with your goal to "transform everything you touch into something finer, worthier, and more useful," as the president of another Virginia college has urged many graduating classes before. In pursuing that goal, you will not only change the lives of others, you will make your own life happier and more fulfilling.

As Albert Schweitzer said, "I don't know what your destiny will be, but one thing I do know. The only ones among us who will be really happy are those who have sought and found how to serve humanity."

You will each discover the unique set of services you can offer to humanity. That service can take many shapes. For some, the contours of your service will be found within your chosen profession. For others, the demands of raising a family may require that you give your greatest gifts within the home for some number of years. I hope that many of you will apply your talents in service to your community on school boards, through civic organizations, through the work of your church, and perhaps as elected officials.

We remember that the lessons from Matthew 25 do not teach us only that we are accountable for how we use our talents. At the heart of the parable is a forceful message about our fundamental obligation to care for our fellow beings:

> For I was an hungered, and ye gave me meat: I was thirsty, and ye gave me drink: I was stranger, and ye took me in: Naked, and ye clothed me: I was sick, and ye visited me: I was in prison, and ye came unto me.

We each have opportunities, daily, to put our talents to use in care and service to those around us.

There is one special category of care and service that I want to highlight—namely, that of teaching. I hope that many members of this graduating class will take up the work of teaching—whether as your chosen profession, as the first and foremost teachers of your children, as tutors to at-risk learners, as Sunday-school teachers, or as mentors to those who follow you in the professions in which you will mature and thrive. Education is one of the greatest gifts we can receive in this life. Insofar as we, as a society, are able to offer that gift, we have a moral duty to do so.

Education carries with it an inescapable stewardship responsibility. As educators, we are charged to aid in developing the talents of the students whose learning is entrusted to us. Having taught nearly continuously for the past thirty years, I know firsthand that teaching offers much joy at the same time that it demands us to give of ourselves liberally, with deep care and respect for the student with whom we engage. I might add that learning, no less than teaching, offers that same opportunity for joy while demanding a giving of oneself. Every teacher knows that we learn from our students even as they learn from us. We grow our talents together.

Each of Virginia's colleges and universities—both public and private—brings its own unique set of talents to these acts of teaching and learning. The talents of a given institution may find their fullest and most ideal expression in the college's statement of mission. The realization of that talent finds its fullest expression in the lives of its alumni.

Our institutions, too, are stewards of talent. We must judge them in the spirit of the parable, as good and faithful servants, when we see that they have added value to each talent entrusted to their care.

At the same time, each institution is itself a talent, entrusted to our stewardship. We will be called to answer for what we have done with each of these talents. If ever you wonder why I devote such effort to talking up Virginia higher education and urging upon it continuous quality improvement, it is because I am determined to add value to the talent entrusted to me, to see the good we enjoy multiplied for the enjoyments of ages to come.

The heart of all education is liberal education. That is the great multiplier that extends skills beyond occupations, raises hopes beyond class and status, and informs opinions beyond prejudices. Our most successful institutions offer students increasing knowledge and confidence in their judgments of their own needs and what is good for them. We praise the doing so. But we ask yet more: that our institutions assure that every graduate will attain not only a clear, critical understanding of his or her own needs and skills but also a sensitive and well-informed understanding of the needs of others. That is the value added that multiplies talents not only at the individual level but at the institutional level as well. That is the heart of quality in higher education.

IV. "The End of Education: Increased Knowledge and Confident Judgment"[7]

Greetings ECPI Graduates! You have arrived in the economic fast lane. Now, fasten your seat belts and get ready for the ride of your life. I bring you news of change swirling swiftly about us, as we navigate our way through daily headlines heralding opportunities and pitfalls in the moving landscape of education and career.

You are uniquely situated to appreciate this picture, benefiting as you do from one of Virginia's most unique educational institutions. ECPI brings a special curriculum to a unique constituency, helping Virginia advance its goal of attaining a highly trained workforce and a well-educated citizen body. I like the fact that its name reflects an evolutionary path of increasing importance. What was the name as the school was incorporated in Virginia thirty years ago (Electronic Computer Programming Institute) became an acronym (ECPI) and then became a first name in the enlarged conception of its mission, ECPI College of Technology. ECPI's capacity for growth was never more important than it is today, when it plays the role of advance scout pointing out paths to future success. You are the beneficiaries of ECPI's success in contributing to Virginia's economic boom, and you can measure that success by a reputation that has spawned increasing competition for ECPI and like institutes from more traditionally organized colleges.

An economic boom adds special punctuation to education's claims to improve human life, and we see this illustrated every day in the form of the headlines that portray this era. Consider some of the headlines from just the past several months:

A few days ago, we read, "Technology, Tourism Power Job Growth" (*Richmond Times Dispatch*, 4/25/99). What a picture—a society that thinks and plays hard, with rich rewards for those who can do both!

On April 11, we read, "Night Moves: More Adults Are Returning to School to Upgrade Their Skills" (*Washington Post*). The picture is that everyone wants to get in on the good times (as I hope they do), and that education holds the passwords.

May 2, we read "Demand for Construction Workers Building" (*Roanoke Times*), which shows prosperity creating new opportunities in the form of demands for life's comforts.

But no one is surprised by these headlines, for we have already seen, "German Tech Firm Plans Area Branch" (*Virginian Pilot*, 3/18/99), "Regional Outlook Focuses on Technology" (*Richmond Times Dispatch*, 1/21/99), and "High Tech Business Sets Up in City Promising Semiconductor Growth" (*Richmond Times Dispatch*, 12/19/98).

These are the reasons for the headlines that say, "Job Opportunities Virtually Unlimited" (*Richmond Times Dispatch*, 5/16/99), "Investments to Create 800 Jobs" (*Richmond Times Dispatch*, 5/18/99), and "Technology Tops Job Gains in 1998" (*Washington Post*, 12/14/98).

The push is on as "the Geeks take flight" (*Washington Post*, 2/15/99), and we are well advised to look out for recruitment ads that read, "Wanted, a Few Good Nerds," because of a "New High Tech Navy Shortage of Wonks" (*Virginian Pilot*, 7/12/98). It is now "Goodbye, Grease Monkey. . . . Hello, Auto Technician" (*Washington Post*, 8/16/98).

And this all results from the effect of "Technology Touted as Equal Opportunity Equalizer" (*Virginian Pilot*, 5/3/98). "High Tech Degrees Open Doors for Students" (*RTD*, 10/4/98); in fact our headlines scream: "Help Wanted High-Tech Jobs Going Begging" (*Virginian Pilot*, 9/9/98).

Because education bars the door to the job waiting to be filled, "Area Tech Education Heats Up by a Few Degrees" (*Washington Post*, 4/29/99). In fact, the jobs can hardly wait for students to graduate: "Students entering the School of Information Technology and Engineering at George Mason University might take five to six years to complete requirements for their four-year undergraduate degree." (*Richmond Times Dispatch*, 10/4/98). As soon as these students learn even a little bit they are snatched up by booming firms and put to work, leaving school a part-time affair.

We see the booming firms all around us: "Nextel Communications, Inc., with headquarters in Reston, plans to hire 700 employees at its new technical and customer support operations center in Hampton" (*Richmond Times Dispatch*, 5/18/99). "AOL Profit Up

Sharply in Quarter; Results Top Analysts Forecasts" (*Washington Post*, 4/28/99). "AOL Plans More Jobs, Buildings; $600 Million Expansion Announced for N. VA." (*Washington Post*, 3/11/99). "MCI Worldcom Posts Rise in Profit" (*Washington Post*, 4/30/99). "IBM Profit Rose 50% in 1st Quarter" (*Washington Post*, 4/22/99).

For all of this we do not lack for portents of concern. On April 25, 1999, Jim Hoagland wrote in the *Washington Post*:

> the global economy created in the 1990s by the spread of markets, information technology and more open trade has yet to prove that it distributes its fruits more evenly than did the system of the Cold War era. The Internet may connect a world in which the rich still get richer and the poor get poorer—only faster. (p. B07)

Such reflections lead us to note the headlines that read, "In Fairfax, A Promise of Jobs Falls Short" (*Washington Post*, 4/23/99); "US Airways Group Posts 50% Drop in Profit" (*Washington Post*, 4/22/99); "Retailers Cope with Worker Shortage" (*Roanoke Times*, 1/20/99); "When Programmers, Managers Have Trouble Staying on the Same Track" (*Washington Post*, 10/4/98); and, finally, "A Block on the Old Chip; Downturn in the Semiconductor Industry" (*Washington Post*, 9/28/98).

Perhaps it is concern about pitfalls as much as enthusiasm about opportunities that leads to headlines such as the following: "Warner Stumps for High-Tech Partnership Program to Solve" the problem that "computer science students at Norfolk State University aren't bombarded with obscene salary offers, laundry service, helicopter rides, or the other tricks corporate recruiters use on techies. . ." (*Virginian Pilot*, 11/14/98). By all means though, concern about the future must inform the headline, "Testing Liberal Arts Waters," which is explained by the note: "Attention, geeks who have read Goethe: Mark Warner is hoping to draw more liberal arts majors into the ranks of the tech work force" (*Washington Post*, 1/14/99).

It is safe to say that we, educators and consumers, have hitched our wagons to the star of technology in a big way. We know that our economic relations are changing in dramatic ways, and we would like to imagine that we can prepare to survive the changes with our humanity, or at least our creature comforts, intact.

Let us pause, then, to ask the question beyond the next question. For you graduates the next question is "what job, what city?" Most of you, I assume, already know the answers, and even if you don't I am confident that you soon will.

So all the more readily I ask you the question next up, namely, *"What will become of you?"*

This is not a religious question, and it is not a philosophical question. The question arises from the trite observation that you are surely going to live and work beyond the job you take next. It will not even be unlikely for you to live and work beyond the career you have now chosen. Are you prepared for your job after the next job, your career after the career you are entering?

Yes, I am raising the ante on the education you have received. I do that without much hesitation because I know that it is above all necessary today for everyone to think in this manner. The education that will help you is the education that prepares you to grow in learning and to survive the changes that will come no less surely in the future than they have come now. I am quite sure that this reality is a source of the inspiration that led ECPI to ask you to study, beyond technical courses, courses in critical thinking, mathematics, social science, writing, and library research.

This beginning on a general education curriculum may well be the most important part of the education you celebrate this evening. For it will remain with you the longest. Its half-life is several generations longer than the half-lives of the programming languages you have learned. It is by virtue of strong, general education programs that our schools avert the fate against which Daniel LeBlanc (president, Virginia AFL-CIO) warned, when he said that schools should not be converted into apprentice shops for industry.

Your journey parallels that of ECPI itself. It did not several years ago provide a curriculum that could remotely be called the beginning of a liberal education. As it has grown, it has observed the need for liberal foundations as the intellectual chassis on which to build the frame of technical competence. I fully expect that its journey will continue, and that it will one day offer full-fledged liberal education.

You, too, may continue. The learning you have begun may grow into a life of learning, where you acquire still more skills but—unlike skills that are worn like suits of clothing—weave them into the flesh and bone of living. For it is only when our skills become like flesh of our flesh and bone of our bone that we know they will grow as we grow. Liberal learning is the fertilizer that forces skills to flower as our own personalities.

Liberal education is at the heart of all education truly worthy of the name, and with these words to you today, I hope I have spurred the growth of the seed of liberal learning which has been planted already in your hearts.

V. "On Becoming a Liberal: Guidance of George Washington"[8]

Your aspiration to develop principled positions through inquiry, reflection, and discourse traces its ancestry back to Socrates and Aristotle. Prominent in the lineage are the founding fathers of this country, who chose ideas and reason—as well as passion combined with self-discipline—as their tools of choice to build this nation. I mentioned earlier the thinking of one of our forebears, Thomas Jefferson. Now I touch upon the life and words of another, George Washington.

The Meaning of "Liberal"

I have titled this address "On Becoming a Liberal: The Guidance of George Washington." There—I have said it. The "L" word. You know as well as I that it is a term that has fallen into disfavor in recent years in many venues. But it is a word with several meanings. One of these meanings has drawn most of the fire. That meaning is the understanding of liberalism that evolved from the New Deal and the Great Society and that seeks to "bring about greater social equality through reliance on the federal government."[9] If we look to alternate—or earlier—meanings of the word, "liberal," I believe we can find within them ideas that inspired the founding fathers of this country, including Washington, and that might still inspire us today.

If we look to its origin in the Latin *liberalis*—meaning "suitable for a freeman"—we immediately can see one reason why liberal philosophy (particularly as developed by Locke and the Scottish Enlightenment) appealed to many of the thinkers in the thirteen colonies. The *Oxford English Dictionary* gives this as its fifth meaning for the term liberal: "Favorable to constitutional changes and legal or administrative reforms tending in the direction of freedom or democracy." The third meaning—"free from restraint; free in speech or action"—is also relevant in this context.

Benjamin Franklin, Thomas Jefferson, James Madison, George Washington, and many of their contemporaries believed, as James Kloppenberg related, that the liberty they held so dear was not a vacation from restraint but a duty to govern. They understood that freedom is inextricably bound to duty—the duty to govern self and the duty to abide by the laws developed by a self-governing people.

Washington certainly lived out his belief in adherence to duty, accepting his countrymen's calls for his services as commander-in-chief of the continental force and, twice, as president—despite personal disinclination. He wrote in his Farewell Address in 1796:

> The acceptance of, and continuance hitherto, in the office to which your Suffrages have twice called me, have been a uniform sacrifice of inclination to the opinion of duty, and to a deference for what appeared to be your desire.[10]

The founding fathers also perceived a close alliance between liberty and virtue. Franklin wrote that "only a virtuous people are capable of freedom."[11] In his Farewell Address, Washington echoed this sentiment with these words: "'Tis substantially true, that virtue or morality is a necessary spring of popular government."

Virtues of Liberalism

In *The Virtues of Liberalism*, Kloppenberg describes how the central virtues of liberalism—as understood in the seventeenth and eighteenth centuries—"descend directly from the cardinal virtues of early Christianity: prudence, temperance, fortitude, and justice." He writes:

> Liberals elevated individual freedom over the acceptance of imposed hierarchy. They conceived of freedom, however, not as license but as enlightened self-interest, not as the ancient vice of egoism but as "self-interest properly understood," in the phrase of Alexis de Tocqueville. Exercising liberal freedom requires the disposition to find one's true good and to choose the proper means to it, which is the meaning of prudence. . . . They conceived of the good life, however, not as gluttony but as moderation in the enjoyment of pleasures. . .
> Liberals elevated the private life over the earlier demands of theocrats and republicans that individual citizens can find fulfillment only in, and thus must sacrifice themselves for, the good of the church or the state. They conceived of the liberal polity, however, as a legal and moral order necessary not only to protect them from each other and adjudicate their conflicts but also to enable them to achieve their goals. The liberal polity could survive only through the faithfulness of its citizens and their persistent loyalty to it—and to its procedures of resolving disputes through persuasion rather than force. . . . Finally, then, liberals elevated the rights of every citizen over the privileges and preferences of an elite. They conceived of such rights, however, as bounded by the firm command that individuals must render to God and to their neighbors what is their due, which is the meaning of justice.[12]

These central virtues of early Christianity and eighteenth-century liberalism—prudence, temperance, fortitude, and justice—are exemplified in the life and writings of George Washington. Indeed, a 1779 portrait of His Excellency General Washington by John Norman depicts Washington's image atop a pedestal on which are inscribed the words "Temperance," "Prudence," "Fortitude," and "Justice."

The liberal virtues lost much cachet in the waning decades of the twentieth century, just as the liberal impulse became blurred. Yet, they remain fundamental components to sustain a self-governing, democratic society.

It is the way he lived his life—even more so than his philosophy and thought—that made Washington a hero in his day and should make him one today as well. Richard Brookhiser made his telling of that life in *Founding Father: Rediscovering George Washington* into "a moral biography, in the tradition of Plutarch."[13] Brookhiser's goal in his work is "to shape the hearts and minds of those who read it—not by offering a list of two-hundred-year-old policy prescriptions, but by showing how a great man navigated politics and life as a public figure."[14] He notes that "When he lived, Washington had the ability to give strength to debaters and to dying men. His life still has the power to inspire anyone who studies it."[15]

Some of those sources of inspiration focus particularly on his intention to guide his countrymen toward the liberal virtues of prudence, temperance, fortitude, and justice.

Justice

Starting with the last on this list, a concern for justice influenced Washington from an early age up to the firm instructions in his Last Will and Testament that "all the Slaves which I hold in [my] own right, shall receive their free[dom]" and his provisions for the continued support of any slaves too old or infirm at the time of his death to support themselves. Like many of his compatriots, Washington chafed under certain British policies toward the colonies, which they saw as contrary to natural justice. Washington's understanding of the origin of justice in natural law was passionately stated in his letter to Bryan Fairfax in 1774: "an innate spirit of freedom first told me, that the measures, which the administration hath for some time been, and now are most violently pursuing, are repugnant to every principle of natural justice. . ."

Washington urged the citizens of the young nation to shape foreign as well as domestic policy in accord with their love of natural justice, writing in his Farewell Address: "Observe good faith and justice towds. [*sic*] all Nations. . . It will be worthy of a free, enlightened, and at no distant period, a great Nation, to give to mankind the magnanimous and too novel example of a People always guided by an exalted justice and benevolence."

Temperance

Temperance was a widely held virtue in eighteenth-century America, conveying not only the meaning mentioned by Kloppenberg—"moderation in the enjoyment of pleasures and a proper respect for the different preferences of others"[16]—but also encompassing diffidence, frugality, and evenly balanced traits of character and intellect. Personal wealth was seen both as a potential source of corruption and the means for a man to secure the independence that might render him less vulnerable to corrupting influences. Washington won great honor and elevated the high regard in which he was held by his decision to serve as commander-in-chief and as president without remuneration. His love of temperance also was exhibited in his steps to minimize or eliminate debt in his personal life and in his warning to the young nation, in his Farewell Address, to avoid "the accumulation of debt, not only by shunning occasions of expence [*sic*], but by vigorous exertions in time of Peace to discharge the Debts which unavoidable wars may have occasioned, not ungenerously throwing upon posterity the burthen which we ourselves ought to bear."

Many of Washington's biographers comment upon his well-rounded competence—his "evenly balanced traits of character and intellect." Barry Schwartz in his book, *George Washington: The Making of an American Symbol*, notes that in Washington's day, excessive intellect—or genius—was suspect, but wisdom was prized. He writes, "Almost everyone who spoke approvingly of Washington's intellect made reference to its wisdom and judiciousness and declared these attributes to be of greater value to the nation than the glittering intelligence. . ."[17]

Prudence

Kloppenberg defines "prudence" as "the disposition to find one's true good and to choose the proper means to it."[18] A more contemporary definition would be "the ability to govern and discipline oneself by the use of reason." Schwartz observes that Washington's self-control was "discovered after America had shifted from the revolutionary to an institutional mood."[19] In fact, it was essential for leading the nation to victory in the war, capturing passion and fervor for a work that had to carry beyond the war—namely, avoiding licentiousness and establishing a new government. "Self-control alone protected liberty from this kind of licentiousness. . .many Americans were quick to focus on Washington's self-control and to find in it the keystone of his character."[20]

The virtue of prudence also involves caution, circumspection, and taking steps to minimize risk. In his Farewell Address, Washington issued several cautions to the country, including the often-quoted advice to "steer clear of permanent Alliances, with any portion of the foreign world." He warns posterity to "resist with care the spirit of innovation upon" the principles of the newly formed government, adding: "In all the changes to which you may be invited, remember that time and habit are at least as necessary to fix the true character of Government, as of other human institutions. . ." His most forceful warning is to hold in check the dangers of factionalism and the tendency for one area of the government to exceed its limit of power. He acknowledged that "There is an opinion that parties in free countries are useful checks upon the Administration of the Government and serve to keep alive the spirit of Liberty." He went on to add, however:

> But in those of the popular character, in Governments purely elective, it is a spirit not to be encouraged. From their natural tendency, it is certain there will always be enough of that spirit for every salutary purpose. And there being constant danger of excess, the effort ought to be, by force of public opinion, to mitigate and assuage it. A fire not to be quenched; it demands a uniform vigilance to prevent its bursting into a flame, lest instead of warming it should consume.

Fortitude

The final of these four virtues, fortitude, in this context pertains to the loyalty of citizens to the government they have created and their intention to resolve difficulties by persuasion rather than force. Washington urges the importance of this virtue eloquently in the Farewell Address:

> This government, the offspring of our own choice uninfluenced and unawed, adopted upon full investigation and mature deliberation, completely free in its principles, in the distribution of its powers, uniting security with energy, and containing within itself a provision for its own amendment, has a just claim to your confidence and your support. Respect for its authority, compliance with its Laws, acquiescence in its measures, are duties enjoined by the fundamental maxims of true Liberty. The basis of our political systems is the right of the people to make and to alter their Constitution of Government. But the Constitution which at any time exists, 'till changed by an explicit and authentic act of the whole People, is sacredly obligatory upon all. The very idea of the power and the right of the People to establish Government presupposes the duty of every Individual to obey the established Government.

Restoring Liberal Virtues and Liberal Education

If, then, we wish to heed Washington's guidance through his life and his words to adopt the liberal virtues of prudence, temperance, fortitude, and justice, how might we today restore their value and practice?

To answer this question, we must look to yet another meaning of the word "liberal," which is the meaning listed first by the *Oxford English Dictionary*. This is the meaning used in the term "liberal arts education." Originally, "liberal" was "the distinctive epithet of those 'arts' or 'sciences' that were considered 'worthy of a free man;' opposed to servile or mechanical." A more current definition of this usage describes "the studies. . .in a college or university intended to provide chiefly general knowledge and to develop general intellectual capacities (as reason and judgment) as opposed to professional or vocational skills."

There is a strong and sure connection between liberal education and democracy—one that was held fast by many American founders. Jefferson's obsession with this connection may burn brightest in the public eye of today. And deservedly so—especially given the excellence of the university that he founded. But other founding fathers also championed the connection between education and democracy, including George Wythe, Benjamin Rush, and George Washington.

We shall not overlook Washington's efforts to establish a national university. While he did not succeed in that project, the funds left in his will for the establishment of a national university did support the founding of Washington & Lee University.

Educational leaders should engender a broad public conversation about the value of a liberal education. Why is this important? Imagine writing a letter to a young friend or relative, providing guidance for his future educational choices. You might say to a youth that education would provide valued skills, extensive knowledge, and enduring discipline to serve throughout life. However, it is still more likely that you would discuss the acquisition of character and judgment that would strengthen the youth's confidence in his own decisions. The cultivation of good habits of decision on sound moral and religious grounds is the single most important gift that education conveys. And a liberal education is the surest way to convey this gift.

In fact, Washington wrote such a letter to his nephew, George Steptoe Washington, on March 23, 1789. He does point young Washington in the direction of training for employment, writing: "The first and great object with you at present, is to acquire, by industry and application, such knowledge as your situation enables you to obtain, as will be useful to you in life." Much of the letter, however, advises the nephew on the development of character—particularly in the virtues of prudence and temperance. It is worth noting that Washington paid for his nephew's education, which leads to the final definition of the word "liberal"—"free in bestowing, bountiful, generous, open-hearted."

Washington was liberal in bestowing the gift of education upon his nephew—through his advice and example and by footing the bill for his formal education. In this, and similar practices and characteristics of Washington's life, we can identify elements that bring the comprehensive understanding of liberalism—not to resemble but—at least into the neighborhood of contemporary liberalism. Stripped of its taste for authoritarianism and a paternalistic disregard for the ordinary judgments of ordinary souls, and purged of its very recent alliance with militantly atheistic social engineering, contemporary liberalism resolves into a generous regard for the well being of our fellows.

George Washington provides the preeminently emulable model for such regard. Throughout his life he displayed large generosity and not infrequently fell susceptible to the hard-luck tale. Just as he embraced as his own mission the future prosperity of all of his countrymen, he easily assisted friends and relatives—and sometimes just fellow citizens—from his own substance. Washington believed that the liberal society would yield not just better citizens but also better human beings—the liberal wish *par excellence*. His plans and exertions to develop the western lands began with defending the rights of the troops he commanded in the French and Indian Wars but ended with his dreams of continent-wide commerce and integrated social and political life for all Americans. Thus, he expressed the liberal wish to perfection, merging the general and the particular in a mission of uplift.

Nowhere does Washington so clearly reveal these motions of his soul as in his meditations on education. As he instructed Jonathan Boucher on the education of Washington's stepson, Jack Custis, one sees him proceed from detailed care for the youth's progress in understanding and character—including a watchful eye on his immediate deportment—to an eventually frustrated attempt to urge dig-

nity and moderation on the tutor himself. Boucher eventually returned a Tory to England, from where he railed against Washington
and the fledgling United States. He had failed Washington not only
by a lax attention to young Jack's deportment but by a greedy demand for pay unearned. Education warrants adequate support, Washington believed. But he also believed that it deserves the reward of
support where it succeeds in advancing the liberal wish and not otherwise.

Washington wrote to Alexander Hamilton in 1796 that, "I mean
education generally as one of the surest means of enlightening and
givg. [*sic*] a just way of thinking to our Citizens. . ." He continued:

> But that which would render it of the highest importance, in my opinion, is, the Juvenal
> [*sic*] period of life, when friendships are formed, and habits established that will stick
> by one; the youth, or young men from different parts of the United States would be
> assembled together, and would by degrees discover that there was not that cause for
> jealousies and prejudices which one part of the Union had imbibed against another part:
> of course, *sentiments of more liberality in the general policy of the Country would
> result from it* [education]. (Emphasis added)

This argument defends Washington's proposal for a national university. No less, though, it reveals the liberal wish as tied to an expectation of "more liberality in the policy of the Country."

Washington also knew how to describe life without the nurture of
the liberal wish. In 1788, while forswearing interest in the new presi-
dency, he took the occasion further to observe the consequence of a
college faltering for lack of cash.

> This is one of the numerous evils which arise from want of a general regulating power,
> for in a Country like this where equal liberty is enjoyed, where every man may reap his
> own harvest, which by proper attention will afford him more than is necessary for his
> own consumption [thus enabling necessary generosity!], and where there is so ample a
> field for every mercantile and mechanical exertion, if there cannot be money found to
> answer the common purposes of education, not to mention the necessary commercial
> circulation, it is evident that there is something amiss in the ruling political power which
> requires a steady regulating and energetic hand to correct and control. . . . if. . .property
> was well secured, faith and justice well preserved, a stable government well adminis-
> tered, and confidence restored, the tide of population and wealth would flow to us, from
> every part of the globe, and with a due sense of the blessings, make us the happiest
> people upon the earth.

The liberal wish provides a compelling, organizing foundation
upon which to erect the public's concern with higher education. That
is the reason we have grown in confidence, that setting forth principles of intellectual and moral growth on grounds of conceded liberty, with expectations of prosperity and generosity, will secure an

education in self-government appropriate to this democracy. Upon reflection, it would be very difficult for anyone who took Washington seriously not to rediscover an impulse toward liberalism and, in the event, learn to celebrate becoming a liberal.

VI. "Women and Education"[21]

Commencement addresses celebrate the gift that members of the graduating class have earned. It may sound odd to speak of earning a gift, for is not a gift almost by definition something that is freely given? And yet, both concepts—something freely given and something earned—apply in this instance. Both matter if we are to honor fully students' substantial attainments and also place their attainments within the wider context of society.

Education *is* a gift—one that each generation offers to its offspring. We see in the education of the young the only gift we have that properly expresses our unconditional love. But education is not a gift that can be passively received. The gift of education that graduates have earned—indeed that they have created—goes far beyond the important development of their expertise. Their education has aided in the development not only of skill and intellect, but also of soul. To succeed as a health care professional, for example, it is critical to have a high degree of technical expertise in order to diagnose, treat, and help to prevent injury to and disease of the body. But the technical expertise, while necessary, is not sufficient, is it? The best health care professionals also attend to the spirit. They respect and care for the essential humanity of the patients they serve. And, they cannot deliver that level of care-giving unless they have first attended to the growth and care-taking of their own souls. Happily, a college education is one of the most fertile mediums we have for growing souls.

One particular aspect of this business of developing human beings calls for special notice—namely, women and education.

A sea change with regard to women's participation in higher education has taken place. This change may be less conspicuous at an institution in which women have long constituted a significant portion of the student body. Nevertheless, between 1970 and 1990, the number of women attending college nationwide more than doubled. In 1996, there were 8.4 million women and 6.7 million men enrolled in colleges and universities across the nation; thus, women now account for 56 percent of the enrollments. The percentage within

Virginia is even slightly higher—at 57 percent. In my prior office, Dean at James Madison College in Michigan, I worked feverishly to attract males into our college of public affairs, for our ratio was two to one. Over six years I could make but marginal progress, for I was fighting against a national tide and not merely a local phenomenon. This disparity exists despite the fact that within the 18-24-year-old age group, men slightly outnumber women. The U.S. Department of Education projects that by the year 2007, the gender gap will widen, with 6.9 million men and 9.2 million women attending college.

An article in the *New York Times* last December pointed out that, "Women outnumber men in every category of higher education: public, private, religiously affiliated, four-year, two-year. And among part-time students, older students, and African-Americans, the skew is much larger." The article speculates about some of the reasons for this gender gap, concluding that "it is probably a confluence of factors, from girls' greater success in high school to a strong economy that may give boys a sense that they can make their way without higher education, whether in computer work or the military."[22]

The focus of this article in the *Times* is on why men are not attending college in greater numbers. We would like to consider, instead, why it is that women are doing so. The social, economic, and psychological factors that lead increasing numbers of women to obtain undergraduate and post-graduate degrees cluster under two broad headings—the pull of opportunity and the push of necessity.

We have come so far as a society that it is hard to remember how limited the opportunities for women were—even so recently as twenty years ago. To be sure, long before these recent years women have demonstrated their capacities in education and in the professions. Until recently, however, few of them have entered the pathways of higher advancement. They had reasons, good reasons, and they had obstacles, bad obstacles. In just the last few decades the exertions of feminists, and still more importantly, the appeal of opportunities, opened the entranceways to profession after profession. Responsible positions are more open to women than they were before. And this progress is a good thing.

At the same time that a new social order has unlatched the doors of opportunity, a new economic order has unleashed the push of necessity. Few families today feel they can afford to rely on the income of a single breadwinner, although many single-parent families do so—not entirely by choice. The economic prosperity we enjoy today may cloud our recollection of the recession of the early 1990s, when, even two-paycheck families found it hard to make ends meet. Further, the recently booming stock market did not obviate the need, in most households, for both partners to work if they are to achieve the level of financial security they desire.

We know well the sacrifices made in families in which both parents must—or choose to—work; at minimum it becomes more difficult to provide the nurturing that children need. We could even debate whether the "fifty-hours-plus" work week that has become the norm in so many professions allows one sufficient time to nurture one's own soul, let alone to be a loving, giving partner or parent. We could also inquire whether the economic, social, and psychological factors that fuel such long work schedules have contributed to an overall decline in our communities. How can we manage, when giving so much time to the office, also to make time for church, neighborhood, and civic responsibilities? Some now ponder the relationships between these questions and the tragedy at Columbine High School.

If we were to debate these questions, we would surely hear compelling arguments both pro and con. There is, however, one question where we might readily reach consensus. Can we not agree that between the pull of opportunity and the push of necessity, women who pursue careers and raise families risk being pulled asunder? Have we, in creating this push/pull nexus, failed to allow a just estimation of the human demands that are placed on all of us, but especially on women? Have we, moreover, unwittingly created a society in which we lead divided lives, and perhaps even exist as divided selves, parceling out our time, energy, and emotion among the compartments in a fashion that leaves us feeling we must rob Peter to pay Paul and ending up by short-changing everyone, including ourselves?

We live in a divided world—one that tends to see either black or white, ignoring all the other colors and shades in between. A world that sees either man or woman. A world that insists on "either/or" rather than "both/and." One that sees reason and emotion, or care and justice, as opposites. Perhaps surprisingly to some but not unexpectedly, feminist thinkers have led the way most recently in articulating the underlying tensions involved in a push/pull world.

Alison Jaggar writes in *Gender/Body/Knowledge: Feminist Reconstructions of Being and Knowing*,

Typically, although again not invariably, the rational has been contrasted with the emotional, and this contrasted pair then has often been linked with other dichotomies. Not only has reason been contrasted with emotion, but it has also been associated with the mental, the cultural, the universal, the public, and the male, whereas emotion has been associated with the irrational, the physical, the natural, the particular, the private, and, of course, the female."[23]

But do we not find that these divisions are contrary to our fundamental human nature?

It may be that we can find answers to these questions by insisting on integrating—rather than compartmentalizing—our lives. Elizabeth Kamark Minnich suggests that "We need not choose between the life of the mind, the spirit, and the body."[24] She, and other teachers, scholars, writers, philosophers, and theologians are exploring ways to integrate our lives. Minnich offers this thought in her essay, "Can Virtue Be Taught: A Feminist Reconsiders":

A picture, a collage, a weave of many strands old and new begins to emerge, suggesting a way of thinking that is resistant, respectful, reflexive, and critical. It refuses dualistic and/or invidiously hierarchical divisions that cannot be breached in favor of distinctions within wholeness. It emphasizes transactional mutuality over oppositional relations. It explores connection, complementarity, relationality within the matrix of experience where we are called to practice both care and justice. And it struggles to retrieve and revalue all aspects of the meaning of being human, from the bodily to the rational to the transcendent, in the name of our fullest unique and common potential.[25]

M. Scott Peck, in his book, *In Search of Stones*, describes it this way:

I don't know who originally coined the term, but a few of us theologians are increasingly exalting "the Holy Conjunction." The Holy Conjunction is the word *and*. Instead of an either/or style of mentation, we are pushing for both/and thinking. We are not trying to get rid of reason but promote "Reason plus." Reason *and* mystery. Reason *and* emotion. Reason *and* intuition. Reason *and* revelation. Reason *and* wisdom. Reason *and* love.

So we are envisioning a world where a business can make a profit and be ethical. Where a government can promote political order and social justice. Where medicine can be practiced with technological proficiency and compassion. Where children can be taught science and religion. Our vision is one of integration. By integration we do not mean squashing two or more things together into a colorless, unisex blob. When we talk of integrating science and faith we are not speaking of returning to an age of primitive faith, where science is discounted, any more than we are arguing for the status quo where a limited science is idolized while faith is relegated to an hour on Sunday. The Holy Conjunction is the conjunction of integrity.[26]

If our goal then is to seek more integration within our lives, how can we best pursue that goal? We can look to women and to education for answers.

In an earlier age, women primarily bore the responsibility for ministering to our daily human needs, while men tended to the worlds of work and scientific and economic progress. While that unnatural division is no longer so rigidly maintained, its prevalence heretofore seems to have imbued women with a sense of the preponderating importance of daily human needs and an insistence that they be met. Thus it is that Barbara Ehrenreich and Deidre English could insist in their book, *For Her Own Good*, "that the human values that women were assigned to preserve expand out of the confines of private life and become the organizing principles of society." Their goal is to create

> . . .a society that is organized around human needs: a society in which. . .the nurturance and well-being of all children is a transcendent public priority. . .a society in which healing is not a commodity distributed according to the dictates of profit but is integral to the network of community life. . .[a society in which] the womanly values of community and caring must rise to the center as the only human principles.[27]

This is not a "both/and" argument. It is not "reason plus." Depreciating the transcendent values of humanity does not ennoble the daily human needs. It rather deprives humankind of worthy ambitions, ambitions to which women no less than men must be open. This opens a world of questions about our familiar conceptions of the differences between men and women. We do not pretend to answer those questions. This brief epitome of expression aims only to invoke earnest labors toward the goal of making the answering of these questions the work of worthy lives. We do not hesitate to pose this challenge, for we are ever mindful of those powerful, heroic influences that shaped our expectations of humanity. They were more often than not women. Mary McCleod Bethune visibly symbolized the value of education. Emma Delaney, at the opening of the twentieth century journeyed into Africa a missionary, with a far greater ambition than the tending of daily needs. She gave her life there in a great enterprise that was, after all, the building of a school whose influence was sustained until very recently, when civil wars engulfed the academy in the flames of discord. Cousin Emma, as she was to William Allen, was a hero to his mother and to him. We have long known that women can be heroes, and it is not amiss to ask them to answer the big questions that haunt us.

We can also look to education for answers. Most people can recall a course, a teacher, a book, or a conversation that radically altered their own understanding of what it is to be a human being and that offered an entirely new insight on the question of "How am I to become all that I might be?" That is an insight to cherish and use as a touchstone when one feels pulled assunder by the divisions of daily life. Moreover, our education about what it means to be a human being has really only just begun by the time of commencement. It is then that we commit to the work and the joy of continuing—throughout life—to explore that question, to learn new and deeper answers, and to put those reflections into action at work, at home, and in community.

We speak of women as though they were men. For these words apply no less fitly to men than to women. Together, men and women can build lives and communities that are whole and undivided. These words of a great educator, Anna Julia Cooper, writing in 1892, underscore this reality:

> . . . 'tis woman's strongest vindication for speaking that *the world needs to hear her voice* [original emphasis]. . . . The world has had to limp along with the wobbling gait and the one-sided hesitancy of a man with one eye. Suddenly the bandage is removed from the other eye and the whole body is filled with light. It sees a circle where before it saw a segment. The darkened eye restored, every member rejoices with it.[28]

VII. "Race in Twenty-First-Century America"[29]

William G. Bowen and Derek Bok wrote *The Shape of the River*[30] in order to draw conclusions regarding the long-term consequences of considering race in college and university admissions. In the long term, as the saying goes, we're all dead. More importantly for us that live now, however, the long term is the twenty-first century. Over the course of this century nothing can be more certain than that the role of race in college and university admission and employment practices must interact with the broader understanding of race in the society at large. As has occurred heretofore, colleges and universities will be as much led as leading. It is therefore timely (if not behind time) to inquire where our deliberations and our practices are leading us.

Of the many studies that have appeared in recent times (one thinks especially of Thernstrom and Thernstrom's *America in Black and White*) surely Bowen and Bok can command pride of place for the most energetic defense of carrying "race sensitivity" forward from the twentieth century into the twenty-first century. This is all the more relevant inasmuch as they endorse the Thernstroms' argument that the real question of race in America is the question of relations between blacks and whites. They do this only tacitly. Nevertheless, *The Shape of the River* is as much structured around such an expectation as is *America in Black and White*. Bowen and Bok, however, defend this as a good thing, building on the assumption that compelling need and desirable consequences suffice as justifications.

We may take Bowen and Bok's account of where we are and how we got there, accordingly, as a meaningful index of the foundation from which we should reason. We may do so all the more inasmuch as they agree with the Thernstroms about the latter question, how we got where we are: namely, a vigorous program of race preferences at least in college admissions. As they do, we will also take their statement as a proxy for where society is today. The goal is to indicate the continuing role that race may play in the next century. To arrive at that view, we will rehearse the course of decisions regarding the present that serve to project future choices.

Everyone concedes a history of racial trauma in the United States. Most concede that much of that racial trauma has been remediated, through trials to be sure, by successive and progressive efforts towards inclusion. However, since at least the mid-sixties many have hotly debated the future course and necessity of continuing efforts of remediation. Much of that debate derives from diverse perspectives about two things. First, some maintain while others doubt that racism—the source of racial traumas—remains a substantial life determining element of American society; secondly, some maintain while others doubt that American blacks can advance within American society only by means of special aids. These two perspectives are the crucial elements for determining policy, although other matters will frequently surface as justification for one or the other policy preference. The best example of the latter is the debate about the "preparedness" of American blacks for participation in society, stemming not from renewed deprivations but from the "lingering effects" of past deprivations. This argument in particular accounts for the passion devoted to the issue of "diversity," although that argument has been generalized to many ethnic and racial groups in order to dilute the divisive effects it has when discussed directly as commentary on the relations between blacks and whites. Thus, the emergence of a "principle" of diversity, while defended within the academy as an independent value, speaks far less to any rigorously demonstrated intellectual proposition than to a moral determination to act upon the basis of conclusions drawn about the relative status of American blacks.

The reasons people choose to defend their postures or policy choices, however, bear far less weight than the consistent actions they take. As Alexander Hamilton remarked in *The Federalist Papers*, we are not privileged to know the interior sentiments of participants in public debates, and we may be quite certain that, whatever their motives, many will be the persons who stand variously on the right and wrong sides of important questions for reasons good and ill. Some will attack affirmative action from the purest motives, some from the worst; still others will defend affirmative action from the purest motives, others from the worst. There is no tool we possess that will enable us to sort them out.

What we can do, accordingly, is to weigh the actual circumstances as far as we can determine them and reason openly about their implications. In that respect we are well advised to begin from the well-founded assumption that the twentieth century closed with a vigorous regime of race sensitivity that has spawned several race-regarding policies and practices. Within colleges and universities this extends from admissions and financial aid to teaching and public service. We do not affect to assess how well these initiatives fare in general with regard to their stated intentions. Rather, we focus on the best claims in their defense and inquire whether, conceding those claims, they suffice to describe a future course to which we ought subscribe.

Bowen and Bok provide those best claims. Looking at twenty-eight highly selective colleges and universities, public and private, they maintain that a *system* of race preferences has served to ameliorate life circumstances for black graduates, to assimilate white graduates and black graduates alike to an integrated culture, and to improve the intellectual climate on these campuses. Their methodology is straightforward: beginning from the acknowledgement that these highly selective institutions admitted students who could not have claimed admissions on their "merits" as normally conceived, they recognize that they have engendered cohorts of students who constitute test pools to determine the effects of such practices. The effects to be tested focus on the contested points of contemporary race theories: stigmatization effects, social cohesion effects, professional development effects, and civic engagement effects, to name the most significant. Moreover, they compared their test cohorts against national coordinates in order to measure the degree of "improvement" they could identify. Thus, preferentially admitted students fared better, they maintain, than they could have done had they rather attended the institutions to which their "merits" had entitled entry.

Now, this picture fairly well sums up where we are. Acknowledging that the face of American society is changing, the argument is that it does so in *some* direct proportion to the strength of deliberate efforts of racial inclusion. Moreover, the tendency of these efforts, according to Bowen and Bok, is gradually to attenuate the need for continuing race sensitivity. They profess themselves agnostic regarding the length of time that will be required for this process to approach evanescence, but it is clear that the path is asymptotic. Still more importantly, they insist that the alternative is persistent and asymmetric separation. They do not answer whether parallel development or growing inequality is the meaning of asymmetric separation, an important question indeed but one that has received no rigorous analysis anywhere. This excluded alternative, parallel development, serves as a useful litmus for assessing where we are. For every argument in favor of inclusion constitutes a denial either of the practicality or the acceptability of parallel development. Historically, of course, assimilation occurs not from efforts of deliberate inclusion but in the context of social "bleedings" across parallel lines—thus the patterns of assimilation among Mexican-Americans in the Southwest and especially in California, but no doubt true of immigrants in general.

The question of where we are today, the era of race sensitivity, is primarily a question, therefore, of whether eventual assimilation or permanent "diversity" is the likeliest consequence. Bowen and Bok implicitly acknowledge this by asking their 1976 and 1989 cohorts from the highly selective colleges and universities whether, while in college, they managed to get to know well "two or more" minority or majority students (in the case where the student was the "other"). As an index of assimilation this is perhaps only slightly less pallid than the old expression, "some of my best friends are. . ." Nonetheless, it does represent the principle that assimilation is the goal. Let us conclude, therefore, that the best way to answer the question of where we are today is in the form of some approximation to a degree of assimilation. Because assimilation necessarily means a declining consciousness of otherness, then the measure would have to be, in some fashion, an assessment of the declining significance of race.

Do colleges and universities today suggest a declining significance of race in the practices and atmospheres of the academy?

Bowen and Bok's own study, measuring cohorts from 1951, 1976, and 1989, shows without ambiguity that the more recent the college experience the greater the sense of racial consciousness that prevails. It takes the form of a desire for "more" rather than "less" emphasis on diversity in college programming and curricula. But "diversity" means simply "difference," and in that context the desire expressed must express rather a heightened than a diminished consciousness of the differences between races. This should not be surprising, for it is manifest in the arguments of Bowen and Bok themselves that they retain a heightened racial consciousness. They make ready judgments about the capacities of black students based on their test scores and grade point averages, even in a work that allows that such indices ought not to be dispositive. In short, they are on the horns of a dilemma. The harder they argue that black students bring other indications of ability than the spare lexical measures admissions offices typically employ, the more they see those "other" measures as evidence of some kind of inferiority. (Thus, it could not have occurred to them, for example, to test the performance of black students with 1100 SAT scores against other students with 1100 SAT scores, which would seem the most reasonable way to assess the relative performance of students specially admitted.) They do not seem able to maintain both that there are "other" measures and that those "other" measures are personal strengths (as opposed to mere environmental data from the knowledge of which white students may benefit). They seem to have trouble seeing blacks as peers, even though they know that the highly selective institutions they studied included in their cohorts black students whose lexical measures placed them at the top of their classes both coming in and going out. It is the heightened sense of racial consciousness, founded in expectations of neediness in black students, that obscures the accomplishments of the strongest students on ordinary measures. Oddly enough, the same thing happened in slavery, where specific superiorities of individual slaves had to be obscured because the fields in which slaves labored had to be constricted and those human attributes were too large for that narrow stage. Where we are today is in a regime of heightened race consciousness that flattens out differences among black students for the sake of social goals.

Much of the argument for diversity today is predicated on the assumption of widening diversity in the future. It is said that America of the twenty-first century will be a nation (or at least a large part of it) with a majority of minorities. That argument, too, abstracts from, if it does not deny, the nature of assimilation. Apart from the refusal to acknowledge increasing rates of interracial marriage (of the sort that leads many thoughtful Jews to wonder if they will disappear as a coherent social group in the United States), the argument operates on the assumption that the changing complexion of society will not, in fact, move in the direction of the major constitutive element of the blend, which remains American whites. It is highly instructive that, until the United States government attracted large numbers of Indians back to reservations with large dollar payments, the population numbers had dwindled drastically. Many who had been away from the reservation—as many who still are—lived ably as white citizens in America. The extraordinary diversity of Hispanic extractions readily enables them to move similarly into the center of white America, and not only on account of intermarriage. In short, what is called "white America" is typically far out of date, leading to false assumptions about what the future may look like. Whatever the typical complexions of individuals may look like, it is far more likely that the vast majority in twenty-first century America will remain "white" than that it will become anything else.

The sole reservation affecting this observation is the incentive-laden preference regime that induces some incontestably "white" citizens to seek recognition as "other" for the sake of competing for benefits or entitlements thus reserved. It is certainly imaginable that a society might "purchase" heightened differentiation among social sub-groups through an incentive structure of that nature. Have we not already observed this phenomenon in microcosm on college and university campuses, on which students not only argue about the legitimacy of theme houses and "interest" groups but also compete to qualify for the recognition? It is fair to say, however, that what we observe on the campuses is only skin deep, and not yet an indication of what the larger society will embrace.

Though it is not inconceivable that society at large could foster differentiation in preference to assimilation, it is questionable whether present tendencies, the inertial thrust toward assimilation encouraged by open intercourse, commercial and otherwise, can be overcome by anything less than a powerful command and control structure dedicated to the purpose. In light of that observation it would not be unreasonable to surmise that America in the twenty-first century will continue lumbering toward assimilation. The pertinent question next in order is the extent to which that process will encompass American blacks. For surely the most powerful and pervasive command structures enforcing differentiation have long been concentrated on American blacks.

This question may not be answered in the context of responding to inquiries about the viability of color blindness. The opposite of race sensitivity is not necessarily color blindness. As we indicated above, this is far more a matter of whether unregulated, parallel development is viable. It is not the color sensitivity of Bowen and Bok that poses a problem; it is the intrusiveness that seeks to direct development. For if that intrusiveness is generalized throughout society, it would surely require the existence of command structures that bear on every aspect of life the same force that the highly selective colleges and universities impose on their campus lives.

Placing matters in perspective, we may ask what are the implications for the 3,000 colleges and universities not included in the Bowen and Bok study. Their claim that they do so much more for black students (because of their elite status) and therefore for America than do the other institutions must surely leave in doubt the no less vigorous regime of racial preferences practiced throughout most of American higher education. Either we are to hold that all such efforts are similarly valuable, though relatively less so, or we are to hold that other institutions are chasing a goal they will never attain. On the model of the elite institutions, they are to pursue a regime of race sensitivity, although they shall never produce leaders, thinkers, and citizens of the same high quality. They are to heighten race consciousness at lower levels of attainment. It is difficult to imagine that this process can eventuate in anything other than a pattern of stratification that strongly resembles segregation, or assignment of place based on race. Remember the Bowen and Bok argument: students who are "entitled" to places in the lesser institutions are being taken into the elite institutions. Correlatively, students being admitted to the lesser institutions must be no less elevated beyond their "entitlements" at least to some degree. And this process continues throughout the system of higher education. At each stage we find, not students making their own way on the basis of their own claims, but students assigned a social place.

This portrait is, of course, overdrawn. It is overdrawn, however, not because it is false to the claims of Bowen and Bok, but because their claims are false. And here is where we find the key to answer the question regarding race in the twenty-first century. In fact, the twenty-eight highly selective colleges and universities represented in *The Shape of the River* do practice extensive racial preferences. They do so in the hope that they are making a contribution to society at large. However, there is no support in this extensive study (the data files are not made available, so we can only reason from the results reported) for the proposition that, by practicing such preferences, they are, in fact, realigning American society. This is intimated in Bowen and Bok's retort to Thomas Sowell's observation that strengthened recruiting could fill their classes with just as many qualified black applicants as the "unqualified" applicants they now admit. Their response is that all colleges use extensive data files and write to every qualified student in the country. That is a surprising and entirely unsatisfactory response. We who know anything about college recruitment and the patterns of visits know quite well how little it suffices merely to write to prospective students, and particularly in the case where the student may not even have envisioned prospects of entering a highly selective institution.

It is a spirit of self-congratulation alone that could persuade serious administrators that their admissions offices are making serious efforts to identify qualified students of special characteristics. The fact is that they spend precious little time at all in *dedicated* efforts to reach such students and tend rather to concentrate their attentions on a relative handful of high schools and known venues for recruiting. Nor do they exert themselves very greatly to fish in waters where it is evident most fish are. In short, their efforts are driven far more by preconceived notions of what constitutes likely sources of recruits and the understandable need to cultivate known sources of continuing enrollments.

Race sensitivity in college admissions proves to be a path of least resistance substitute for real effort to identify qualified students. In that sense it suggests, unfortunately, that a good deal of the talk about inclusion is more rhetoric than real. That unfortunate result, however, holds good news for America and race in the twenty-first century. The fact that institutions and their leaders are not, in fact, doing what they claim to do suggests that they may prove, in the end, to be less harmful to social mores than would otherwise appear to be the case. In a very real sense, they are less intrusive than they could be, and have adopted a de facto "let them be" policy.

Whatever hope there is for America in the twenty-first century probably derives far more from the likely failures of ill-conceived social initiatives in the twentieth century than from any positive results to be expected from those initiatives. A society dedicated to the proposition that all men are created equal cannot long endure on the supposition that some men cannot rise to the challenge of equality. In the society at large every indication is that this lesson begins to take root. The emerging pattern of court decisions on affirmative action suggests that the Powell fig-leaf of "diversity" will soon lose its power to hide the reality of affirmative action erected in higher education and elsewhere. The likelihood that voters elsewhere will eventually follow the California Proposition 209 pattern seems sufficiently founded to suggest that we will, as a society, look for new ways to ground our fondest social hopes. In that context, what the twenty-first century offers is the prospect of renewed deliberation, with the ground now laid to make respect rather than assumptions of inferiority the basis of that deliberation.

As the twenty-first century closes race should have receded as a meaningful social datum in the United States. The reason for this is that the society—like higher education—will have abandoned nostrums of declining social value in favor of more direct pursuits. It will become more important to justify education in terms of its intrinsic worth rather than as a totem of social rectification. The Bowen and Bok at the end of the next century will be far less concerned with whether black students and white students knew each other than with whether they studied and learned. Institutional performance will replace institutional profession as the index of value. Nor, for that matter, will it be likely that the succeeding presidents of Princeton and Harvard in the twenty-first century will be in much position to orchestrate their student bodies to indulge favored social theories— at least, they will not be able to do so and at the same time remain educational leaders in a world that has been shaped by emerging technologies and knowledge applications that are quite unforgiving of unessential distractions.

The country it seems is leading higher education rather than the reverse. Ordinary citizens will likely have voted out racial preferences long before any college or university declares that it intends to operate without them. That is itself a most chilling reflection, given the pretensions that we have long nursed in higher education. The University of Massachusetts at Amherst's recent announcement in this respect, we are reminded, follows only upon a calculated decision by litigants not to appeal a court decision that invalidated racial preferences in a Boston school and was binding on the University.

It is of some moment for us now to reflect on what will become of important social matters that colleges and universities have handled so badly, as they are being taken out of their hands. The greatest danger we face is that, when we lose the struggle to defend the maximum argument (complete race sensitivity in academic programming), that we will abandon even the minimal decencies. The minimal decencies include acknowledging that law and justice require the commitment of resources and energies to assure that equal opportunity operates not only abstractly but also in practice. That means moving beyond self-congratulation and establishing vital links with extensive communities that can communicate the existence of opportunity. Colleges and universities must substitute principles and practices of attraction for the lazy practice of preferences in order to assure, not diversity but real opportunity for talented students of all backgrounds to benefit from their offerings. For example, it is rather remarkable that institutions that were so generally founded by and in churches should betray so obtuse an ignorance of this most pervasive foundation in our society as a recruiting ground. It is permitted to offer hope. One only needs to imagine that hope may be an incentive to worthy conduct in order to benefit from it. Race in the twenty-first century will recede as an issue in proportion as hope emerges as a promise.

VIII. "Doing Good by Knowing What You Are Doing"[31]

Honors convocations, perhaps more than any other venue, can join non-ironically in Abraham Lincoln's Gettysburg claim, that the "world will little note nor long remember what we say here today." The world should long remember, however, the high efforts that inspire such moments. For they give rise to serious reflection on the topic, "doing good by knowing what you're doing."

First of all, do no harm.

There is perhaps no more awe inspiring professional ethic. This foundation of the Hippocratic Oath tells us more than that benevolence is a guiding star of human regard for other humans. It speaks not only to intentions that are well founded but also to the standards of knowledge and understanding that must inform the best intentions. To gain confidence that in any endeavor affecting other human beings one's effort will do no harm, one must also attain knowledge sufficient to warrant such confidence.

We are mindful of this powerful oath—not because we have any reservations about your intentions but because we are much aware of the ends to which we dedicate learning. We seek to learn most of all in order to strengthen capacities to do good. We act on the assumption that we understand that goodness is the offspring of knowledge. Experience, however, often belies the assumption.

It is altogether conceivable that ignorance is what accounts for the gap between experience and intention. But it requires only a little learning to come to appreciate that. However knowledge informs action, there is no knowledge sufficient to ward off every eventuality, whether from chance or from the diversity of human sentiments and understandings. Or, to put the matter more concretely, we will sometimes do harm to others even when we try hardest to avoid doing any harm. There are none of the human frailties that mere knowledge alone can improve upon, for we are fallible and will err even in our best moods.

Why, then, do we celebrate distinctive accomplishments with honor, if we know that our actions are often as nearly sad failures as they are happy successes? We celebrate them to foster our resolve. With Abraham Lincoln, we believe that what counts in human life is far more the honor deserved than the honor received. When we have so conducted ourselves as to deserve honor, no degree of failure can tarnish the honor we shall have earned. Nor will unhappy consequences do so, for personal happiness is not the standard of honor. Before we celebrate successes, therefore, let us recall that it is far less the accomplishment or the success than the effort brought to it that qualifies for this honor. So it was with the brave few at Thermopylae, the dozen or so Spartans who warded off the thousands of Xerxes until finally those brave few fell. Their honor lay not in their success (though they purchased precious time for the Greeks) but in their sacrifice.

No one can reflect upon the honors won by the Spartan soldiers without recognizing that there is some tension between honor and mere personal happiness. When happiness becomes not the reward of a life well lived but the immediate goal of our every exertion, we are least of all likely to embrace self-sacrifice in an hour of need. Yet, what would the mother be who could not give her life itself for the sake of her child? Nor could a mother capable of such sacrifice ever be regarded as thinking nothing more important than personal enjoyments. In this case we behold the true measure of honor: it results from those attainments (or at least the efforts to reach them) by which we measure not our own happiness but the excellences before which we bow. Honor we behold clearly only when we revolve it in the light of human ends greater than ourselves. Because there is never any shame in seeking ends greater than ourselves, we may win honor even when we fail of our goal. It is the goal we seek that distinguishes our effort. It is the sacrifice we are willing to make that secures our effort.

Nor should honor be confused with fame. While honor brings good reputation, good reputation does not bring honor. A youth perhaps more nerdy than desired, might avoid the attentions of honor and reputation, on the fear that it was a kind of contemptible braggadocio. Eventually one learns, however, that one can scarcely become meaningfully human without being moved by the desire for honor. For to be so moved is to bow before the claims of human excellence as a test of one's own right to exist. Honor invokes those aspects of the soul that tamp out the distractions of mere enjoyments. To that extent it needs no fame to maintain its claim. When it does, in fact, win fame, as this convocation in a small way acknowledges, that gives testimony only that humanity cannot fail to be compelled by honor. The Spartan soldiers won fame not by seeking it but by being truly Spartan. Perhaps they failed to stop the Persians, but they did not fail to uphold the virtue of Sparta.

When we recognize all of the efforts that deserve honor, including those that do not eventuate in mentioned prizes, we press upon higher education heightened standards of accomplishments. In fact, we should take a cue from athletics, in which we habitually push individuals to the point of failure in order to take the measure of their abilities. Our champions work hardest and longest, never stopping until they fail (which is generally long after everyone else has failed). What we accomplish with such standards is improved performance from everyone.

Where improved performance counts most is in life trials, those occasions on which even we cannot sustain our devotion to cherished ideals, when the race outruns us. To meet with divorce and yet maintain a commitment to the moral standard that abhors divorce; to err with childbirth out of marriage and yet refuse to justify it by denying the knowledge that it is wrong; and to slip in attention to moral duty without ducking the knowledge that we knew better: that is to retain the capacity to deserve honor.

Nor are such considerations merely personal. All of our lives are intertwined with those important moments of community and national decision-making that make us alternately benefactors and scourges of mankind. First of all, do no harm, we say. But nowhere do we find it so difficult to avert the likelihood of doing harm as in those occasions when our sentiments sustain policies that degrade or injure our fellows. There, too, the standard of knowledge must prevail if we are to adhere to a steady course of moral development—and what else is education for if not for consistent moral development? For Americans that challenge is often framed in international crises. May we mention Rwanda? Kosovo? One must question not only what the official presentations suggest, but also what the likelihood of human affairs entails. Recall the case of American intervention in Haiti, which was preceded by deliberate but unavowed efforts on the part of American officials to generate a refugee crisis that would provide a pretext for intervention. We must ask what our obligations are in such cases.

Similarly, in the case of affirmative action we observe that the University of California has now approximated the levels of enrollment for black students it previously attained while practicing preferences. Although the people of California ended preferential admissions, the University has discovered the means to maintain opportunities for black students. More importantly, those students now are even better prepared for college than were the students previously admitted. The key to the situation seems to be the redoubled effort the University has had to undertake in the form of outreach and the careful review of student files. They simply have been forced to pay more attention to the human beings, as if they really cared about them.

These results suggest that not all was well with the practice of racial preferences, that perhaps it was a remedy embraced too readily with the intention of doing good and with too little attention to the injunction to do no harm. This is a case in which knowledge of the people whom we affect to influence, direct, or control bears most importantly on our ability to act for good while avoiding harm. It demonstrates that the knowledge of the race to be run counts for as much as, if not more than, the ability to run the race.

An honors convocation is indeed a celebration, but not a trivial matter. Rather, nothing in our academic lives bears greater importance, for nothing else bears so importantly on the purpose of academic endeavors. Higher education engages all of us in the necessary work of celebrating honors attained, but doing so in an atmosphere that reminds us constantly of the importance of nurturing the human gifts that make such honors possible. In turn, that entails conveying a vision of the future of higher education that will redeem the very efforts by which we might distinguish ourselves.

Notes

1.   Remarks delivered to the Faculty of the Virginia Commonwealth University Library, University Student Commons, Virginia Commonwealth University, Richmond, Virginia, May 20, 1999.
2.   S. Schielfelbein, "Editor's Odyssey: Gleanings from Articles and Editorials by N. C." *Saturday Review* (April 15, 1978): 12-20.
3.   Gertrude Himmelfarb, "Revolution in the Library," *The American Scholar* 66 (Spring 1997): 203.
4.   Delivered to the Foreign Language Association of Virginia, Fairview Park Marriott, Falls Church, Virginia, November 6, 1998.
5.   Commencement Address, E. Stuart Grant Convocation Center, Averett College, Danville, Virginia, December 12, 1998.
6.   Thomas Wolfe, *The Web and the Rock* (London: Heinemann, 1969), 431.
7.   Commencement Address, ECPI College of Technology, Chrysler Hall, Virginia Beach, Virginia, May 22, 1999.
8.   Atlas Economic Research Foundation, 30th International Workshop: "New Technologies and Public Policy," Farmington Country Club, Charlottesville, Virginia, August 29, 1998. Previously published in *The Locke Luminary* 2 (Summer 1999): 3-14, and reprinted here with permission.
9.   James T. Kloppenberg, *The Virtues of Liberalism* (New York: Oxford University Press, 1998), 10.
10.   All Washington quotations in this address are taken from Allen, *George Washington: A Collection.*
11.   Kloppenberg, 35.
12.   Ibid., 5-6.
13.   Richard Brookhiser, *Founding Father: Rediscovering George Washington* (New York: The Free Press, 1996), 11.
14.   Ibid., 12.
15.   Ibid., 13.
16.   Kloppenberg, 5.
17.   Barry Schwartz, *George Washington: The Making of an American Symbol* (New York: The Free Press, 1987), 162.
18.   Kloppenberg, 5.
19.   Schwartz, 167.
20.   Ibid., 167.
21.   Commencement Address, College of Health Sciences, Roanoke Civic Center Arena, Roanoke, Virginia, May 14, 1999.
22.   "Women Increasingly Outnumber Men at Colleges and Universities," *New York Times* (6 December 1998): I, 1-3.

23.   Alison M. Jaggar, "Love and Knowledge: Emotion in Feminist Epistemology," in Alison M. Jaggar and Susan R. Bordo, eds., *Gender/Body/Knowledge: Feminist Reconstructions of Being and Knowing* (New Brunswick, NJ: Rutgers University Press, 1989), 145.

24.   Elizabeth Kamarck Minnich, "Can Virtue Be Taught? A Feminist Reconsiders," in Barbara Darling-Smith, ed., *Can Virtue Be Taught?* (Notre Dame, IN: University of Notre Dame Press, 1993), 79.

25.   Ibid., 81.

26.   M. Scott Peck, *In Search of Stones: A Pilgrimage of Faith, Reason, and Discovery* (New York: Hyperion, 1995), 369.

27.   Barbara Ehrenreich and Deidre English, *For Her Own Good: 150 Years of the Experts' Advice to Women* (Garden City, NY: Anchor Press/Doubleday, 1978), 292.

28.   Anna Julia Cooper, *A Voice from the South* (New York: Negro Universities Press, 1969), 121-23. Quoted in Minnich, 83-84.

29.   Presented at the National Conference of the American Association of Higher Education, Washington, D. C., March 22, 1999.

30.   William G. Bowen and Derek Bok, *The Shape of the River: Long-Term Consequences of Considering Race in College and University Admissions* (Princeton, NJ: Princeton University Press, 1998).

31.   Honor's Convocation, Chicago Hall, Saint Paul's College, Lawrenceville, Virginia, April 14, 1999.

Bibliography

"Actual Versus Predicted Institutional Graduation Rates for 1100 Colleges and Universities." *Postsecondary Education Opportunity* 58 (April 1997): 1-8.

Adelman, Clifford. *Answers in the Tool Box.* Produced for the U.S. Department of Education, Office of Education Research and Improvement. Jessup, MD: Education Publications Center, 1999.

_____. "Crosscurrents and Riptides." *Change* 31 (January/February 1999): 20-27.

_____. "Diversity: Walk the Walk, and Drop the Talk." *Change* 29 (July/August 1997): 34-46.

_____. "To Help Minority Students, Raise Their Graduation Rates." *Chronicle of Higher Education* 45 (September 4, 1998): B8.

_____. "What Proportion of College Students Earn a Degree?" *AAHE Bulletin* 51 (October 1998): 7-9.

Allen, W. B. "The Challenges of Academic Leadership." *The Clarion* 4 (November/December 1999): 12-35.

_____. "Excellence in Judgement: The Curriculum." In Herzberg, A. M., and Krupka, I., eds. *Statistics, Science and Public Policy. V. Society, Science and Education.* Proceedings of the Conference on Statistics, Science and Public Policy, Herstmonceux Castle, Hailsham, U.K., April 26-29, 2000. Kingston, Ontario: Queen's University, 2001.

_____. *George Washington: A Collection.* Indianapolis: Liberty Classics, 1988.

_____. "On Becoming a Liberal: Guidance of George Washington." *The Locke Luminary* 2 (Summer 1999): 3-14.

_____. "Taking the Final Steps in Raising Academic Standards." *Virginia Issues and Answers* (Winter 1998): 18-21.

_____. "The Truth About Citizenship: An Outline." *Cardozo Journal of International and Comparative Law* 4 (Summer 1996): 355-372.

American Academy for Liberal Education. "The Academy's Education Standards." <http://www.aale.org/edstand.htm> (October 23, 2001).

American Association of State Colleges and Universities. *The 1999 Public Policy Agenda.* New York: AASC&U, 1999.

Anderson, Charles W. "Pragmatism, Idealism, and the Aims of Liberal Education." In Orrill, Robert, ed. *Education and Democracy: Re-imagining Liberal Learning in America.* New York: The College Board, 1997.

Armour, Richard. *The Academic Bestiary.* New York: William Morrow & Company, Inc., 1974.

231

Balch, Stephen, and Rita Clara Zurcher. *The Dissolution of General Education, 1914-1993*. Princeton, NJ: National Association of Scholars, 1996.

Baldwin, James. "A Talk to Teachers." *The Saturday Review* 46 (December 21, 1963): 42-44, 60.

Baliles, Gerald L. "In Mills Godwin's Legacy: Lessons for Today's Virginians." *The Virginia Newsletter* 74 (July 1998).

Barnett, Ronald. *Higher Education: A Critical Business*. Bristol, PA: SRHE and Open University Press, 1997.

Baron, Brita. "Summary of the Country-Specific Issues or Concerns." Paper delivered at the conference on "Global Higher Education: Common Benefits, Common Responsibilities," organized by the Academy for Educational Development and the Institute for Higher Education Policy. Washington, D. C., August 19, 1999.

Barton, Paul E., and Richard J. Coley. *Growth in Schools: Achievement Gains from the Fourth to the Eighth Grade*. Princeton, NJ: Educational Testing Service, 1998.

Bateson, Mary Catherine. *Composing a Life*. New York: Penguin Group, 1990.

Benjamin, Robert, et al. *The Redesign of Governance in Higher Education*. Rand Corporation, February 1993.

Bledstein, Burton J. *The Culture of Professionalism: The Middle Class and the Development of Higher Education in America*. New York: W. W. Norton & Company, 1970.

Bloom, Allan. *L'Âme désarmée*. Translated by Paul Alexandre. Paris: Julliard, 1987.

————. *The Closing of the American Mind*. New York: Simon & Schuster, 1987.

Bonevac, Daniel. "Leviathan U." In Dickman, Howard, ed. *The Imperiled Academy*. New Brunswick, NJ: Transaction Publishers, 1993.

Bowen, Roger W. "The New Battle Between Political and Academic Cultures." *Chronicle of Higher Education* 47 (June 22, 2001): B14-15.

Bowen, William G., and Derek Bok. *The Shape of the River: Long-term Consequences of Considering Race in College and University Admissions*. Princeton, NJ: Princeton University Press, 1998.

Boyer Commission on Undergraduate Education. *Reinventing Undergraduate Education: A Blueprint for America's Research Universities*. Stony Brook: State University of New York, Stony Brook, 1996.

Brigham Young University. *The Mission of Brigham Young University and the Aims of a BYU Education*. Provo, UT: Brigham Young University, 1955.

Brookhiser, Richard. *Founding Father: Rediscovering George Washington*. New York: The Free Press, 1996.

Buchanan, James M., and Nicos E. Devletoglu. "Students: Consumers Who Do Not Buy." In Buchanan, James M., and Devletoglu, Nicos E., eds. *Academia in Anarchy*. New York: Basic Books, 1970.

Burke, Joseph C., and Shahpar Modarresi. *Performance Funding and Budgeting: Popularity and Volatility*. The Third Annual Survey. Albany, NY: The Nelson A. Rockefeller Institute of Government, 1999.

Butler, Nicolas Murray. "A University Defined." *The Reference Shelf* 7. Edited by James Goodwin Hodgson. New York: H. W. Wilson Company, 1931.

Buxbaum, Peter A. "Lower Costs, Fewer Choices." *Transportation & Distribution* 36 (December 1995): 48-54.

Callan, Patrick M., and Joni E. Finney, eds. *Public and Private Financing of Higher Education: Shaping Public Policy for the Future.* Phoenix, AZ: Oryx Press for the American Council on Education, 1977.

Callan, Patrick M. "Reframing Access and Opportunity: Problematic State and Federal Higher Education Policy in the 1990s." In Heller, Dolnald E., ed. *The States and Public Higher Education Policy: Affordability, Access and Accountability.* Baltimore: John Hopkins University Press, 2001.

Characteristics of Excellence in Higher Education: Standards for Accreditation. 1994 ed. Philadelphia: Commission on Higher Education Middle States Association, 1994.

Cheney, Lynne V. *Fifty Hours: A Core Curriculum for College Students.* Washington, D. C. : National Endowment for the Humanities, 1989.

Coffin, Henry Sloan, "Timeless Elements in Education." In Fairchild, Henry Pratt, ed. *The Obligations of Universities to the Social Order.* New York: New York University Press, 1933.

Cole, Luella. *The Background for College Teaching.* New York: Farrar and Rinehart, 1940.

Coles, Robert. *The Call of Service: A Witness to Idealism.* Boston: Houghton Mifflin Co., 1993.

The College Board. *Trends in Pricing, 2000/01.* New York: The College Board, 2000. <http://www.collegeboard.org/press/ cost00/html/Trends inPricing2K.pdf> (June 23, 2001).

The Commonwealth Foundation of Virginia. "Assessment of Higher Education Enrollment Estimates in the Commonwealth of Virginia." (February 1, 1995).

"Controversy over Charges by Stanford Prompts Critical Review of Entire Indirect-Cost System." *Chronicle of Higher Education* 37 (April 3, 1991): A22.

Cooper, Anna Julia. *A Voice from the South.* New York: Negro Universities Press, 1969.

Council for Aid to Education. Commission on National Investment in Higher Education. *Breaking the Social Contract: The Fiscal Crisis in Higher Education.* N.p.: Rand Corporation, 1997.

Darvas, Peter. "Higher Education Reform in Hungary: Current Priorities and Strategies." Paper delivered at the conference on "Global Higher Education: Common Benefits, Common Responsibilities," organized by the Academy for Educational Development and the Institute for Higher Education Policy. Washington, D.C., August 19, 1999.

Davies, Gordon K. "Education is Not a *Trivial* Business, a *Private* Good, or a *Discretionary* Expenditure; It is a Deeply *Ethical* Undertaking at Which We *Must* Succeed if We Are to Survive as a *Free* People: Twenty Years of Higher Education in Virginia." Richmond: State Council of Higher Education for Virginia, 1997. <http://www.schev.edu/wumedia/gordon.html> (April 13, 2001).

Diamond, Robert M. "Broad Curriculum Reform is Needed if Students Are to Master Core Skills." *The Chronicle of Higher Education* 43 (August 1, 1997): B7.

Dickman, Howard, ed., *The Imperiled Academy*. New Brunswick, NJ: Transaction Publishers, 1993.

"Discounting and Its Discontents: The Cost of Maintaining Enrollment." *Change* 26 (July-August 1994): 33-37.

Drucker, Peter. "The Information Executives Truly Need." In *Harvard Business Review on Measuring Corporate Performance*. Cambridge: Harvard Business School Press, 1991 [1998].

DuBois, W. E. B. *Darkwater: Voices from Within the Veil*. New York: Schocken Books, 1972.

_____. "The Hampton Idea." In Aptheker, Herbert, ed. *The Education of Black People*. Amherst: University of Massachusetts Press, 1973.

Eccles, Robert G. "The Performance Measurement Manifesto." In *Harvard Business Review on Managing Corporate Performance*. Cambridge: Harvard Business School Press, 1991 [1998].

"Education: Investment in Human Capital." First National City Bank of New York *Monthly Economic Letter* (August 1965). In Lineberry, William P., ed. *Colleges at the Crossroads*. New York: The H. W. Wilson Company, 1966.

Ehrenreich, Barbara, and Deidre English. *For Her Own Good: 150 Years of the Experts' Advice to Women*. Garden City, NY: Anchor Press/Doubleday, 1978.

Fife, Jonathan D., and Steven M. Janosik. "Defining and Ensuring Quality in Higher Education in Virginia." *Virginia Issues and Answers* 6 (Spring 1999): 22-27.

Finifter, David, et al., eds. *The Uneasy Public Policy Triangle in Higher Education: Quality, Diversity and Budgetary Efficiency*. New York: American Council on Education and Macmillan Publishing Co., 1991.

Finn, Chester E., and Bruno V. Manno. "What's Wrong with the American University?" *Wilson Quarterly* 20 (Winter 1996): 45-60.

Finn, Jeremy D. "Opportunity Offered—Opportunity Taken: Course-Taking in American High Schools." *ETS Policy Notes* 9 (Spring 1999): 1-7.

Francis, John, and Mark Hampton. "Resourceful Responses: The Adaptive Research University and the Drive to Market." *The Journal of Higher Education* 70 (November/December 1999): 625-42.

Freedman, James O. *Idealism and Liberal Education*. Ann Arbor: University of Michigan Press, 1996.

Gaff, Jerry G. *General Education: The Changing Agenda*. Washington, D.C.: Association of American Colleges and Universities, 1999.

Gaff, Jerry G. *Twelve Principles for Effective General Education Programs*. Washington, D.C.: American Association of Colleges and Universities, 1994.

Giroux, Henry A. "Liberal Arts Education and the Struggle for Public Life: Dreaming About Democracy." In Gless, Darryl J., and Smith, Barbara Herrnstein, eds. *The Politics of Liberal Education*. Durham, NC: Duke University Press, 1992.

Glazer, Nathan. "In Defense of Multiculturalism." *New Republic* 205 (September 2, 1991): 18-22.

Goldberg, Maxwell H. "Liberal Learning and the Land-Grant System: Futures and Optatives." In Anderson, G. Lester, ed. *Land-Grant Universities and Their Continuing Challenge*. East Lansing: Michigan State University Press, 1976.

Grey, Thomas C. "Civil Rights vs. Civil Liberties: The Case of Discriminatory Verbal Harassment." In Franke, Ellen et al., eds. *Reassessing Civil Rights*. Cambridge, MA: Blackwell Publishers for the Bowling Green Social Philosophy and Policy Center, 1991.

Hauptman, Arthur M. "Reforming the Ways in Which States Finance Higher Education." In Heller, Donald E., ed. *The States and Public Higher Education Policy: Affordability, Access and Accountability*. Baltimore: Johns Hopkins University Press, 2001.

Hauptman, Arthur M. "Trends in the Federal and State Financial Commitment to Higher Education." In Finifter, David H. et al., eds. *The Uneasy Public Policy Triangle in Higher Education: Quality, Diversity and Budgetary Efficiency*. New York: American Council on Education, 1992.

Heller, Donald E. *The States and Public Higher Education Policy: Affordability, Access and Accountability*. Baltimore, MD: Johns Hopkins University Press, 2001.

Henry, William. *In Defense of Elitism*. New York: Doubleday, 1994.

Higher Education: Tuition Increasing Faster Than Household Income and Public Colleges' Cost. Washington, D.C.: General Accounting Office, August 1996.

Himmelfarb, Gertrude. "Revolution in the Library." *The American Scholar* 66 (Spring 1997): 197-204.

Horn, Laura J., and Xianglei Chen. *Toward Resiliency: At-Risk Students Who Make It to College*. Washington, D.C.: U.S. Department of Education, 1998.

Horowitz, Helen Lefkowitz. *Campus Life: Undergraduate Cultures from the End of the Eighteenth Century to the Present*. New York: Alfred A. Knopf, 1987.

Hutchins, Robert Maynard. *The Higher Learning in America*. New Haven, CT: Yale University Press, 1962.

Ikenberry, Stanley O., and Hartle, Terry W. *Taking Stock: How Americans Judge Quality, Affordability, and Leadership at U.S. Colleges and Universities*. Washington, D.C.: American Council on Education, 2000. http://www.acenet.edu/bookstore/pdf/taking_stock.pdf> (July 5, 2001).

Immerwahr, John. *Taking Responsibility: Leaders' Expectations of Higher Education*. San Jose, CA: National Center for Public Policy and Higher Education, 1999.

Isetti, Ronald. "The Future of Liberal Arts Colleges: Commercialization or Integrity?" *Liberal Education* 60 (December 1974): 539-47.

Jaffa, Harry V. *Crisis of the House Divided*. Chicago: University of Chicago Press, 1959, 1982.

Jaggar, Alison M. "Love and Knowledge: Emotion in Feminist Epistemology." In Jaggar, Alison M. and Bordo, Susan R., eds. *Gender/Body/Knowledge: Feminist Reconstructions of Being and Knowing*. New Brunswick, NJ: Rutgers University Press, 1989,145-171.

Jennings, Marianne M. *The Dissolution of General Education: A Review of Arizona's Three State Universities' Programs of Study and Degree Requirements.* n.p.: Arizona Association of Scholars, 2000.

Johnston, J. B. "How Shall the College Discharge Its Obligation to Society?" *The Reference Shelf* 7. Edited by James G. Hodgson. (1931): 101-113.

Kenny, Robert W. *Reinventing Undergraduate Education: A Blueprint for America's Research Universities.* New York: The Boyer Commission on Educating Undergraduates in the Research University, 1998.

Kernan, Alvin. *In Plato's Cave.* New Haven, CT: Yale University Press, 1999.

Kerr, Clark. *The Uses of the University.* 3d. ed. Cambridge: Harvard University Press, 1982.

Keynes, John Maynard. *The General Theory.* New York: Harcourt Brace, 1936.

Kloppenberg, James T. *The Virtues of Liberalism.* New York: Oxford University Press, 1998.

Kluge, P. F. (Paul Frederick). *Alma Mater: A College Homecoming.* Reading, MA: Addison-Wesley Publishing Co., 1993.

Krutsch, Phyllis M. "The Passive Culture of Public Boards." *Trusteeship* 6 (March/April, 1998): 22-25.

Lapovsky, Lucie, and Hubbel, Loren Loomis. "An Uncertain Future." *Business Officer* (February 2001): 25-31. <http://www.nacubo.org> (July 1, 2001).

Lederman, Douglas. "Persistent Racial Gap in SAT Scores Fuels Affirmative-Action Debate." *Chronicle of Higher Education* 45 (October 30, 1998): A36-37.

Lederman, Marie Jean. "Consumer Evaluation of Teaching." *Liberal Education* 60 (May 1974): 242-48.

Lindemann, Lynn W. "Why Faculty Object to Accountability in Higher Education." *Liberal Education* 60 (May 1974): 175-80.

Lineberry, William P., ed. *Colleges at the Crossroads.* New York: The H. W. Wilson Company, 1966.

Losco, Joseph, and Brian L. Fife, eds. *Higher Education in Transition: The Challenges of the New Millennium.* Westport, CT: Bergin & Garvey, 2000.

Lovett, Clara M. "State Government and Colleges: A Clash of Cultures." *Chronicle of Higher Education* 47 (April 27, 2001): B20.

Lucas, Christopher J. *Crisis in the Academy: Rethinking Higher Education in America.* New York: St. Martin's Press, 1996.

Machiavelli, N. "The Administrator: Notes on the Academic Manna Game." *Liberal Education* 20 (December 1974): 500-04.

MacTaggart, Terrence J., ed. *Seeking Excellence Through Independence.* San Francisco: Jossey-Bass Publishers, 1998.

Marchese, Ted. "Assessment and Standards." *Change* 30 (September/October 1998): 4.

Martin, Jerry L., and Anne D. Neal. *The Shakespeare File: What English Majors Are Really Studying: A Report.* Washington, D.C.: The Forum, 1996.

Maritain, Jacques. *Education at the Crossroads.* New Haven, CT: Yale University Press, 1943 [1978].

Matlock, Thao P. "The Overlap Group: A Study of Nonprofit Competition." *Journal of Law and Education* 23 (Fall 1994): 523-47.

McAndrew, William. "Doubting the Deans." *The Reference Shelf* 7. Edited by James G. Hodgson. New York: H. W. Wilson Company, 1931, 130-142.

McGuinness, Aims C., and Peter T. Ewell. "Improving Productivity and Quality in Higher Education." *AGB Priorities* 2 (Fall 1994): 1-4.

McKeown-Moak, Mary P. *Financing Higher Education in the New Century: The Third Annual Report from the States*. Denver, CO: State Higher Education Executive Officers, June 2001. <http://www.sheeo.org/finance/fin—00—report.pdf > (August 13, 2001)

McPherson, Michael S., and Morton Owen Schapiro. "Financing Undergraduate Education: Designing National Policies." *National Tax Journal* 50 (September 1997): 557-72.

_____. *The Student Aid Game: Meeting Need and Rewarding Talent in American Higher Education*. Princeton, NJ: Princeton University Press, 1998.

_____. *The Student Finance System for Undergraduate Education: How Well Does It Work?"* Discussion paper-11. Williamston, MA: Williams Project on the Economics of Higher Education, 2000. <http://www.williams.edu/wpehe/abstracts.html#dp-11> (June 13, 2001).

Minnich, Elizabeth Kamarck. "Can Virtue Be Taught? A Feminist Reconsiders." In Darling-Smith, Barbara, ed. *Can Virtue Be Taught?* Notre Dame, IN: University of Notre Dame Press, 1993, 69-85.

Moore, John H. "Higher Education and the Burger King Society." *Vision & Values* 8 (November 2000). <http://www.gcc.edu/ alumni/vision-moore2.asp> (December 8, 2000).

Moore, Stephen, and Julian Simon. *It's Getting Better All the Time*. Washington, D.C.: The Cato Institute, 2000.

"More First-year College Students Return for Second Year; Fewer Students Graduate in Five Years." *ACT Newsroom* (April 26, 2001). <http://www.act.org/news/releases/2001/04-26-01.html> (June 7, 2001).

Mortenson, Thomas G. "Postsecondary Participation of Students from Low Income Families." Tables presented to the Round Table Meeting of Advisory Committee on Student Financial Assistance. Boston: Boston University, April 12, 2000. <http://www.ed.gov/ offices/AC/ ACSFA/mortenson.pdf> (August 13, 2001).

National Association of College and University Business Officers. "Interim Report of the Ad Hoc Committee on College Costs." Washington, D.C.: NACUBO, February 2001. <http:// www.nacubo.org/public_ policy/cost_of_college/> (July 1, 2001).

National Center for Education Statistics. *Condition of Education, 2001*. Washington, D.C.: NCES, 2001. <http://nces.ed.gov/pubsearch/pubsinfoasp?pubid=2001072> (June 12, 2001).

_____. *Digest of Education Statistics*. Washington, D.C.: NCES, 2001. <http://nces.ed.gov/pubs2001/digest/dt185.html> (May 13, 2001).

National Commission on the Cost of Higher Education. *Straight Talk About College Costs and Prices*. Phoenix, AZ: Oryx Press, 1998. <http://www.acenet.edu/programs/DGR/costreport.HTML> (May 20, 2001).

Neal, Anne D., and Jerry L. Martin. *Losing America's Memory: Historical Illiteracy in the 21st Century*. Washington, D. C.: American Council of Trustees and Alumni, 2000. <http://www.goacta.org> (August 13, 2001).

Neusner, Jacob, and Noam M. Neusner. *Reaffirming Higher Education*. New Brunswick, NJ: Transaction Publishers, 2000.

New Millennium Project on Higher Education Costs, Pricing, and Productivity. *Reaping the Benefits: Defining the Public and Private Value of Going to College*. Washington, D.C.: The Institute for Higher Education Policy, March 1998.

New York Association of Scholars and Empire Foundation for Policy Research. *SUNY's Core Curricula: The Failure to Set Consistent High Academic Standards*. New York: The Association, July 1996.

Newman, John Henry. *The Idea of a University*. New Haven, CT: Yale University Press, 1996.

Nisbet, Robert. *The Degradation of the Academic Dogma*. New York: Basic Books, 1971.

Nussbaum, Martha. *Cultivating Humanity*. Cambridge, MA: Harvard University Press, 1997.

Oakeshott, Michael. "The Idea of a University." In Fuller, Timothy, ed. *The Voice of Liberal Learning: Michael Oakeshott on Education*. New Haven, CT: Yale University Press, 1989.

_____. *Rationalism in Politics*. Indianapolis, IN: Liberty Fund, Inc., 1991.

Ortega y Gasset, José. *Mission of the University*. Edited and translated by Howard Lee Nostrand. New York: W. W. Norton & Co., Inc., 1994.

Palmer, Parker. Foreword to Mary Rose O'Reilly. *Radical Presence: Teaching as a Contemplative Practice*. Portsmouth, NH: Boynton/Cook Publishers, 1998.

_____. "The Heart of a Teacher." *Change* 29 (November/December 1997): 15-21.

Pascarella, Ernest T., and Patrick T. Terenzini. *How College Affects Students: Findings and Insights from Twenty Years of Research*. San Francisco: Jossey-Bass Publishers, 1991.

Pattenaude, Richard L. "Administering the Modern University." In Losco, Joseph, and Brian L. Fife, eds. *Higher Ecucation in Transition: The Challenges of the New Millennium*. Westport, CT: Bergin & Garvey, 2000, 159-176.

Peck, M. Scott. *In Search of Stones: A Pilgrimage of Faith, Reason, and Discovery*. New York: Hyperion, 1995.

Peel, Malcolm L., and Leo L. Nussbaum. "The Core Course Redivivus." *Liberal Education* 20 (December 1974): 478-88.

Petersen, John C. *Internationalizing Quality Assurance in Higher Education*. Council for Higher Education Accreditation, Occasional Paper. Washington, D. C.: CHEA, July 1999.

Phipps, Ronald. *College Remediation: What It is; What It Costs; What's at Stake?* Washington, D. C.: Institute for Higher Education Policy, 1998.

President's Commission on Higher Education. *Higher Education for American Democracy*. Washington, D.C.: Government Printing Office, 1947.

Proctor, Samuel D. "Land-Grant Universities and the Black Presence." In Anderson, G. Lester, ed. *Land-Grant Universities and Their Continuing Challenge*. East Lansing: Michigan State University Press, 1976.

Public Agenda Online: The Issues-Education, "People's Chief Concerns." <http:// www.publicagenda.org/ issues_pcc_ detail. cfm?issuetype=education&list=13> (August 6, 2001).

Redd, Kenneth E. *Discounting Toward Disaster: Tuition Discounting, College Finances, and Enrollments of Low-Income Undergraduates.* Indianapolis, IN: USA Group Foundation, 2000.

Reid-Wallace, Carolynn. "The Promise of American Education." In Alexander, Lamar, and Finn, Jr., Chester E., eds. *The New Promise of American Life.* Indianapolis, IN: Hudson Institute, 1995.

Report of the Commissioners for the University of Virginia, Assembled at Rock-Fish Gap, in the County of Augusta, August 1, 1818. Charlottesville: C. P. McKennie, 1824.

Reynolds, Noel B. "On the Moral Responsibilities of Universities." In Thompson, Dennis L., ed. *Moral Values and Higher Education: A Nation at Risk.* Provo, UT: Brigham Young University Press, 1991.

Richmond, Julius B., and Rushi Fein. "The Health Care Mess: A Bit of History." *JAMA: Journal of the American Medical Association* 273 (January 4, 1995): 69-70.

Roney, Lois. *Academic Animals: A Bestiary of Higher Education Teaching and How It Got That Way.* Philadelphia: Xlibris, 2001.

Saltrick, Susan. "Through a Dark Wood." Paper presented at the Conference on Learning Communities, University of Miami, January 9, 1998. Distributed to AAHESGIT mailing list, November 20, 1997. <http:// www.tltgroup.org/resources/ rdarkwood.html> (April 20, 2001).

Schielfelbein, S. "Editor's Odyssey: Gleanings from Articles and Editorials by N. C." *Saturday Review* (April 15, 1978): 12-20.

Schwartz, Barry. *George Washington: The Making of an American Symbol.* New York: The Free Press, 1987.

Scott, Robert A. "Lay Bare the Questions Hidden by Answers." *The College Board Review* No. 184 (Spring 1998): 20-25.

Selingo, Jeffrey. "Questioning the Merit of Merit Scholarships." *The Chronicle of Higher Education* 47 (January 19, 2001): A20-22.

Shaw, Kenneth A. "Helping Public Institutions Act Like Private Ones." In MacTaggart, Terrence J., ed. *Seeking Excellence Through Independence.* San Francisco: Jossey-Bass Publishers, 1998.

Sheehan, Colleen. *The Core Curriculum of Pennsylvania's State System and State-Related Universities: Are Pennsylvania's Students Receiving the Fundamentals of a College Education?* Harrisburg, PA: The Commonwealth Foundation for Public Policy Initiatives, September 1998.

Shils, Edward. "The Idea of the University: Obstacles and Opportunities in Contemporary Society." In *The Calling of Education,* 237-38 [reprinted from *Minerva XXX/2* (Summer 1992), Kluwer Academic Publishers].

Smith, Barbara Herrnstein. "Hirsch, Literacy, and the 'National Culture.'" In Gless, Darryl J., and Smith, Barbara Herrnstein, eds. *The Politics of Liberal Education.* Durham, N.C.: Duke University Press, 1992, 75-94.

Smith, Adam. *An Inquiry into the Nature and Causes of the Wealth of Nations*. Edited by R. H. Campbell and A. S. Skinner. Indianapolis, IN: Liberty Classics, 1976.

Smith, Charles W. *Market Values in American Higher Education: The Pitfalls and Promises*. Lanham, MD: Rowman & Littlefield Publishers, Inc., 2000.

Spafford, Ivol. *Building a Curriculum for General Education: A Description of the General College Program*. Minneapolis: The University of Minnesota Press, 1943.

State Council of Higher Education for Virginia. *Advancing the System of Higher Education in Virginia: 1999 Virginia Plan for Higher Education*. Richmond: State Council of Higher Education for Virginia, 1999. <http://www.schev.edu/html/ reports/ 99vaplanfinal.pdf> (March 18, 2001).

_____. *General Education in Virginia: Assessment and Innovation—A Challenge to Academic Leadership*. Richmond: State Council of Higher Education for Virginia, 1999. <http://www.schev.edu/html/reports /gen ed study.pdf> (February 12, 2001).

State Higher Education Executives Organization. "State Accountability Reports." <http://sheeo.org/account/act-reports.htm> (August 6, 2001).

State Higher Education Executive Officers. "State Strategies that Support Successful Student Transition from Secondary to Postsecondary Education: Symposium and Briefing." February 17-19, 1998.

Stoke, Harold W. *The American College President*. New York: Harper & Brothers Publishers, 1959.

Strauss, Leo. *Liberalism Ancient and Modern*. New York: Basic Books, 1968.

Swenson, Craig. "Customers and Markets: The Cuss Words of Academe." *Change* 30 (September/October 1998): 33-38.

Tocqueville, Alexis de. *De la démocratie en Amérique*. Paris: Garnier-Flammarion, 1981.

Trachtenberg, Stephen Joel. *Speaking His Mind*. Phoenix, AZ: American Council on Education and The Oryx Press, 1994.

United States Department of Education. Advisory Committee on Student Financial Assistance. *Access Denied: Restoring the Nation's Commitment to Equal Educational Opportunity*. Washington, D. C.: Department of Education, February 2001. <http://www.ed.gov/offices/AC/ACSFA/access_denied.pdf> (August 13, 2001).

University of Virginia Rector and Visitors Petition to the United States Congress. "Petition to Abolish Tariff on Scientific Books Imported from Abroad." File draft, November 30, 1821. Printed: *Central Gazette*, 4 January 1822. (Mss # 3734, Thomas Jefferson Papers, The Albert and Shirely Small Special Collections Library, University of Virginia Library).

Vaughn, Ernest Vancourt. "The Origins and Early Development of Universities." *The Reference Shelf* 7. Edited by James G. Hodgson. New York: H. W. Wilson Company, 1931.

Vedder, Richard. "Higher Education at Lower Cost." *Wall Street Journal* (31 August 1998): A17.

Veysey, Laurence. *The Emergence of the American University*. Chicago: University of Chicago Press, 1965.

Virginia Business Higher Education Council. *Virginia First 2000—Business and Higher Education: Partners for the Learning Economy.* (no date or place of publication. Address of Council: 800 East Leigh Street, Suite 106, Richmond, Virginia 23219. Tel. 804-828-2285).

Wallin, Jeffrey D. "Is Civic Education Compatible with Liberal Education?" *On Principle* 5 (April 1997): 3 < http:// www.ashland.edu/ashbrook/ publicat/onprin/v5n2/wallin.html > (August 6, 2001).

Wayland, Francis. *A Memoir of the Life and Labors of Francis Wayland.* Edited by F. Wayland and H. L. Wayland. New York: Sheldon and Co., 1867.

Weiler, Hans N. "States, Markets and University Funding: New Paradigms for the Reform of Higher Education in Europe." *Compare* (October 2000): 333-39.

Western Interstate Commission for Higher Education and The College Board. *Knocking at the College Door: Projections of High School Graduates by State and Race/Ethnicity, 1996-2012.* Boulder, CO: WICHE and The College Board, 1998.

Winston, Gordon C., and Ivan C. Yen. *Costs, Prices, Subsidies, and Aid in U.S. Higher Education.* Discussion Paper-32. Williamston, MA: Williams Project on the Economics of Higher Education, 1995. <http:// www.williams.edu/wpehe/abstracts.html#dp-32> (June 13, 2001).

Winston, Gordon C. *A Guide to Measuring College Costs.* Discussion paper-46. Williamston, MA: Williams Project on the Economics of Higher Education, 1998. <http://www.williams.edu/wpehe/ abstracts.html#dp-46> (June 13, 2001).

_____. "Is Princeton Acting Like a Church or a Car Dealer?" *Chronicle of Higher Education* 47 (February 23, 2001): B24.

_____, and David J. Zimmerman. *Where is Aggressive Price Competition Taking Higher Education?* Discussion paper-56. Williamston, MA: Williams Project on the Economics of Higher Education, 2000. <http:// www.williams.edu/wpehe/ abstracts.html#dp-56> (May 21, 2001).

_____. "Where is Aggressive Price Competition Taking Higher Education?" *Change* 32 (July-August 2000): 10-18.

Wireman, Billy. "Productive Careers and Noble Lives: A New Mandate for Liberal Arts Education." *Vital Speeches of the Day* 63 (December 15, 1996): 135-38.

Wolfe, Thomas. *The Web and the Rock.* London: Heinemann, 1969.

"Women Increasingly Outnumber Men at Colleges and Universities," *New York Times* (6 December 1998): Section I, 1-3.

Zemsky, Robert, Susan Shaman, and Maria Ianozzai. "In Search of Strategic Perspective: A Tool for Mapping the Market in Post-Secondary Education." *Change* (November/December 1997): 23.

Zumeta, William. "Public Policy and Accountability in Higher Education: Lessons from the Past and Present for the New Millennium." In Heller, Donald E., ed. *The States and Public Higher Education Policy: Affordability, Access and Accountability.* Baltimore: Johns Hopkins University Press, 2001.

Index